F418

Clare of Assisi

MARCO BARTOLI

Translated by
SISTER FRANCES TERESA OSC

Foreword by
BRIAN PURFIELD OFM

DARTON · LONGMAN + TODD

First published in Italian in 1989 by
Institut Storico dei Cappuccini, Rome

English translation first published in 1993 by
Darton, Longman and Todd Ltd
1 Spencer Court
140–142 Wandsworth High Street
London SW18 4JJ

ISBN 0–232–52026–7

A catalogue record for this book is available
from the British Library

Unless otherwise stated scriptural quotations are from
The Jerusalem Bible published and copyright 1966,
1967 and 1968 by Darton, Longman and Todd Ltd and
Doubleday and Co. Inc. Quotations from *The Writings of Francis and Clare*
copyright 1982 the Missionary Society of St Paul the Apostle in the State
of New York are used by permission of Paulist Press.

Cover: Illustration: *Saint Clare of Assisi*, Poor Clare Workshop,
Kamonyi (Rwanda). Used by permission of the Protomonastery
of St Clare, Assisi, Italy. Design: Jeremy Dixon.

Typography by Humphrey Stone

Phototypeset by Intype, London
Printed and bound in Great Britain
at the University Press, Cambridge

Contents

Contents

Contents

Foreword

For centuries the life and writings of Clare of Assisi were not really known, even in the Franciscan world. Happily this situation changed in the second quarter of this century, but it is only recently that there has been serious study of their content. Against this background, it gives me great pleasure to introduce this translation by Sister Frances Teresa OSC of the work of Marco Bartoli. The English-speaking world now has a well-documented and very informative life of Clare. Taken together with the invaluable work of Father Regis Armstrong OFM CAP, who translated the writings and early documents, we now have important tools for our study of the life and charism of Clare. The light that is Clare can now shine out even more brightly for the Church and the world of today, and the figure of the woman of Assisi can emerge in her own right from the shadow of Francis, where perhaps she has been mistakenly placed for too long.

Clare's life and writings indicate, among other things, that she was a strong, persistent, determined, holy, loving and skilful woman who had a vision. She articulated that vision in her life and writings; she spent herself tirelessly in pursuit of it; she left that vision to countless women who would desire and attempt to follow in her footprints. The passion that characterised her living and loving spans centuries and cultures and urges us to live as passionately our vocation in our world and time.

Clare made a unique contribution to the Franciscan movement. She made the Franciscan way of life work in an enclosed setting. The freedom characteristic of the Franciscan finds a home within four walls. Where Francis emphasises preaching, with Clare it is praying. Where Francis speaks of fraternity, Clare speaks of community. For Francis the apostolate is extensive and mobile. For Clare, it is intensive but diffusive. Clare does not speak of exercising the apostolate, but of *being* apostolic. Clare gives the Franciscan vision its feminine expression. Her way of life complements Francis' vision. After Francis died, and the friars struggled over their way of life, Clare maintained a clear vision of what Francis was about. These pages bring out how heroically faithful Clare was to the legacy of Francis.

Bartoli aims at a reconstruction of the life of Clare in historical terms. In giving us his historical account of the life and spirituality of Clare, he subjects the acts of the process of canonisation to careful and searching analysis. This source provides us with indispensable firsthand information concerning the life and death of Clare. The author also makes a valuable contribution to our knowledge of the life of Clare by weaving his information on her into the realities of early thirteenth-century central Italy.

A great deal has been written in recent years on medieval women and on religious women at the time of Clare. Bartoli uses these studies, together with general information about the Middle Ages, and draws out the meaning of these events in the life of Clare. He has synthesised and presented clearly the fruit of much recent research. The references at the end of the work to sources and further literature will enable us to continue our research into questions about the life and charism of this remarkable woman.

This is an invaluable reference work for those who wish to have at hand the most up-to-date historical scholarship on the life of Clare. Sister Frances Teresa is to be congratulated for her painstaking translation and for making the work available to a wider audience during the celebration of the eight hundredth anniversary of the birth of Clare. We have a rich heritage steeped in history as this present volume so clearly indicates. Our task is not to leave it in the pages of history, but to live it!

BRIAN PURFIELD OFM
Franciscan Study Centre
Canterbury, Kent

Translator's Preface

This book was first placed in my hands by Father Dario Pili OFM, at a time when he was delegate from the Friars Minor to the Poor Clare nuns, with the earnest wish that I should translate it into English. When I began to read it, I realised that it was indeed an example of something that has been rather lacking in biographies of Clare, namely, a objective study of her by a professional historian, albeit an admiring one, as distinct from reflections on Clare by someone within the Order seeking to live by her precepts. As far as I know, this is the first time such a study has been written, or the first such modern study, and Marco Bartoli has approached his task with two main sources of information. One is Clare's own writings and the contemporary or near contemporary documents, such as Celano's accounts of her life and that of Francis. The other source is historical, particularly the light cast by our constantly increasing knowledge of the position of women and women's religious movements in the thirteenth century. Recently our growing understanding of the Beguine movement has in its turn – as always – cast new light upon old information, so that what we already knew about some of the poverty movements of the time, and the extraordinary upsurge of experimental women's religious communities, has been greatly enhanced.

It is almost a truism to say that there are a number of parallels between the thirteenth and the twentieth centuries, but like most truisms, it is also partly true. The parallels can be traced in the shift of economic forces, the growing nationalism, the emergence of more and more vernacular languages in serious literature, the increasing power of banking, the expansion of international trade and the concomitant urbanisation, the way in which the rich were getting richer and the poor becoming poorer, the (so far successful) fight of the governing classes to retain their power – to name a few points, most of which will have a familiar ring to us today. Another resemblance between the two periods can be seen in the changing position of women within society, for the emergence of a new merchant class was enabling women to develop a much more involved and a far freer life-style than would have been possible for a young aristocratic girl such as Clare. For her, the future would still largely have been governed by the family's political commitments and aspirations in which marriage alliances played an important part. A young woman like Clare who was beautiful, healthy and cultured would have been seen as an important resource, and even in the most loving of families her own wishes would not have been the first consideration.

As Raoul Manselli, Bartoli's revered master, is at pains to stress in his study of Francis,[1] part of our difficulty is that terms such as class, bourgoisie, education must not be understood simplistically to mean exactly the same then as now. It is the historian's task to help us understand such differences and nuances as well as the major shifts and trends of influence, and this Bartoli does well. Although he is a specialist, his book is not a specialist study for experts, even though it necessarily presupposes some familiarity with the period and with religion.

The fact that Bartoli is not a Franciscan himself has perhaps enabled him to approach the story of Clare from a fresh angle. His examination of Clare's famous dream, for instance, made in the light of modern psychological expertise, yet without imposing any anachronistic interpretations, is masterly. In many respects, Bartoli has done for Clare what Manselli did for Francis. He has given us a historical appreciation which makes no pretence at being the last word but which has certainly opened up the study of Clare and moved it on to a still more professional level. For this alone, quite apart from the interest of the book, the whole Order must stand in his debt.

In this translation, I have taken one or two liberties which should be noted. I have consistently translated *fraternita* as 'community' when it referred to the sisters, and as 'fraternity' when it meant the brothers. Again, Bartoli often uses the phrase

donna di Assisi, meaning Clare. After some thought, I settled
for 'woman of Assisi' rather than 'lady of Assisi'. I did this
because it seemed to me that here Bartoli was not referring to
Clare as one of the *maiores*, that is, the powerful and aristocratic, but as she herself chose to be, one of the *minores*, one
of the little folk, who yet attained a special place in Assisian
hearts by virtue of what she was in herself, not by virtue of her
rank or status. However, there is no English word which exactly
conveys all the nuances of the Italian *donna*, such is the torment
and the challenge of translation. Similarly, the Italian *sposa*,
like the Latin *sponsa*, falls differently on the ear than does the
English 'spouse'. After much hesitation, I decided, rightly or
wrongly, to translate *sposa* by 'darling' or 'beloved', in the
belief that these words convey to our hearts and minds something much nearer to what would have been in Clare's heart
and mind as she wrote.

For the Rule and letters of Clare, I have made my own
translation and, like Bartoli, followed the verse numbering given
in the definitive Latin text published in 1985 by Les Editions
du Cerf under the title *Écrits*. This numbering differs from that
in the *Writings*, but the text in the *Early Documents* has been
corrected to tally with the Latin. This is all a bit confusing but
one hopes that, given time, the discrepancies will be ironed out.
For the Rule and writings of Francis, I have used the translation
of Father Regis Armstrong OFM CAP, printed in *Writings of
Francis and Clare* in the Classics of Western Spirituality series.
The text of the canonisation process, the Rules of Hugolino
and Innocent are taken from *Clare of Assisi: Early Documents*,
also translated by Father Regis Armstrong and published by the
Paulist Press. Quotations from 1 and 2 Celano are to be found
in the *Omnibus of Sources* published by the Franciscan Herald
Press.

It remains only to express my gratitude to all those who
have helped or encouraged me in this work, particularly my
community who listened patiently to the text in various stages
of incompletion and whose comments were always helpful. As
the whole Order celebrates the eighth centenary of Clare's birth
in 1993–94, let us hope that this book will be one contribution

towards making a most remarkable and original woman far more widely known than she is at present. Not only was Clare the first woman to write a Rule for other women, but she was for many years the embodiment of all Francis' teaching and insight. Without her, Francis cannot be fully understood, and it is still true to say that the Franciscan charism cannot be expressed in its fullness today without the loving voice of Clare calling us and guiding us to a radical reappraisal of all our values.

SISTER FRANCES TERESA OSC
Convent of Poor Clares
Arundel

Introduction

Clare, daughter of Favarone, died in Assisi on 11 August 1253. All the people from the city and the villages came to the monastery where she had lived for more than forty years. The fame of her holiness had already spread far and wide, and both devout and curious came together to pay her their last respects and to assist at the translation of her body,[1] so much so that the city authorities thought it necessary to provide an armed escort headed by the mayor in person. Even the pope, Innocent IV, finding himself in Assisi with his curia, was drawn to San Damiano by the event.[2]

A remarkable thing happened during the ceremony of moving Clare's body to San Giorgio and conducting the funeral service (San Giorgio is a church within the city walls where, on an earlier occasion, the body of St Francis had also been laid to rest). When the Friars Minor began the Office for the dead, the pope stopped them and invited them instead to celebrate the Office for holy virgins.[3] This gesture of the pope which probably arose from nothing more than an emotional impulse, helped to hasten the canonisation of Clare; but even in those days a canonisation process was a task for the Roman curia. It had to ensure that a person was only recognised as a saint after a detailed and searching inquiry. The celebration of the Office of virgins during the solemn translation of Clare's body to San Giorgio would have had only one meaning: the *ipso facto* recognition of the sanctity of Clare.[4] One who was well aware of the precedent which would have been set by such a procedure was Rainaldo, the cardinal of Ostia and protector of the Order. He begged the pope to be prudent and to have the Office of the dead recited in the usual way.[5]

THE ACTS OF THE CANONISATION PROCESS

Innocent IV, who had known Clare personally, did not give up the idea of bringing her quickly to the honours of the altar. Scarcely two months later, when he had hardly resettled himself in Rome, he dictated a letter on 18 September to Bartolomeo, archbishop of Spoleto, who was the promoter for the regular process of canonisation.[6] In this letter the pope invited Bartolomeo to investigate Clare's 'life, her conversion and her conversation as well as the aforesaid miracles and the truth of every circumstance, and to do so diligently and solicitously in accordance with the interrogation which I command you to make by this our seal'.[7]

Thus the process for the canonisation of Clare of Assisi was formally begun. Bartolomeo chose the commissioners who would help him with this stage of the investigation and then he sought out those religious who would oversee the regular unfolding of the process itself. Finally, he looked for a notary to write down the words of the witnesses in the required way.[8] Within a month, on 24th November, the first sitting was held in the cloister of San Damiano in the presence of the same Bartolomeo, archbishop of Spoleto,[9] of the archdeacon Leonardo, of the archpriest Giacomo of Trevi, of Brother Marco the visitator to the sisters of San Damiano and in the presence of two of the most faithful companions of Francis and Clare, Angelo and Leo. Lastly, the notary Ser Martino was there.

The process lasted until 29 November – at least in so far as we can gather from the only extant manuscript. There were sixteen depositions from the sisters of San Damiano (fifteen were given by individuals and one was a collective testimony). Three more were given by notable men from the city, one by a woman who had been a friend of Clare since childhood and the last by a servant, a *famiglio* from her paternal home.

These acts of her canonisation process make an extremely interesting document. Even though they are mediated through questions put by the commissioner or the notary's translation of the replies, we hear in them the living voice of people who had actually known her.[10]

A canonisation process does not end with the reconstruction of the life story of the person under consideration, but with the ascertaining of their holiness.[11] The commission charged with the task had to draw up a schema of questions, so formed as to bypass any unhelpful digressions on the part of the witnesses.[12] Unfortunately the 'questions' which Innocent IV drew up in his bull have not been preserved, but from the witnesses' replies we can see clearly that their responses fitted into a previously established format. This dealt with Clare's *life* in her father's house; her *conversion*, that is her choice of religious life; her *conversation*, that is her conduct during the years at San Damiano and finally her *miracles*, the signs which demonstrated her holiness.[13] This schema was the one generally used for canonisation processes at that time and was certainly familiar to Bartolomeo, archbishop of Spoleto, for only the year before he had presided at the canonisation process of Blessed Simone da Collazzone.[14] On the other hand, this schema of questions which channelled the answers through a previously established format was not particularly preoccupied with historical data, but was more concerned to establish certain juridical conditions. For this reason the *forma interrogatorii* provided that, after the witnesses had been sworn in, they were to be questioned about how they knew the facts to which they were bearing witness, about when the events happened (with day and month), about where they happened and about who was present.[15]

At the same time, those who gave witness certainly did so with every intention of proving the holiness of Clare. The very thing which makes her canonisation process so interesting is the way in which those charged with conducting it and those giving evidence had such manifestly different ideas about sanctity. They both wanted to proclaim Clare a saint, but the requirements of one group did not always coincide with the evidence of the other.[16] This harmonious discord adds to the interest of reading the acts of the process, particularly if one bears in mind that the witnesses were using Italian while the notaries were recording in Latin. We must also remember that the only manuscript which preserves the text of the process does not report the original Latin but a fourteenth-century translation. In spite of all these obvious limitations, the process is one of the most vital sources through which we can hear the thoughts of that group of women and those three knights from central Italy in the thirteenth-century.[17]

That part of the process which records the acts was contained within a circle of five days, spent in the cloister of San Damiano and the church of San Paolo of Assisi; probably there was other evidence to follow but which has not been preserved for us.[18] In any case, both the institution and the conclusion of the process took place within the very short span of two years, so that in spite of the death of Innocent IV, the saint of Assisi was solemnly canonised in the cathedral of Anagni in August 1255. The Roman curia had unanimously agreed to inscribe Clare among the saints. Alexander IV, Innocent's successor, and the pope who actually proceeded to the canonisation, was in fact that same Cardinal Rainaldo who two years earlier had urged Innocent to prudence. The bull *Clara claris praeclara*, in which he proclaimed her sanctity, developed the basic themes of her life and then presented a brief synthesis of the ideals of female holiness which the Roman curia was offering to the world of the time.[19] The pope himself then took his share in writing the Office of the new saint.[20]

THE *LIFE OF ST CLARE THE VIRGIN*

Part of every canonisation process is the writing of a life, to be approved by the curia. This makes use of the information gathered during the process and forms the basis for composing a proper Office for the new saint.[21] In the case of Clare two such *legenda*, or lives, were written, one in verse and the other in prose.[22] Down the centuries the prose version is the one which has been read the most, the so-called *Life of St Clare the Virgin*. For a long time this hagiographical composition was thought to have been written by St Bonaventure[23] but nowadays almost everyone attributes it to Thomas of Celano.[24] This attribution is perfectly acceptable – at least provisionally, while we await a new, critical edition which may well throw fresh light on the matter – bearing in mind that the author seems to have been an educated Franciscan and an expert in this *genre* of hagiography.

The author was commanded to undertake the work by Innocent IV. He had first-hand material in the acts of the process and also such direct evidence as he had collected for himself.[25] By and large he kept to the sources although he developed them somewhat in his elaborations and interpretations. The *Life* needs to be read in the light of the evidence given at the process and then we can see how Celano offers us a third level from which to understand the life of Clare.[26] This means that as well as the commissioners charged with seeing to the canonisation process and as well as the witnesses who, at that same process, gave evidence of their own ideas about Clare's holiness, we now have an educated man whose gifts had already been demonstrated in three similar compositions about Francis of Assisi. As with other works in this literary *genre* of hagiography, the works of Thomas of Celano were not meant to be an historical biography of the person concerned.[27] The *Life* was written for edification; Clare is presented as a mirror, a model of sanctity. Above all she was to be imitated by those women who formed part of a movement, characteristic of the time, which has been called 'the women's religious movement of the thirteenth century'.[28] In a certain sense, the circle was now closed, because although this official *Life* was indeed a work of learning, it was destined for a popular public not all that different from the very sisters whose evidence is the basis of all writings on Clare.[29]

Yet, when we have finished tracing the development which spiralled out from the sources on Clare, we finally come to ask: where is Clare herself? In other words, is it possible to draw a trustworthy historical profile of the woman of Assisi through the fog of hagiography? The very difficulty of the task goes a long way towards explaining why there is such a dearth of historical studies on Clare of Assisi.[30] By any reckoning the number is small, but particularly so when we compare it with the amount written about Francis of Assisi.[31] Yet, for the historian, Clare's case is especially interesting, not only because we have both the canonisation process and the *Life* preserved for us but still more so because we have several writings of

Clare herself. Obviously these represent a source of outstanding importance.[32]

Although Clare was not a particularly cultured woman, she is still one of the few medieval women whose writings have come down to us. Unlike the situation with Francis, we are not talking about a whole *corpus* of writings, or at least no such collection of manuscripts has yet been found. Nevertheless, we are talking about work of undoubted value, not least because the Rule which she wrote for her sisters is the first known example in the history of the Church of a Rule for religious life written by a woman for other women.[33]

Clare's known writings consist of a Rule, a Testament, a Blessing and five letters. In these there are very few biographical details beyond reference to her choice of life, but they do give us a clear picture of her mind and spirituality.

The Rule which Clare wrote in the last years of her life, for her sisters present and to come, was the product of a long and difficult juridical passage. In the course of this she rejected all the other normative texts given her, including those given by the pope. As well as defining the norms of the life, Clare's Rule also includes a number of passages quoting directly from Francis' Rule for the friars. Clare, in her Rule, has gathered together all those points which seemed to her to be the essentials of her choice of life, and the Rule clearly shows that, for her, the most significant thing of all was '*to live according to the perfection of the Gospel*'.[34] In chapter 6 she carefully inserts the instructions which Francis had given the sisters. This is the chapter which holds the heart of the experience of Clare and her companions.

The themes of chapter 6 are taken up again in her Testament.[35] At the start of this century more than one scholar doubted the authenticity of this text, yet the whole document is very similar to the Testament of Francis, particularly in its character of spiritual exhortation. Neither Testament sets out to be a new legislative document but seeks instead to record the fundamental, basic religious experiences undergone by Francis and Clare. However, any doubts about its authenticity have now been finally removed by the discovery of three codices, in Messina, Madrid and Upsala respectively.[36] In these codices we also find the Blessing of Clare so that this, too, is now unanimously accepted as authentically hers.[37] The result is that anyone who wants to come close to the mind of Clare now has two extremely interesting documents, both of which give a very exact idea of her awareness of and reflections upon her own human and religious experience.

The final category of the writings of Clare is made up of the letters which she wrote to Agnes of Bohemia who had founded a monastery at Prague modelled on that of San Damiano. To Agnes, Clare had written words of comfort and encouragement with a strong insistence on the themes of poverty, of mystical marriage with Christ, and fidelity to the Franciscan spirit of her own vocation. The only Latin manuscript of these letters was not published until 1924.[38] Here, too, there is no longer any doubt about its attribution; on the contrary, it is quite obvious from these four letters that they are just a part of the correspondence between these two women.[39] It is highly likely that Clare's correspondence was far wider than this, particularly since we have several replies sent to her: from Francis; from Cardinal Ugolino, then Pope Gregory IX; from Clare's sister, Agnes. The Supplement to the *Annales Minorum* tells us that Clare wrote two letters to Ermintrude of Bruges[40] of which a text has come down to us that is probably a synthesis of these two letters. In its present form it cannot be attributed to Clare although it does have echoes of a spirituality very similar to that of the letters sent to Agnes of Bohemia.

The letters Clare received were sent back to her correspondents. During her lifetime she was, in fact, very widely known and a number of documents either mention her or else her experiment in community at San Damiano. Of the replies mentioned above, the two from Francis are certainly authentic and these Clare inserted, fittingly enough, into her Rule. Further research will be able to shed more light on the letters from Cardinal Ugolino and Clare's sister, Agnes.[41]

THE DOCUMENTS OF THE THIRTEENTH CENTURY

The thirteenth-century documents relevant to the study of Clare can be subdivided into two groups: witnesses and normative texts. In the first group, witnesses, must fall the writings of Jacques de Vitry, Thomas of Celano and several other hagiographical works. The second is composed of the *Privilege of Poverty* in its two redactions, the Constitutions of Cardinal Ugolino and the Rule of Innocent IV.

Jacques de Vitry was a prelate of Belgian origin, from Oignies in Brabant where he had known the woman penitent Mary of Oignies. After her death he wrote a life of her in which he presented her as the spearhead of the women's movement in northern Europe. Jacques came to Italy during 1216, immediately after the death of Innocent III, and he was disgusted by the behaviour which he saw among the members of the Roman curia. On that trip, his only comfort was his meeting with certain brothers and sisters, *minores*, of whom he wrote most positively in a letter from Genoa in that same year.[42] He makes no explicit mention in this letter of San Damiano or of Clare, but Assisi's proximity to Perugia (where Innocent III had died) suggests that it was to her and her community that Jacques referred.

Thomas of Celano's evidence took the form of the official biography or *Life* of St Francis of Assisi which he had been commissioned to write immediately after that saint's death.[43] When Celano came to speak of San Damiano and the rebuilding of the church by Francis, he inserted a whole chapter dedicated to the poor ladies (as he called them) who were living there.[44] The interest of this chapter derives from the fact that it was written in 1228 when Clare was still in the prime of life. His description of Clare, the first ever written, deserves to be quoted in full:

Of it [San Damiano] the Lady Clare, a native of the city of Assisi, the most precious and firm stone of the whole structure, was the foundation. For when, after the beginning of the Order of Brothers, the said Lady was converted to God through the counsel of the holy man, she lived unto the advantage of many and as an example to the countless multitude. She was of noble parentage but she was more noble by grace; she was a virgin in body, most chaste in mind; a youth in age but mature in spirit; steadfast in purpose and most ardent in her desire for divine love; endowed with wisdom and excelling in humility; Clare by name, brighter in life and brightest in character.[45]

Thomas of Celano was then charged with writing a *Second Life* of Francis and in this one he lingered even longer over the relationship between Francis and the sisters of San Damiano.[46] Many of the episodes in the *First Life* in which he speaks of Clare and her companions are also found in other works, notably the *Legend of Perugia*.[47] Much of the material for this came from the circle of those closest to Clare and it was written when the woman of Assisi was not only alive but when she was also the most important person in the minorite movement.[48]

To these hagiographical testimonies can be added the letter of notification of the death of Clare which was probably written by one of the clerics in the chancellery of Cardinal Rainaldo, protector of the Order. It was modelled on the letter written by Brother Elias on the death of Francis.[49]

With regard to the juridical sources, the *Privilege of Poverty* is especially interesting. This is a completely original document for which Clare herself sought approval from several popes. Until just a few years ago it was thought that the text of the original, granted to Clare by Innocent III, had been lost and even its existence was questioned. All these doubts have now been cleared up by the discovery of the text in the three documents already mentioned, those of Messina, Madrid and Upsala.[50] It would be hard to overestimate the value of this document which is, in fact, the first papal document ever granted to the Franciscan movement.[51] The *Privilege of Poverty* was also confirmed by Gregory IX in a slightly different version.[52]

Finally among the juridical sources, we must mention the Constitutions of Ugolino and the Rule of Innocent IV.[53] Whether these two normative texts were ever made use of by the community at San Damiano is an open question. What is certain is that Clare herself felt the need to write a Rule of her own into which she would place some passages from each of these two texts.

These, then, are the principal sources at the disposal of anyone wanting to try to reconstruct a biographical profile of Clare of Assisi. To them we must add two short works of hagiography from the thirteenth century and the by no means negligible works of iconography which came into being during the years immediately after Clare's death.

This material could be classified in various ways: a first listing might be a strictly chronological one, in which case the list of available sources, including those of doubtful authenticity, would be:

1. *Privilege of Poverty* (1216 version of Innocent IV)
2. Letter of Jacques de Vitry (1216)
3. Letter of Cardinal Ugolino dei Conti di Segni (about 1220)
4. *First Life* of Thomas of Celano (1228)
5. Letter of Gregory IX (1228)
6. *Privilege of Poverty* (version of Gregory IX, 1228)
7. Constitutions of Ugolino (dating back to 1218–19, but the version which has come down to us is that of 1228)
8. Letters of Clare to Agnes of Bohemia (1234–53)
9. *Second Life* of Thomas of Celano (1246–47)
10. Rule of Innocent IV (1247)
11. Testament and Blessing of Clare (1253)
12. Rule of Clare (1253)
13. Letter of notification of her death (1253)
14. Process of canonisation (1253)
15. Office of St Clare (1254)
16. *Rhyming Life* (1254–55)
17. Bull of the canonisation of Clare: *Clara claris preaclara* (1255)
18. *Life of St Clare the Virgin* (1255)

To this list must also be added the writings of Francis to the sisters at San Damiano which Clare inserted into her Rule and Testament, and also those Franciscan hagiographical writings which were not official. In most of these, the passages which refer to Clare all have parallels in the *Second Life* of Thomas of Celano.[54]

On this documentary base, it is quite possible to attempt to reconstruct a biography of Clare of Assisi, and to do so in terms which are historical rather than apologetic. To this end, the sources will be analysed not only chronologically but also in the light of their greater or lesser relevance to the aims of this research. Accordingly, one would rearrange the material in the following way:

1. Writings of Clare: Rule, Testament, Blessing and letters
2. Process of canonisation
3. Contemporary witnesses: *First* and *Second Life* by Thomas of Celano; letter of Jacques de Vitry; letters of Cardinal Ugolino; *Legend of Perugia*; etc.
4. Juridical sources: *Privilege of Poverty*; Constitutions of Cardinal Ugolino; Rule of Innocent IV
5. Hagiographical sources: letter of notification of her death; bull of canonisation; *Rhyming Life*; *Life of St Clare the Virgin*; etc.

This comparative analysis will allow us to lay bare that spiral around which the sources themselves have developed. It will also allow us to assess the internal contradictions and the influences of one source upon another. In this way we can build up a reliable reconstruction of the culture and mind, not only of Clare herself, but also of the people who knew and talked about her, whether they were educated ecclesiastics like Ugolino or Thomas of Celano, or whether they were unlettered nuns like the sisters at San Damiano.

ONE

The Courtly Culture of Knighthood
and Models of Sanctity

C lare's whole life was spent near Assisi and her name is so
closely bound up with that of her city that, in order to
draw together the basic threads of her story, we must first
briefly recall some of the basic social and political facts about
life in this Umbrian town.

ASSISI IN THE FIRST HALF OF THE THIRTEENTH CENTURY

In the first half of the thirteenth century, Assisi was a small
town of medium importance.[1] It was situated in the heart of
the Umbrian valley, and knew all the same disturbances as the
larger towns of the duchy of Spoleto. It was drawn into the
alternating fortunes of the dispute between pope and emperor,
particularly in the years after 1197–8, following the death of
Henry VI. This death created a power vacuum, within which
the city did everything it could to establish its political and
economic autonomy.[2] As a result, the city went through all the
various phases that contributed to the formation of an Italian
commune at that period: the domestic in-fighting between the
maiores or landowners and the *minores* or men of the people;[3]
the struggle of the local feudal lords to have their authority in
the area recognised;[4] and finally the struggle with the neighbouring towns (Perugia in particular) who threatened the city's
political autonomy and even its economic survival.[5]

This continual state of belligerence within and without the
city was kept alive and was fed by the tensions between the
emperor Frederick II and the popes. Together they made central
Italy, and especially Umbria, their chosen battleground.[6] On the
other hand, this condition of perpetual war did not hinder a

demographic and economic growth such as had not been seen for some centuries.[7]

For the peasant farmers in the area, this signalled a change in their social and economic dealings, because simultaneously with the declaration of the commune, a huge stratum of the populace also became free from such centuries-old feudal bonds as the *hominitium* (i.e. the personal subjection to the lord). This led to the forging of new bonds and new economic forces.

At the beginning of the century, Assisi was still a typical Italian agricultural community, basing its prosperity on the local economy. We must not, however, forget the exceptions, merchants who carried on an international trade – men such as Pietro Bernadone, father of Francis of Assisi. By the end of the century various trading activities had been established as well as a solid middle class composed of merchants, notaries, doctors, butchers, excisemen, cobblers, stonemasons, tailors, bakers, millers, barbers, and so on.[8]

Clare's family, unlike that of Francis, did not come from this newly emerging class. On the contrary, she was a member of that group of *maiores* who fought and hindered the development of the *homines populi*, the men of the people.

THE HOUSE AND FAMILY OF CLARE

Clare, says the *Life of St Clare the Virgin*, was born from a 'truly noble family'. Her father was a knight, a *miles*, as were all her family on both sides.[9] The official biography says no more; this was enough to enable the thirteenth-century reader to site Clare in a well-known scheme of things, that of the holy noble lady.[10]

The nobility of Clare's family was not just a literary device used in the *Life* but is attested to by the other sources as well. Research into the archives of Assisi has brought enough documents to light for us to be able to reconstruct Clare's family fairly accurately.[11] First of all, we must be clear that we are not talking about a great feudal lordship and that there were greater families in Assisi, the Gliserios for example; but we are talking about one of the families of *maiores* in the city. These *maiores* formed part of the urbanised aristocracy, having their own house within the city walls but with their real power base out in the country. There they had castles and farms from which they drew both men and resources in order to maintain their town palaces and their military panoply.[12] There were not more than twenty such families in Assisi. Their very effective power is shown by the way in which they managed to hold their ground in the difficult internal war with the citizens of Assisi between 1198 and 1210. This was made possible by a network of alliances and support, particularly from Perugia.

Clare's father was a *miles*, that is, to use the corresponding term in English, a knight,[13] and he belonged to the family of descendants of Offreduccio. The head of the family was Clare's uncle, Monaldo, who was probably the eldest. After him came Favarone and then the other brothers, each of whom had his own estates and men, his own family of wife and children. The family group appears as a flexible but tightly-knit social grouping, rigidly organised along the line of male descent.[14]

The house where Clare was born was an aristocratic *domus* or homestead, typical of a town in central Italy. For more than fifty years, her family had been woven into the fabric of Assisi and their house was on a site of particular relevance, right in the heart of the town. San Rufino, in fact, was the aristocratic centre of Assisi and members of the town's most illustrious families were among its chapter. This was in contrast with the new piazza del Comune, situated much lower down in a part of the town directly under the control of the bishop.[15]

If the building's situation in the town was a clear statement of its aristocratic character, then even more so was its architecture.[16] Clare's house, of which only traces remain to us, must have been one of the typical aristocratic buildings of the thirteenth century, far more like a country castle adapted for defence than a residential house in a town. The very construction of the house, made of stone with only the one door, easily defended by the armed men of the household, was designed for a situation in which armed attack was always a possibility – as indeed it was in the turbulent life of twelfth- and thirteenth-century Italian cities.[17]

In the structure of an aristocratic *domus* or household, there was an area reserved for the women.[18] Clare first saw the light in these women's quarters. They were made up of just a small number of rooms and here the women would spend the greater part of their day. Here, almost exclusively in the company of women, she would have spent the early years of her life, and among these women the one who would certainly have exercised the strongest influence on the young Clare was her mother.[19] Ortolana was far from being a woman of no importance. She had herself come from an aristocratic family and been given in marriage to Favarone, a member of one of the most important families of Assisi. In addition to this, she was well travelled. She had been to Rome, to St James at Compostella, to St Michael at Monte Gargano, and finally to the Holy Land.[20] These were the traditional pilgrimages of the twelfth and thirteenth centuries. In the wake of the ardour of the crusades, western Christianity was still on the move. Pilgrimages, including that to the Holy Land, had never completely died out during the High Middle Ages, but it was with Ortolana's generation that the whole of western Christendom appeared to be seized with a collective enthusiasm for pilgrimage-making.[21]

In Pisa, in central Italy, not far from Assisi, there lived a woman named Bona who organised travel by land and by sea, thus gaining a reputation for holiness. Had her fame travelled as far as Ortolana? It is impossible to know. What is certain is that the lady of Assisi shared the enthusiasm for pilgrimages so characteristic of the religious and evangelical awakening of the twelfth century.[22] These voyages were long and hazardous and full of unforeseen happenings and a woman could only risk them if she knew she could rely on her companions and on the support of the other women. Ortolana set out in the company of some of the women who frequented her house – her servants, her friends, women who had houses in the same piazza of San Rufino and were therefore members of the same 'group'.[23] Attached to and surrounding these magnates' homes would have been a whole network of solidarity made up of the members of this group, of families bound together by economic, matrimonial and political ties. As a result the whole life of the family would have been contained and supported within a wider system of belonging. Ortolana seems to have held a pre-eminent position within this circle of relationships, and when she went on pilgrimages she was accompanied by younger neighbours who probably would also have had the task of performing some personal services for her.

While in the *Life* Clare's father is only a background figure, Ortolana stands out clearly in all her importance. It was Ortolana who chose to call her daughter Clare, a name completely unknown in the family until then. It was Ortolana who watched sympathetically over Clare's new way of life. Finally, it was Ortolana who, after a number of years, followed her daughter to the new monastery of San Damiano. This probably took place after she had been widowed and when she would, in consequence, have moved into a far more vulnerable social position.

In the personal life of Ortolana, we can see the history of a generation. Her marriage, which would have been arranged as an alliance of families, encompassed her life as wife and mother with three or more children and a large number of men and women servants, and when finally she entered widowhood, her future would have been full of uncertainties, because women of that period lacked any effective juridical guarantees. Throughout all these stages, Ortolana's vitality and questing spirit expressed themselves in the only field allowed to her by the society of the time – religion. Her pilgrimages would seem to indicate a need for freedom and she sought it in faraway places. Her works of mercy and her good deeds in the service of the poorest were a concrete way of leaving the confines of the house, seeking interests in the life of the town where poverty and mendicancy were present to an extent never seen in preceding generations. To bring her life to its close at San Damiano represented a final statement of freedom; she would not stay in a family where she may not have been well cared for and where she would probably have been seen as a guest, but nor did she return to her father's house from which she was now separated by many years of autonomous living. Instead, she went to a community which her daughter had founded in opposition to the family.[24]

Clare would have seen a number of other women as well as Ortolana. With some of them, for example the daughters of Guelfuccio, she formed friendships which were to last for the whole of her life. All these women would have lived, for the most part, retiring lives and if they did go out into the town, it would only have been in order to take part in religious ceremonies in and around the cathedral. One notes in them a thirst for news, an eagerness for human relationships; it was not by chance that the preachers of the period saw curiosity as one of the main vices of women.[25] Gossip, rumour, good and bad news – these were the means by which the city, and even the whole world, crossed the boundaries of the household.

At the same time, the city outside the walls of the home was changing rapidly. Economic, demographic and social developments all imposed new cultural models and new scales of values. The group of aristocratic women living in the home of Offreduccio's descendants were living a contradiction. On the one hand, they were at the top of the social scale, respected and envied by everyone; on the other hand, they were enclosed, not only physically, in a way of life which allowed them very little scope. Other women, less rich and perhaps less noble than they, lived much freer lives, filled with responsibilities. These women collaborated with their husbands in tending the shop; they conducted their own small businesses and took their part in the economic and social growth of their city.[26]

There were certain moments when even the group of women living near the piazza of San Rufino were caught up in the life of their city. The civil wars of Assisi split its citizens into two. Clare's family sided with the *maiores* against the *minores* who by now formed the greater part of the population. The collision was violent and sooner or later all the *maiores* and their families were driven into exile.[27] Favarone and his family, too, had to leave. They chose the neighbouring town of Perugia, anxious to play their part in the civil war which had also weakened this rival to Assisi. The war was long and cruel. In one sense, the *maiores* were the stronger side and with Perugia's help, defeated the army of the commune at Collestrada. This was the battle in which Francis, son of Pietro Bernadone, also fought.[28] However, it was by no means a decisive battle and Clare was forced to wait yet some time before she could return to her home in Assisi.

We know nothing of her stay in Perugia except that she would have found there a number of the aristocratic families of Assisi. What we do know is that when, much later on, she chose to bring a new kind of religious community into being, she found her first and most faithful companions among the young women with whom she had made friends during her Perugian exile. It is highly likely that the very privations which were a part of exile had bound these young aristocratic girls together with bonds of solidarity, all the stronger in that they were forced to live so precariously, and that these bonds of solidarity and friendship endured across the years.

COURTLY CULTURE AND KNIGHTHOOD

In this warring society in which conflict was a condition of daily life, even the education of young women reflected this warlike quality.[29]

The term *miles cavaliere* or knight-on-horseback, which had come into use at the start of the eleventh century, was the term *par excellence* to indicate the aristocracy. In its Latin form, it indicates the military calling, while in the vernacular it recalls that symbol of power for this class of people, namely the horse. It also suggests the status of lord and all the power that goes with it. It was from within this aristocratic class, starting in Aquitaine at the beginning of the eleventh century, that the courtly culture arose.[30] The tales of the deeds of the knights of Charlemagne or King Arthur would have livened the afternoon and evening, helping the work of the house along. Many place-names bear witness to the spread of various cycles of stories of knightly courtesy in Italy during the eleventh and twelfth centuries. Names of towns, of places, of districts, are all evidence of the impression made by tales of the deeds at Roncevalles or of the Knights of the Round Table, indicating how deeply the culture was penetrated by these stories.[31] This was the first secular culture in the history of the western Middle Ages. It was a culture in which, for the first time, those who wrote and enjoyed the tales were not ecclesiastics but the aristocracy themselves (even though some of the clerics helped in the elaboration of the stories); and at the very heart of this culture of knighthood was, predictably, war, the primary activity of the knights.

After war, in these tales of ancient honour, came love.[32] It is more than probable that Clare, like the other young girls of good family in the region, had listened to the stories of the loves of Isold and Guinevere. She too was destined to wed a knight, a man of arms, through whom she would find her place in a line of descent even more important than her own.

It has been said that this courtly culture represented an exaltation of love and women. In reality, while it is true that woman is indeed placed on a pedestal, it was always a man who put her there; it was always a man to whom she owed her exaltation.[33] The place of an aristocratic woman was always within the house of her lord. When she left this house, a woman of good family would have had a companion and would have shunned any communication with strangers.[34] In these stories, passed on by word of mouth and only written down much later, the knight would sometimes meet a woman in an open clearing of the forest, but this would either be a woman of bad reputation or else one of lower social status.[35] There can be no doubt that such tales of tournaments and love would have had an educative function, for through them the young women would have been led to accept the retirement in which they had to live, at least until marriage set them free. In this way, there was established a close relationship between the life they lived and the life they dreamed about, between daily life and imaginary fantasy. The virtues demanded of women were always the same, prudence, silence, reserve, humility.[36] All these made a 'gentlewoman', that is a woman who would make a wife of a 'gentleman', one of a good aristocratic family.[37]

MODELS OF SANCTITY

Side by side with this 'lay' culture, Clare would have known another, equally rich in characters and ideas. This was the world of saints. Tales of the deeds of the saints were part of an oral culture every bit as rich as the one which told of the deeds of King Arthur and his companions. Saints, like knights, were heroes who went into battle and triumphed for the faith and for the good of the weak. The sources are silent about Clare's education in her father's house, and it is no longer possible to reconstruct accurately the cultural resources which would have been available to her. It is possible, though, to reconstruct a cultural context which would most certainly have influenced her.

We can be sure she would have shown great interest in the story of San Rufino whose church stood in the same piazza as her home. The legend of the holy bishop had been written down some time during the twelfth century, that is just before Clare was born. Among other things, the legend speaks of two women of easy habits, Nicea and Aquilina, who were put in prison in order to try to seduce the champion of the faith, but when they saw Rufino, they were themselves brought to the faith and baptised. This is a typical hagiographical situation. There is one almost the same in the acts of St Christopher. Yet, it is very interesting that in thirteenth-century Assisi, as part of the story of San Rufino's life, one heard of prostitutes being converted and martyred and so becoming focal points for veneration.[38]

It was because the emperor had tried to prevent a *cultus* from developing that the body of San Rufino had been lost after his martyrdom. According to the legend, which here repeats another typical hagiographic detail, it was the saint himself who, many centuries later, showed a peasant the place where his body had been thrown into the river. This allowed the body to be rediscovered and the basilica built and dedicated to his honour. In this way, a new cult was born, poised between its close rapport with the world of the peasants and its new relationship with the city in which the church had been built.

This is clear in a prayer which is one of the oldest to have come down to us from that period:

O San Rufino, always defend us, your servants; O San Rufino, hear your people.

Protect from an unprovided death all those who keep your festival today.

May they not be overwhelmed by hailstones or pestilence; may they not be condemned either to hunger or to the fire which devours.

May the sorrows of war be far from them; convert all the citizens to peace, remove all litigation and drive away the sorrows of war.

Let the fields never lack a harvest nor the vines lack grapes, for you can save all things.

You who are loving and good, just, innocent and kind and our salvation. You, who are loving and good.[39]

These words give us some idea of the social and human context in which Clare lived. They show us the precarious nature of the life lived by people daily threatened with illness, famine and the uncertainties of weather, a people whose one prayer on a feast day was that they might be preserved from horrible death. Life in Assisi at the start of the thirteenth century was hard. They were subjected to all the hazards which could endanger the productivity of their fields. Above all, they were subjected to the threat posed by a continuing fratricidal war which split the town in half with innumerable lawsuits and conflicts.

The culture of knighthood exalted courage, strength and war. In this prayer, however, and in the accounts of the miraculous cures worked at San Rufino's intercession, what we see emerging is a culture of the conquered, of the poor, of all those who, in the end, had to bear the consequences of war and the weight of the uncertainties of life. Around Rufino's tomb, we catch a glimpse of the huge mass of poor people crying their appeals for peace and healing. The accounts of healing, spread by word of mouth, all contributed to build up the fame of the sanctuary. In the case of Assisi, these accounts were gathered together at the start of the thirteenth century by order of Bishop Guido and made into a lectionary in which even today we can read about the healings that have taken place at the tomb of San Rufino.[40] These stories of suffering and liberation from suffering formed the natural background to the education of a young girl like Clare who lived nearby in the parish of San Rufino.

In such accounts of miraculous healings we hear the voices of those who are rarely heard in medieval documents, and, among them, the voices of women. Here, in contrast to the romances, the woman is often the protagonist. We also find women among those who are healed, such as the young woman possessed by a demon who was carried into the cathedral one Holy Thursday. There, with great shouting and to the fear of all present, she was set free. There are also the women who seek and find justice. The lectionary, for instance, tells of the victory of one Berta, daughter of Ermanno di Clesia, who was accused by her father and brother of having sinned through love with a certain young man. As a result, the father and brother threatened to kill the young man. Berta saved her reputation and the lad's life by thrusting her arm into a cauldron of boiling oil and invoking the help of San Rufino. With his aid, she drew her arm out of the oil, healthy and unburned.

Finally, there are the holy women. Obviously it is not possible to know for sure which tales of the saints were known to Clare as a young girl, but it is practically certain that she did know several. We may hazard a guess that from her very young days she was particularly familiar with the story of the virgin martyr, Agnes. Agnes had promised all her love to the Lord and, in order to remain faithful to this promise, she refused the love of a number of illustrious people and, finally, was faced with martyrdom. This saint is the only one whom Clare mentions explicitly in her writings, and hers was also the name taken by Clare's sister, Catherine, when she followed Clare in her choice of religious life.[41]

Basically, hagiography offered an even more negative view of women than did courtly culture. Woman, for the medieval church writer, was the gateway of the Devil and the cause of original sin.[42] However, in spite of this negative context, the cult of sanctity offered medieval women an alternative to subjection first to their fathers and then to their husbands. This was the alternative represented by choosing religion. We are not necessarily talking about a total renunciation; the option for chastity was only the final stage of the life of perfection. Before coming to such a choice, and side by side with it, there was ample room for a whole range of exercises of devotion and charity open to all women. Ortolana herself is an example of just how much freedom was available, even though a woman was married.[43]

These two frames of reference, that is, the world of knights and the court, and the world of the life of holiness, would then probably have defined the cultural limits for Clare and her companions, whether they were in Assisi or in exile in Perugia. Both these universal ideals would have exercised a profound influence on the way in which she saw life and conducted herself towards her neighbour. The first would have taught her the virtues of a 'noble' lady; the second would have opened her mind to the possibility of other choices.

In order to discern the ways in which these two cultural models specifically affected and influenced the actual life of Clare, it is very interesting to read the acts of the canonisation process and the *Life* of Thomas of Celano in the light of each other. Thomas of Celano and the process have a shared vision of the world and unite their ideals of nobility with those of sanctity, but Celano slides over a number of aspects which, with an international readership in mind, he judges to be of little interest. The canonisation process, however, sees things from a much more 'local' point of view and is particularly rich in details which we would not otherwise know about.

THE YOUTH OF CLARE – THREE GROUPS OF WITNESSES

The most interesting information about the first eighteen years of Clare's life comes from the canonisation process. In her writings, Clare herself tells us nothing about her life before she entered religion,[44] but the sisters and the other witnesses were explicitly questioned about this. What kind of things do we learn from them? We learn that Clare had been a saint from the first years of her life or even from the womb of her mother. This would be in accordance with the concept of sanctity as something the person possesses from birth.[45]

The replies of the sisters did not deflect the papal commissaries from starting with a group of witnesses who could tell about life within Clare's actual home. Sister Cecilia, daughter of Gualtieri Cacciaguerra da Spello and one of Clare's first companions, recalls the actual words of Clare's mother herself:

This witness declared that she had heard the mother of St Clare say how, when she was expecting this child and was standing before the Crucifix praying for help in the dangers of childbirth, she heard a voice which told her that she was to bring forth a great light which would greatly enlighten the world.[46]

There is also the evidence of Clare's second, and youngest, blood-sister, Beatrice, who followed her to San Damiano in 1229:

Under oath, she said that this witness was a sister by blood to the Lady Clare of blessed memory, and that from childhood, her life had been most angelic; she was a virgin and always remained so and she always performed the good deeds of holiness, so much so that her good repute spread among all those who knew her.[47]

However, the one who gives us the most detailed picture of life in Clare's home was Giovanni di Ventura di Assisi, the old servant. He testifies that:

This witness lived in the house of the Lady while she remained in her father's house as a child and as a maid, for he was a watchman for the household. The Lady Clare grew to about eighteen or so, and was of the most noble parentage in Assisi, both on her father's side and on her mother's. Her father was called Messer Favarone and her grandfather Messer Offreduccio de Bernardino. And that child had been so good, both in her life and in all she did, as if she had been in a monastery all the time.

Asked about her manner of life, he replied:

Although the household had been one of the largest in the city, and that great sums of money were spent in it, yet she, even though she was fed in a manner appropriate to a great house, still asked that the food she had been given to eat and which she had set aside and kept, be sent to the poor. Asked how he knew this, he said that he had lived in the house and that he saw these things and had also been told them and so firmly believed them.

While she was still living in her father's house, she wore rough cloth under her other clothes. He also said that she fasted, prayed and did other works of piety as he himself had seen, and he was of the opinion that right from the beginning she had been inspired by the Holy Spirit.[48]

These three witnesses, with their different lines of approach, give us a detailed picture of the life of the household of Offreduccio. In the first place, there is the old man of arms, so proud to belong to the court of one of the greatest families in the city, for, in a world divided into *maiores* and *minores*, simply to belong to a great family was, in itself, grounds for boasting. This is why he underlines the way in which, in Clare's home, they had eaten 'in a manner appropriate to a great house'. Here we see the shrewd assessment of a serving man who knew very well the difference between what happened outside his patron's house and what happened inside where food never lacked but was, rather, served in abundance.[49] It seems that Clare, too, was aware of what went on outside the house; she knew that outside the door there were poor people, that there were many folk who lived precariously, and she was concerned about how they would manage. Therefore she had food taken out to them. It was probably an analogous concern which urged her to choose a garment of coarse cloth to wear under her festive dress. This cloth was in fact unbleached wool which was used to make clothes for the servants and the poor. The servant who said this probably meant that Clare was a friendly girl who did not demand rich clothing; although she could have been dressed in silk or cotton she was, quite simply, content that she too should dress as the servants did.

Her sister Beatrice also starts her evidence with a judgement; from childhood Clare had been 'angelic', as can be seen from two virtues, namely that she was a virgin and that she practised the works of holiness. By this she probably means exercises of devotion as much as works of mercy. The most interesting point in Beatrice's evidence is her reference to the 'good repute' in which Clare was held in the city. It was a matter of major concern for women enclosed in the signorial household so to act that both they and their household were held in high esteem. Here we see one way in which these women's lives could be both closed off and yet very exposed to the world around them. Reputation, the voice of public opinion, was central to the life of a medieval city and it exercised a power far beyond the narrow boundaries of the signorial palace.[50]

Last of all we have the witness of Ortolana herself, as reported by Sister Cecilia. It conveys the whole essence of this woman who, her life at risk and confronting her first childbearing,[51] turns to the cross.[52] Here Ortolana reveals herself as a woman of the new religious piety, for she does not turn to some saint or other, but directly to the crucifix. Is it possible that this was one of the fruits of her pilgrimage to the Holy Land? That Ortolana heard a voice speaking directly to her was considered fairly normal. The rapport between the visible and the invisible worlds, between Heaven and earth, was seen by Ortolana and those who heard her as one of continual exchange, the one world concerned with in the other.[53] The voice said to her that the daughter whom she was carrying would be like a light which would illumine the whole world.[54] There is an extraordinary breadth of vision about this Assisian woman; the ambitions she conceived for her daughter were global ambitions. This typifies the contradiction of Ortolana; she was the mother of a family, bound by her duty to that family, and for most of her life she was enclosed within the narrow boundaries of the walls of her husband's house, and yet her hopes knew no bounds. When her daughter was born, the name she wanted her to have – 'Clare' – preserves the memory of this voice and of these unlimited hopes of Ortolana.

A second group of witnesses is made up of the wider family: Sisters Amata and Balvina, called in the canonisation process Clare's 'blood-relatives', were daughters of a cousin, Messer Martino da Coccorano.[55] Together with them must be read the first witness, Sister Pacifica de Guelfuccio, who had known Clare from her childhood since when she was in the world, she had been her neighbour and a distant relative, also between her own house and that of the virgin Clare there was nothing but the piazza and this witness often talked with her.[56]

Bona, Pacifica's sister and also an intimate childhood friend of Clare, was the seventeenth witness. Then there were the two sisters who knew Clare from the time of exile in Perugia. These were Sister Benvenuta of Perugia and Sister Filippa di Leonardo de Gliserio who was a member of one of the noblest Assisian families and among the first who were obliged to flee.[57] However, of all these witnesses, it was the Lady Bona di Guelfuccio who best described Clare's early life. Bona had been a friend from childhood, living next door (for she, too, had a house in the piazza San Rufino):

She said that at the time of [Clare's] entry into religious life, she was a discreet young girl of about eighteen who always stayed in the house, and that she kept herself hidden, not wanting to be seen, and she so lived that she was not seen by those who passed by the house. Also she was very kind and was careful about the other good works.[58]

In these witnesses we can clearly see how the courtly culture of knighthood not only offered a literary model but how, at the same time, it also used the model to impose definite patterns of behaviour to be observed by the young women who heard these imaginary tales. Like a true feudal lady, Clare always had to live hidden away from the gaze of strangers, enclosed within the signorial palace.[59] It is clear from the account given by her friend Bona that Clare never showed herself at the window, but neither would any other young girls of her age and class have done so, for they never allowed themselves to 'be seen by those who passed by in the road'. This does not mean that Clare would have had no contact with the world outside; quite the contrary. From this group of witnesses, too, we find the importance of public reputation coming to the fore once again, as for instance in the evidence of her niece Amata:[60]

Before she chose religion, she was considered to be holy by all who knew her. This was because of the great grace and the virtues which God had given her, and this was the reputation which she had in public.[61]

Sister Filippa says the same thing:

Before St Clare had entered religious life, she was held to be a saint by all who knew her. This was because of the great integrity of her life and her many virtues and graces, all of which the Lord God had placed in her.[62]

'Reputation' is the word the sisters use for 'the fame of her holiness', thus revealing a certain hagiographical awareness, because the reputation for holiness was in fact, one of the conditions required by the religious authorities for the creation and recognition of a *cultus*.[63] Clare is presented here as the saint of the whole city since everyone recognised the signs and virtues of holiness in her, in this case very precociously if from her earliest childhood she was held to be a saint. The inference is that the bond between this city and this woman was one of long standing. It is clear from their answers that Sister Balvina and Sister Filippa were well aware of the expectations of those conducting the process, that they wanted to hear that Clare had been a saint from her birth. The element of originality in the sisters' testimonies lies in the connection they make between this 'precocious holiness' and Clare's public reputation, that is, between the saint and her city.

The third group of witnesses comprises two noblemen from Assisi. Their evidence is grouped separately because they look at things from the point of view of those who had come to know Clare when she was still in her father's house, even though they always saw her, so to speak, from the outside, that is from outside the signorial household.

Messer Ranieri de Bernardo of Assisi testifies that he

knew the Lady Clare when she was a young girl in her father's house, [he said] she was a virgin and, from the very beginning of her life, had begun to pay attention to deeds of holiness as if she had been made holy from her mother's womb. Because she had a beautiful face, a husband was considered for her. Many of her relatives begged her to accept them as a husband but she never wanted to consent. Indeed, the witness himself had many times asked her to be willing to agree to this, and she did not even want to hear him; what is more, she preached to him about despising the world.

Asked how he knew these things, he replied; because his wife was a relative of the Lady Clare and because the witness conversed confidentially with her in her house and saw her good deeds.[64]

Pietro de Damiano's evidence, too, centred around Clare's refusal of marriage:

He and his father lived near St Clare's house and that of her father and other members of her family. He knew Lady Clare when she was in the world and knew her father, Lord Favarone, who was noble, great and powerful in the city – he and others of his household.

Lady Clare was noble, of a noble family, and of an upright manner of life. There were seven knights in her household, all of whom were noble and powerful. Asked how he knew these things, he replied that he had seen her because he was her neighbour. At that time the Lady Clare was only a young girl and she lived a very spiritual life, as was believed. He saw her father, mother and relatives who all wanted her to be married magnificently to someone great and powerful in accordance with her nobility, but the young girl, at that time about seventeen or so, could not be convinced by any means because she wanted to remain in her virginity and to live in poverty, as she demonstrated since she sold all her inheritance and gave it to the poor. She was considered by all to have a good manner of life.

Asked how he knew this, he replied: because he was her neighbour and knew that no one could ever convince her to bend her spirit to worldly things.[65]

It was not a case of bringing two men into the canonisation process in order to underline the issue of marriage. These two witnesses had come from the same social background as Clare, and to them the natural thing for a young girl would have been marriage with someone else of good family. Incidentally, it is worth noting that these two witnesses were the only ones to record in the process that Clare was physically beautiful as well. In their view, all her good breeding, her courtesy, even her loveliness could have only one function: to enable the House of Favarone to make a marriage alliance with some other family every bit as powerful.

THOMAS OF CELANO ELABORATES

Such information on Clare's childhood as was afforded by the canonisation process was gathered together and reworked by

Thomas of Celano. The first paragraph of the official biography centres around the figure of Ortolana. Thomas of Celano tells us nothing about Clare's father except his name but gives us detailed particulars about her mother. Why this choice? Thomas' work was primarily focussed on women and his plan was to give them models to imitate. In this setting, his decision to describe Clare's mother rather than her father is perfectly logical.[66]

His portrait of Ortolana is a kind of miniature life of a saint, written with the intention of furnishing a model for women who were not able to follow Clare in her fullness of choice because they were married and living 'in the world':

[Ortolana], although she was bound by the bond of marriage and was burdened by the cares of the family, none the less devoted herself as much as possible to divine worship and applied herself to works of piety. She therefore devoutly travelled with pilgrims beyond the seas and after surveying these places which the God-man had consecrated with his sacred footprints, she afterwards returned home filled with joy. She set out again to pray to St Michael the Archangel and visited with even more devotion the basilicas of the Apostles. What else? A tree is known by its fruits and the fruit is recommended by its tree. The richness of the divine generosity preceded in the root so that an abundance of holiness would follow in the branch.[67]

All Thomas of Celano's theology of women is concentrated in that 'although' at the beginning. Ortolana lived a holy life *although* she was married and had to think about the needs of the household. It is as if he had said that it was normally impossible for a woman to live a full Christian life. The needs of the family made demands on her which allowed no room for the life of faith, and anyway the high road to salvation lay through monastic life and included the choice of chastity. This was traditional thinking about women. On the other hand, Thomas did belong to a new generation, he was also a Franciscan and not a monk, and he had come into contact with all the new ideas fermenting among the laity. In addition to this, he had lived for a good many years in Germany where, even then, a number of women from good families were choosing to live their lives of faith in a new way and not in traditional monastic structures. Through this new form and manner of life they gave birth to what has been called 'the women's religious movement of the thirteenth century'.[68] These women, who were beginning to be known as 'Beguines', were often married women or widows, and they continued to live in contact with 'the world'. There can be no doubt that they were in Thomas' mind when he drew this portrait of Ortolana 'the woman of faith although she was married'.[69]

However, while speaking of Ortolana, Thomas meant above all to begin speaking about Clare, and in this passage he begins to reveal her idea of holiness. Thomas always seems to be poised between what we might call the 'high medieval' idea of holiness and another idea, in those days a more 'modern' one. The first is the notion of holiness as *virtus*, strength, as if holiness were a divine force mysteriously present in someone. The second is the notion of a more interiorised holiness in which religious feeling was manifested in external signs and the Gospel choice made evident by miracles.[70] In this instance, it is the first idea which predominates: the holiness of Clare was not only hers right from her mother's womb but was even prepared for by the holiness of Ortolana herself, so that holiness seemed like a kind of sap, rising from the root and spreading through the trunk and all the branches.[71] Such a holiness is transmitted in the blood. With this approach, it is no chance that so much weight was given to lineage, for this holiness was tightly bound in with nobility.

The link between holiness and nobility of blood is a constant in this kind of hagiography and had been put forward in Clare's case, too, in the *First Life* of Thomas of Celano, where she was described as noble by birth and more noble by virtue. This literary model sprang from the conviction that nobility of birth was a kind of privileged factor in holiness. This is why all the women canonised during the thirteenth century were of noble birth, if not actually royal. Clare's nobility was certainly not royal. Hers was a small family of knights whose wealth was only noteworthy when compared with those around them. If we read between the lines we see that at a certain point her biographer makes this clear: 'Her home was rich and they had abundant means in relation to the general condition of the country.'[72]

The scheme which Celano followed rested firmly on this base of nobility of blood and had to do so if he were to present Clare as a model of sanctity in a way which could be exported to every European country. This is why he continually under-lines that Clare 'took her origin from a family already suf-ficiently illustrious' and that 'her father was a knight, and on both sides of her family all her relatives belonged to the knightly class.'[73]

Thomas of Celano, however, also had another, more interior, ideal of holiness. Personal virtue was of fundamental import-ance to him, and it is not by chance that the *Life* starts with the words: 'The wonderful woman, Clare, [shining] by name and by grace.'[74] Within this perspective, even Clare's childhood was seen as a model of virtue to be offered as an example. Ever since she was a baby and once she had 'received the first rudiments of the faith from her mother's lips', Clare had been known for three particular virtues: compassion, the practice of prayer, and virginity. With regard to compassion, Thomas refers to an episode told by at least four of the witnesses at the canonisation process[75] in which Clare set aside some of her own food to send to the poor in the city. Clare probably repeated this gesture more than once, and on one of these occasions she may perhaps have sent food to Francis and his companions while they were working, like the poor, on the reconstruction of St Mary of the Portiuncola (although the *Life* is silent on this detail).[76]

The way in which Thomas develops his material is very interesting. He searches for biblical texts which could be adapted for his purpose, and he finds one in a passage from Job and another in the last chapter of the Book of Proverbs.[77] This last quotation (Prov. 31:10–31) is particularly indicative: it is a passage which describes the qualities of the ideal woman as if she were the wisdom of Israel, as a model offered by the Church to all medieval women. The verse quoted (v. 20) deals with alms-giving: she opened her hand, it says, to the needy and stretched out her hand to the poor. This whole chapter of the *Life* seems to have that passage of Proverbs in mind which ends with words more complimentary to women than any others in the Bible:

> She holds out her hand to the poor,
> she opens her arms to the needy . . .
>
> Charm is deceitful and beauty empty;
> the woman who is wise is the one to praise.
>
> Give her a share in what her hands have worked for,
> and let her works tell her praises at the city gates.[78]

Thomas of Celano does not content himself with setting the evidence of the process in a biblical context, he also gives a personal reading of the episodes under discussion. For example, he says:

In order that her sacrifice would be more pleasing to God, she would deprive her own body of delicate foods and, sending them secretly through intermediaries, she would nourish the bodies of the poor.[79]

In this way, the inner meaning of what happened is substantially altered. We are no longer talking about a simple gesture of caring for the poor who lived in such numbers and such conditions of want, often right outside the doors of Clare's house. We are now talking about an exercise of penance, a sacrifice which the child Clare imposed on herself in order to please God. What a sad idea of Clare emerges from these words! And what a sad idea of God – a God who is appeased by the sacrifices of a child![80] To understand something of this concept of Thomas of Celano, we must remember that we are dealing here with an idea which is, in some ways, quite modern. The original concept of sacrifice, as is well known, is that of offering a victim on an altar.[81] It is only in the New Testament, and above all in the Letter to the Hebrews, that the word begins to be used about a person. In Hebrews, it speaks of Christ who gave his life 'as a sacrifice' to God.[82] It is emphasised over and over again in Scripture that there is now no need for any sacrifice because Christ has offered himself once and for all. He alone is 'the perfect sacrifice, pleasing to God'. However, during the

Middle Ages, and especially after the Crusades which awoke a keener Christological awareness in people, we find the idea growing that we can associate ourselves with the sufferings, passion and sacrifice of Christ.[83] When Thomas speaks of Clare as a 'sacrifice more pleasing to God', he has all these things in mind. He is not speaking about a bad God who is pleased when people suffer, but of a God who became human and who suffered himself because of the sins of everyone. He is also speaking of those few, that is the saints, who unite themselves with him and who freely deprive themselves so as to imitate Christ and to share his sufferings.

The difference between the theology of Thomas and that of the witnesses at the process can also be seen in the matter of virginity. The sisters underline the virginity of Clare, as much before as after her entry into the monastery of San Damiano, and Thomas takes up the theme, adding: 'Under her costly and soft clothes she wore a hair shirt, blossoming externally to the world, inwardly putting on Christ.'[84] Here Thomas is improvising somewhat. At the canonisation process, the old serving man of Clare's household had stated that she wore a rough garment, that is one of undyed wool, under her other clothes[85] but this was only a statement about her moderation and her lack of affectation in her clothing. In the words of her biographer, however, this is transformed into an act of corporal punishment. Even her hair shirt was nothing more than a piece of rough cloth such as pigskin or something similar. It may be that Clare had indeed chosen such penances many years later when she lived 'in religion', but certainly her biographer steps beyond the evidence if he wants to anticipate this form of self-punishment right from her earliest youth. It is quite likely that what we see here reflected in Thomas of Celano is that widespread ambivalence about the body so characteristic of the profoundly dualistic medieval society. Or it could have been that he, who was usually so measured, abandoned himself for once to the demands of a hagiography which considered this kind of heroic activity to be the norm.

The portrait which Thomas of Celano paints of the child Clare is that of a heroine of penitence and sacrifice who right from the first years of her life lived according to the virtues and way of life which were to be hers at San Damiano.[86] The finishing touch is given to this portrait by the idea that Clare was in some way reserved or set apart. She is presented as a 'chest of many perfumes' which 'even though closed reveals its contents by its fragrance'.[87] Here we no longer have the little girl who stayed within her house taking care lest the passers-by see her at the windows; we have the nun in embryo who by living in seclusion lent credence to the fame of her virtues.

The image of Clare, the young girl, which emerges from behind that drawn by her biographer or by the evidence of the canonisation process, comes into focus with a few broad out-lines. Clare was born at the end of the twelfth century into a city torn by social strife. Her own family was an aristocratic one and a member of the *maiores* of the city. Clare was the first-born of the younger branch of this family, she was beautiful and had been educated with a view to a good marriage. This education had two major points of reference, the courtly culture and the culture of sainthood. Clare was not a nun in miniature; she was simply a young girl who had been brought up according to the principles of an aristocratic education, knowing both the fatigues and the problems of war and exile. The only con-clusions we can draw about the childhood of Clare, in reference to her future holiness, come from the figure of her mother, Ortolana. In all the sources Ortolana emerges as a woman who was characteristic of the religious renewal taking place at the end of the twelfth century and the start of the thirteenth.

TWO

The Search for an Alternative

We have already seen that Pope Innocent IV wanted to proceed as quickly as possible to the canonisation of Clare and that he wrote to this effect to Bartolomeo, the archbishop of Spoleto, inviting him to institute a true and proper process, to interrogate the witnesses about the *life, conversion, conversation and miracles* of the lady of Assisi.[1] The first term, *life* meant that period which Clare had spent living in her father's house, in other words her youth. The second term, *conversion*, meant her passage from life 'in the world' to life 'in religion'. *Conversation* covered the period she spent at San Damiano and the last item *miracles*, covered the proofs of holiness both before and after her death. In this way the sanctity of Clare was to be studied in four distinct sections, each with its own ideal point of reference.

THE CONVERSION OF CLARE

Of these four aspects of Clare's life, the second is certainly the most dramatic. Her conversion means the actual moment when she moved from life in her father's house to a new life which was to be lived in a style and by a rule as yet untried. Clare was about eighteen when she made this life-changing choice. In what spirit did she set out on this road? With what intentions? From the sources, we can reconstruct the development of events fairly accurately and some of the evidence at her canonisation process is very relevant here, particularly that given by her sister Beatrice and by her friend Bona.[2] The official biography devotes three whole chapters to telling the story of her conversion, chapters entitled: 'Meeting and friendship with the blessed Francis'; 'How, through the work of the blessed Francis, she changed her life and passed from this world to the religious life'; and 'How she firmly resisted the violence of her family'.[3] Before we proceed to trace the unfolding of Clare's conversion, however, it would be good to reflect on the attitudes and intentions she would have had as she approached her decision.

In her writings, Clare often speaks about conversion. The actual word is used six times; three in reference to the conversion of Francis and three to her own conversion. Let us look first at those dealing with Francis. Francis himself, in fact, does not use this word in his writings, not even in his Testament when he talks about his passage from life in the world or about his choice of faith. He prefers the expression 'I began to do penance':

The Lord granted me, Brother Francis, to begin to do penance in this way: while I was in sin, it seemed very bitter to me to see lepers. And the Lord Himself led me among them and I had mercy upon them. And when I left them that which seemed bitter to me was changed into sweetness of soul and body; and afterward I lingered a little and left the world.[4]

All the same – whether he uses the word itself or not – there can be no doubt that in Francis' personal story, conversion means the precise moment of turning away from his former life.[5] Probably the Poverello did not want to use the word 'conversion' because with the passage of centuries it had lost some of its primitive evangelical meaning of a changed manner of life and instead it had acquired the more strictly juridical meaning implying a 'change in status' or 'entry into a religious Order'.[6] At the moment when Francis left the world he did not belong to any Order nor enter any monastery. All he wanted was to live according to the Gospel. From a juridical point of view, he became a 'penitent', which meant a lay person who subjected himself to particular disciplines in order to gain forgiveness for his own sins.[7] The first name given to Francis' companions was: the penitent men of Assisi.[8] In the light of this we can see that when Francis says in his Testament, 'I began to do penance', he was using this phrase in a very precise way. It is an especially apt phrase for the radical, evangelical character of his choice.

Clare was much struck by Francis' decision. The dramatic thoroughness of the saint's conversion impressed her greatly and it always remained her model for her own choice of life. This is why Clare insisted on recording his conversion in her own writings. We must not forget that Clare was only about twelve or thirteen when Francis concluded his journey of conversion by stripping himself of everything in front of the bishop of Assisi. This episode, in which he returned his clothes to his father, took place in the piazza not far from Clare's home and it would certainly not have passed without comment in that household.[9]

Clare saw conversion as a break which signified the beginning of a completely different life. This is why, in her own writings, her conversion serves as the moment of beginning, as if she had been newly born, and she dates the most important events from this point of reference: 'A little after his conversion . . . I promised him obedience'.[10] Francis' conversion had taken place in the winter of 1206 and another five or six years were to pass before Clare made her decision to break with her family and her former way of life so as to live according to the Gospel. It is true that in her writings she says, 'after a short time'; perhaps those years passed quickly for her as she waited to be able to make the same choice as Francis. Certainly they were years which did not seem to amount to much in Clare's eyes when, in her old age, she wrote her Testament and could look back on decades of fidelity to her choice.

Having looked at the intentions and feelings with which Clare probably approached her conversion, it becomes possible to follow her through the four steps which the sources detail for us. These are: her meeting and talks with Francis; the breach and conflict with her family; her consecration at the Portiuncola where she received the tonsure from Francis, and finally her choice to live the life of poverty at San Damiano.

HER MEETING WITH FRANCIS

More than five years lie between Francis' conversion and that of Clare. During this time they were in close contact with each other. Which of them took the initiative for such meetings? The sources disagree,[11] and at the canonisation process the witnesses themselves were uncertain about this. Clare's sister Beatrice, who is probably the most important witness about her sister's journey of conversion, is quite clear that it was Francis who took the initiative:

After St Francis heard the fame of her holiness, he went many times to preach to her, so that the virgin Clare acquiesced to his preaching, renounced the world and all earthly things, and went to serve God as soon as she was able.[12]

However, the evidence of Bona di Guelfuccio, who had been Clare's friend since childhood and who had had no small part to play in the first meetings between Francis and Clare, always gave Clare the honour of initiating the contact:

Lady Clare was always considered by everyone a most pure virgin and had such fervour of spirit she could serve God and please him. Because of this, the witness many times accompanied her to speak to St Francis. She went secretly so as not to be seen by her parents.[13]

In this case, the initiative for the meetings would have sprung from Clare's own spirit of religious quest. This impression is strengthened by another episode recounted by the same Bona shortly afterwards:

Lady Clare, while she was still in the world, also gave the witness a certain amount of money as a votive offering and directed her to carry it to those who were working on St Mary of the Portiuncula so that they could sustain the flesh.[14]

Here we see an example of one of Clare's many works in favour of those poorer than herself, in this case dating right back to the time when she was still in her father's house. This time, as it happened, the poor in question were 'those who were working on St Mary of the Portiuncula' which in all probability meant Francis and his companions.[15] Their poverty, then, had impressed the young noblewoman. Like her mother, she would have been accustomed to practising works of mercy, but, unlike her mother, Clare wanted to overcome the barriers themselves that separated her from the poor; she did not want simply to confine herself to giving alms to the poor but wanted to share their life with them as well.

This episode can probably be dated 1210 or 1212; Clare was now no longer a child but a young woman who knew what she was doing. A young woman of Assisi would certainly have attained her majority by the age of sixteen[16] and, among her other qualities, Clare had already shown a strong spirit of initiative. That great spirit of fervour to serve God and please him, of which Bona had spoken during the canonisation process, was expressing itself in her intense involvement in works of mercy. She went out freely in search of the poor, and the fame of her holiness had already spread among her fellow-citizens.[17]

Ortolana too was dedicated to works of mercy; she too had let herself be touched by the needs of the poor of Assisi. The difference between her choice and Clare's is obviously that for Clare it was not enough to help from afar; she chose to make the life of the poor her own life.[18] Before she could implement this choice, Clare had to overcome a number of barriers separating her from the poor and even, indeed, from Francis and his companions. These were the barriers of her social position, hindering her from contact with those on a different social level; barriers of a social convention which would never look kindly on any woman who took such an initiative; and the barriers which surrounded her simply because she was a woman and thus someone to whom the intinerant and uncertain life led by Francis and his companions was absolutely forbidden.

That a young girl, alone, could overcome all these obstacles and make such a choice seemed utterly impossible. In all probability, the family would instantly have laid the responsibility for such a scandal at Francis' door and have attributed all the initiative to him. The evidence given at the canonisation process by Beatrice, Clare's sister, may have attributed a rather larger role to Francis in this than he took in reality. Perhaps she was moved by family loyalties, for her evidence is usually extremely helpful in reconstructing the chain of events.

In her own writings, for example in her Testament, Clare herself had to speak about the beginnings of her religious life in order to throw into relief the role which Francis took as founder of her community and father of her choice in life. She could say nothing less than:

After the most high, heavenly Father saw fit in his mercy and grace to enlighten my heart to do penance according to the example and teaching of our most blessed Father Francis, shortly after his own conversion, I, together with the few sisters whom the Lord had given me soon after my conversion, freely promised him obedience, since the Lord had given us the Light of his grace through his holy life and teaching.[19]

Clare, then, who had always spoken of herself as the 'little plant of the blessed Father Francis' still insisted, so many years later, that he had been the one to whom she had freely promised obedience. Nobody had forced her to, least of all Francis.

The *Life*, too, underlines the fact of Clare's role:

hearing of the then celebrated name of Francis who like a new man was renewing with new virtues the way of perfection forgotten by the world, she immediately desired to see and hear him.[20]

Thomas of Celano, then, also considered that the initiative for the meeting between the two saints of Assisi came from Clare, immediately after she had learnt about Francis' way of life. Even if the *Life of St Clare* says no more about Francis the poor man than that while he and his companions worked at the Portiuncula they had nothing to eat, yet it says much about a Francis who was 'then celebrated', whose holiness was no longer laughed at but recognised and valued by all. Celano was anxious to specify that Clare was 'moved by the Father of the spirits whose initiative each one had already accepted'.[21] Each one here means both Francis and Clare. It seems that while Brother Thomas was anxious to protect the independence of his saint, he was also concerned that both Francis and Clare should be, so to speak, equal and level:

No less did he desire to see and speak with her, impressed by the widespread fame of so gracious a young lady, so that in some ways he who was totally longing for spoil and who had come to depopulate the kingdom of the world would also be able to wrest *this* noble spoil from the evil world and win her for his Lord.[22]

Thomas was very interested in the story of how that friendship had begun which was so to bind together the lives of Francis and Clare and he took up a rather equivocal position because he was aware of his readership, and particularly of the sisters. In the end he even attributed his own concern to Francis himself:

He visited her and she more frequently him, moderating the times of their visits so that this divine pursuit could not be perceived by anyone nor objected to by gossip. For, with only one close companion accompanying her, the young girl, leaving her paternal home, frequented the clandestine meetings with the man of God, whose words seemed to her to be on fire and whose deeds were seen to be beyond the human.[23]

Obviously a friendship between the Poverello and the eldest daughter of one of the main families in the city could have given rise to comments which would have been far from kindly, especially in Assisi where public reputation was so important. Francis, on any number of occasions, had shown that he himself cared nothing for either the risk or the reality of a negative judgement by the crowd, but it is more than likely that he was worried by Clare's request. A woman wanting to share his way of life was certainly no small problem: how could she share the poverty and mendicancy of the Poverello and his first companions? About ten years later when he was putting his Rule into writing, Francis warns his brethren not to receive women into the fraternity:

Absolutely no woman should be received to obedience by any brothers, but once she has been given spiritual advice, let her perform a penance where she will.[24]

In Francis' view, if women were to join the fraternity, this would risk completely changing its character, quite apart from creating considerable problems:

All of us must keep close watch over ourselves and keep all parts of our body pure, since the Lord says: Anyone who looks lustfully at a woman has already committed adultery with her in his heart, and the Apostle says: Do you not know that your members are the temple of the Holy Spirit? Therefore, whoever violates God's temple, God will destroy him.[25]

Presumably these injunctions arose from experience gained during the first years of the Franciscan community, but they also seem to have been a component of Franciscan spirituality right from the start. The responsibilities of his choice actually imposed upon Francis an attitude towards chastity which was every bit as radical as his attitudes to poverty and obedience.

Clare was probably more concerned about public comment than Francis was. As Bona di Guelfuccio[26] relates, she went to Francis 'secretly so as not to be seen by her parents'. However, her concern was not, as Thomas of Celano believed, to protect her reputation. It was something far more practical: to avoid the opposition of her family, which could have stopped her from realising her plans.

CONFLICT WITH HER FAMILY

The opposition of Clare's relatives was far the greatest obstacle placed in the way of her choice. The family had had quite other plans for their eldest child; Clare was to have been married to someone worthy of her rank[27] and it was this life already mapped out for her which formed the biggest barrier that Clare had to overcome before she could share the life of Francis and his companions. It was because she was forced into real conflict with the family that her choice had such a dramatic quality. Even Thomas of Celano in his biography tells about the family's matrimonial plans for Clare, but he chooses to do so after he has given his account of her flight from her father's house. As a result, her flight loses that strong note of conflict and its expression of a radical change in the direction of her life.[28]

Leaving the house, the city, her relatives, and leaving alone,[29] Clare came to St Mary of the Portiuncula. The brethren were waiting for her with lighted torches to show the way and together they all went into the church. Here, at the hands of the brothers, Clare's hair was cut off and she left behind her the adornments of this world.[30]

In the canonisation process there is only a slight hint of all this. Even Bona di Guelfuccio, who had certainly accompanied Clare on her visits to Francis, can say no more in evidence than:

St Francis cut off her hair in the church of St Mary of the Portiuncula, as she had heard, because she, the witness, was not present since she had already gone to Rome to observe Lent.[31]

In this case Thomas of Celano is the more reliable witness and he uses sources other than the canonisation process, inserting them into a liturgical context:

The Solemnity of the Day of the Palms was at hand when the young girl went with fervent heart to the man of God, asking him about her conversion and how it should be carried out.[32]

The information that the day of her flight was Palm Sunday[33] is extremely interesting, even though we are not told this any-where other than in the *Life*. Palm Sunday introduces Holy Week and is usually called 'the first Sunday of the Passion'. In the West, before the custom of infant baptism was established, the catechumens were baptised on Palm Sunday. The liturgy of this day begins with Jesus' entry into Jerusalem and ends with a reading of the Passion.[34]

Celano's whole account seems to recall the structure of the liturgy. Clare, at Francis' command, clothed herself 'richly and elegantly' and went, with the whole city, to celebrate the joy of the Lord's entry into Jerusalem, but then during the night, she was to abandon this joy by stripping herself of her rich clothes and following the Lord, just as she had seen him change the joy of entering the city into the sorrow of the Way of the Cross.[35]

The extreme precision of the details ('the brothers received the virgin Clare with lighted torches')[36] leads us to believe that the episode was not just a literary embellishment on the part of her biographer but that this is an exact account of how Clare fled from her father's house. Then again, Thomas of Celano himself says in the dedicatory letter at the beginning of the *Life* that he had listened to other eyewitnesses, among whom were Francis' brethren. It is quite possible that one of these early friars had given Thomas the details of Clare's flight, even though his evidence had not formed part of the canonisation process. There can be no doubt that it was as the *Life* tells us – that Francis himself prepared this 'liturgical flight'. It was he, with his own hands, who cut off Clare's hair and, by this act, consecrated her to the Lord.[37] That we are dealing with a liturgical act is beyond doubt; a slight perplexity does arise because the *Life* fails to use the word 'tonsure' which was the technical term for the cutting of hair during the consecration of virgins. On the other hand, this is the exact word used in the bull of canonisation: *Clara claris praeclara: Et ipso beato Francisco, sacra ibi recepta tonsura* ('she received the holy tonsure from blessed Francis himself').[38]

Perhaps because he was so aware that the circumstance was extremely unusual, Thomas of Celano avoided stressing that it was Francis who gave her the tonsure on that Palm Sunday night. Clare was not an ordinary young girl leaving her parents to enter monastic life; rather she was a young woman who had run away from home, going forth to meet contempt and disapproval from everyone. Nor was Francis a bishop – to whom the consecration of virgins was normally reserved. In fact, he was not even a priest but only a layman, and yet he took upon himself the right to consecrate Clare to the Lord.[39]

In the light of the customs of the time, it is quite obvious that Clare's gesture and Francis' decision in her regard were both extraordinary.[40] In order to underline this, Francis himself wanted to give a liturgical dimension to her flight. One could even say that he 'invented' a new liturgy so that he might receive Clare worthily in the name of the Lord. It was a liturgy encompassing the whole span of that day and one which well expressed the religious imagination of the holy architect of the Greccio 'liturgy of the crib'.[41] Over and above this, however, the uniqueness of the event is borne out in the same *Life* when it goes on to tell of the reaction of Clare's family when they learnt about her flight. They, *conglobati in unum*, 'banding together as one', ran to the monastery where Clare had taken refuge and by alternate threats and promises tried to make her give up such a 'worthless deed' (*huiusmodi vilitas*) which had no precedent in the area.[42] Clare's choice was a scandal. Yet, many young girls, from the nobility as she was, had left the world to retire into a Benedictine monastery just like the one where Clare's family had gone to find her. So what was the element of scandal in Clare's choice? What was the *vilitas*, the worthlessness of her act, which made it so unbecoming to her class and never before seen in the district?

The bull of canonisation says that 'for the love of Christ, Clare turned all her goods into alms and distributed them among the poor'.[43] The canonisation process adds some more details when Sister Cristiana di Bernardo da Suppo says:

In selling her inheritance, Lady Clare's relatives wanted her to give them a better price. She did not want to sell it to them, but sold it to others so the poor would not be defrauded. All she received from the sale of the inheritance, she distributed to the poor. Asked how she knew this, she replied: because she saw and heard it.[44]

All the *vilitas* of Clare was in this gesture, that she sold her inheritance and gave the proceeds to the poor. There can be no doubt that this act was a definite breach with the family. Clare herself preferred to sell her inheritance for less rather than to rob her gesture of its quality of challenge. She was making a statement about a change in the conditions of her life, affirming that her own inheritance belonged to the poor. To act out the opposite, to return her inheritance to her family, would have been to deny the poor their rights.

IN THE MONASTERY OF SAN PAOLO DELLE ABBADESSE

After Clare had been consecrated to the Lord in the little church of St Mary of the Portiuncula, she was conducted by some of Francis' companions to the monastery of San Paolo delle Abbadesse. This was one of the most important and richest monasteries in the area. Clare presented herself there as a poor woman; she had no dowry such as young aristocratic ladies who chose (more or less willingly) to enter monastic life were accustomed to bring.[45]

Clare had sold her goods, she had distributed the proceeds to the poor, and only then had she presented herself at the monastery. This sequence of events is testified to quite clearly by her sister Beatrice:

She sold her entire inheritance and part of that of the witness and gave it to the poor. Then St Francis gave her the tonsure before the altar of the Virgin in the church of the Virgin Mary called the Portiuncula, and then sent her to the church of San Paolo delle Abbadesse.[46]

The value of this first-hand evidence lies in Beatrice's own clarity about what had happened to the inheritance. Clare had sold her inheritance but had not then divided it up, carefully and exactly; in fact, in order to have more to give to the poor, she had also sold part of her sister's inheritance. What was the content of this inheritance? We can be sure it consisted of the dowry which the family had set aside for the marriages of Clare and Beatrice. Within the aristocratic families of central Italy during the twelfth and thirteenth centuries, there had been a definite transition away from the system of a marriage portion, by which, at the moment of marriage, the husband gave the wife a notable part of his patrimony. Instead of this, the dowry system was becoming the custom, whereby that part of the paternal inheritance due to the daughter was given to her in advance. The object of this was to enhance her chances of making an advantageous marriage, with all the consequences for the family which would accrue from that. This transition from a marriage portion to a dowry parallels another development for women at that time, in which the dominant control of the husband was exchanged for a system in which the father's control predominated. As a result, the role played by the wife with regard to her sons shifted correspondingly and began to decline in importance.[47]

Thus it is highly likely that Clare, in accordance with the custom of the time, would have received her dowry before she fled from her father's house. Not only this, but the fact that Beatrice also had access to her dowry leads one to think that it had been given at a very young age, for at the time of Clare's flight Beatrice was very young indeed. Clare's 'crime' was that she refused to use her dowry to procure a good marriage, although this would simultaneously have guaranteed her security for life and reinforced the social position of the family. Instead of this, she alienated it and distributed the proceeds to the poor.[48]

Once again Thomas of Celano chooses to reverse the order of events. He first speaks about Clare's choice of life, about her consecration at the Portiuncula and her arrival at San Paolo delle Abbadesse, and only then, when she had already realised her ideal, does he come back to the theme of poverty. This is the point at which he tells how she sold her inheritance and gave the proceeds to the poor. Why did he decide to do this? Almost certainly because of the internal organisation of his text, since he places this whole account in his chapter on the poverty of Clare.[49] Yet when he makes poverty nothing more than one of the other virtues, he betrays his own ideas as well, even if he does make it the most important virtue. Thomas was, after all, a Franciscan himself. For Clare, poverty was a condition of life; it was the indispensable precondition for realising her religious ideal. In this, Clare is perfectly in line with the ideal proposed by Francis[50] and which he felt it necessary to record in his Testament when he said:

Those who came to receive life gave to the poor everything which they were capable of possessing and they were content with one tunic, patched inside and out, with a cord and short trousers. And we had no desire for anything more.[51]

So Clare was the complete Franciscan when, having chosen to sell her inheritance and given the money to the poor, she presented herself at the doors of San Paolo delle Abbadesse as a poor woman seeking to live according to the Gospel.

Her situation at San Paolo delle Abbadesse cannot have been easy. When her family got to know about it, they did everything they could think of to make her change her mind, a sign that the condition of Clare was wretched indeed. The word *vilitas*, which the *Life* uses here, not only referred to what she had done but also to the condition in which she was living. Not content with giving her goods to the poor, she had become one of the poor herself, assuming the condition of a servant and renouncing the status of her noble birth.[52]

San Paolo delle Abbadesse was a great monastery with lands and sources of income spread throughout the region. Life there was regulated so as to serve a community of nuns, all of them members of the nobility who had dedicated themselves to prayer. Under them, they would have had men and women servants, wearing a different habit, doing different work and of a different social level. These servants were responsible for the material affairs of the community. They would have been bound to the monastery by various kinds of bonds, some as personal servants, some as lay sisters or brothers and others as tenants.[53]

When Clare knocked at the doors of this monastery she was not seeking to be received as the nun which her social status would have permitted, but as the servant which her new social condition demanded. She no longer had any dowry to give the monastery as was the custom, and so she presented herself to them as a poor woman in order to live there as one of the servants.[54]

It is most likely that Clare wanted to follow Francis' example at this, the very first, moment of her new life outside the family. He too had had to confront the hostility of his family, and it could be that the first news Clare ever had of him was when the town crier publicly announced that Francis had been summoned to judgement before the bishop for the offence of abandoning his father's house and squandering the family property. Immediately after the famous episode of disappropriation before Bishop Guido, Francis had left Assisi and 'at length coming to a certain cloister of monks he spent several days there as a scullion'.[55]

In this monastery, near Gubbio, Francis had assumed that condition of a servant or lay brother which he had already experienced when staying with the priest at San Damiano; in this type of source, 'servant' and 'lay brother' mean much the same thing. It is highly likely that Clare would have followed Francis' example and, therefore, that her position at the monastery of San Paolo delle Abbadesse would have been that of a servant. This would have been the 'crime' which her family wanted her to renounce.

The monastery of San Paolo was under the protection of the bishop of Assisi and, more importantly, it had been granted numerous privileges, among which were very wide-ranging rights of asylum. These rights had been recognised by Innocent III in 1201 and would have been able to protect Clare from her family's eventual reaction. In spite of this, however, the conflict did take place and was particularly violent. Her sister Beatrice takes up the story:

When her parents wanted to drag her out, Lady Clare grabbed the altar cloths and uncovered her head, showing them that she was tonsured. In no way did she acquiesce, neither letting them take her from that place nor remaining with them.[56]

The same story was told during the process by Messer Ranieri de Bernardo and the watchman, Giovanni di Ventura, who said he knew this because it was public knowledge.[57] The most detailed account of the attempts made by Clare's family to drag her back to her home is given in the *Life*:

But after the news reached her relatives, they condemned with a broken heart the deed and proposal of the virgin and, banding together as one, they ran to the place, attempting to obtain what they could not. They employed violent force, poisonous advice and flattering promises, trying to persuade her to give up such a worthless deed that was unbecoming to her class and without precedent in her family. But taking hold of the altar cloths, she bared her tonsured head, maintaining that she would in no way be torn away from the service of Christ. With the increasing violence of her relatives, her spirit grew and her love – provoked by injuries – provided strength. So, for many days, even though she endured an obstacle in the way of the Lord and her own relatives opposed her proposal of holiness, her spirit did not crumble and her fervour did not diminish. Instead, amid words and deeds of hatred, she moulded her spirit anew in hope until her relatives, turning back, were quiet.[58]

Only Thomas of Celano records that the struggle lasted for several days and this detail suggests that once again he was drawing on sources other than the canonisation process.

All this time Clare was alone – or at least, the sources present her as being alone. The nuns of San Paolo delle Abbadesse were not concerned to defend her by enforcing their right to grant asylum. Bishop Guido, who certainly knew about Clare's intentions and who was the superior of the nuns of San Paolo, did not seem anxious to oppose a family as powerful as the descendants of Offreduccio. As far as we can tell from the sources, even Francis took no part in the story. It could be that he was away. If the flight had taken place in 1211, then that was the summer when Francis had set sail on his first attempt to reach the Holy Land. If, on the other hand, the flight had been in 1212, it is quite likely that he had gone to Rome to tell Pope Innocent III about the development of his fraternity. It is more likely, however, that having once taken Clare to San Paolo delle Abbadesse, Francis thought that he had fulfilled his obligations in the confrontation. That would have been quite in line with his own advice to his brethren in the *Regula non bullata* quoted above.[59] After he had given Clare his spiritual counsel, he would then have left her to go and do penance in any place she chose. Clare in her Testament seems to allude to something of this nature:

But when the blessed Francis saw that although we were physically weak and frail, we did not shirk deprivation, poverty, hard work, distress or the shame or contempt of the world – rather, as he and his brothers often saw for themselves, we considered all such trials as great delights after the example of the saints and their brothers – he rejoiced greatly in the Lord. And, moved by compassion for us, he promised to have always, both through himself and through his Order, the same loving care and special solicitude for us as for his own brothers.[60]

So there would have been a period when Francis had not been willing to assume pastoral and spiritual responsibility for Clare. He never had any wish to collect women under his obedience. Only the perseverance and insistence of Clare would have persuaded him to consider her in exactly the same way as he did his brethren.

For all these reasons, Clare was left to carry through this hard stuggle with her family all alone. Her resistance was extraordinary. In the street, local gossip quickly heard all about it, as Giovanni di Ventura testifies. Thus were born the first stories about Clare's remarkable strength, stories which filtered through the walls of her home, thanks to the indiscretion of some of the servants. One such story was recounted during the canonisation process by Sister Cristiana di Bernardo da Suppo:

The virgin of God, Clare, left the worldly house of her father in a wonderful way. Because she did not want to leave through the usual exit, fearing her way would be blocked, she went out by the house's other exit which had been barricaded with heavy wooden beams and an iron bar so it could not be opened even by a large number of men. She alone, with the help of Jesus Christ, removed them and opened the door. On the following morning, when many people saw that door opened, they were somewhat astonished at how a young girl could have done it.[61]

According to this account Clare, all by herself, had had to move the heavy beams of wood which blocked the exit of this secondary door if she were to flee from her father's house. These beams which impeded her flight were like a symbol of all the difficulties, not just the material ones, which she had had to overcome in her decision to leave her family. In the wonder of the people when they saw the door the next morning, we see a reflection of popular admiration for Clare, that 'young girl' who had done what many men together could not have done.

So conversion, in the life of Clare, is that moment when her dialogue with Francis gathered perhaps its maximum force and intensity. Without Francis, Clare would not have chosen to break with her family. Without him she would not have sold her inheritance and given it to the poor. Without him she would not have dreamt of a radical Gospel, living so far beyond the devout life lived by her mother. Yet Clare's conversion is one of those moments in her life when her own exceptional greatness of personality stands out. Francis on his own would not have had the determination to sustain such a conflict. That same determination enabled Clare not only to resist her family but also to lay claim to her full place in the community of the *lesser ones*.

THREE

The Privilege of Living without Privileges

San Paolo delle Abbadesse was the most important monastery of Benedictine women in the diocese of Assisi.[1] It also had a certain political influence, which was why even the popes concerned themselves with it. By a bull dated 1201 Innocent III had granted it a number of privileges, among which was the one already mentioned of giving asylum. This was a privilege of some importance, since it granted protection to everyone who lived on the monastery's land, and in those years of open warfare between Assisi and Perugia, this was very opportune. Also, the monastery was wealthy; its lands and possessions were as rich as, if not richer than, those of the bishop of Assisi himself, although the monastery was subject to him in other matters.[2]

After a certain period of time, however, Clare left this monastery. One might wonder if the asylum offered by the monastery had been insufficient to protect her from the reactions of her family, for they had come intent on a complete sequestration of her and her goods, although Clare had resisted them by hanging on to the altar cloth.[3] The author of the *Life* suggests that her family, seeing that their enterprise was in vain, declared that as long as Clare remained at San Paolo delle Abbadesse, then they were defeated. Why, in that case, did she leave?

In this period immediately after her flight from her father's house, Clare appeared to have been unsettled. The radicality of her choice, sanctioned by receiving the tonsure in the little church of St Mary of the Portiuncula, was beyond question, but she did not know at this stage what should or could be her way of life. She did not know just what that life was to which the Lord was calling her.

AT SANT'ANGELO IN PANZO

So the decision to leave the monastery of San Paolo could not have been the result of external pressure but the personal conviction of Clare herself. Among other things, only this would explain why she chose instead to go to the community of Sant'-Angelo in Panzo, a group of religious women living on the slopes of Monte Subasio, nearer to Assisi and therefore even more exposed to any further action from Clare's family.[4]

Why then did Clare leave San Paolo delle Abbadesse? Why could she not content herself with her condition as a servant? The sources are silent on this point. This may have been partly because many years later, when Clare had become famous and San Damiano a house where cardinals and popes visited, San Paolo had become one of the monasteries attached to the Damianite movement. This meant that it was part of that fellowship which bound the monasteries together by the spiritual bond of shared experiences, in spite of their histories and Rules. Yet in that case, why do both the canonisation process and the official *Life* of Clare mention these early differences at all? Their later silence does seem to spring simply from good motives, so there only remains the problem of why Clare left the monastery.

Hers was an action, a journey, not without precedent, for Francis himself had not stayed long at the abbey of San Vere-condo near Gubbio, which was where he had at first worked as a servant.[5] Other great monastic reformers before him, men like St Romuald, had also chosen to leave pre-existing institutions in order to put into practice their new insights about a more radical following of the Gospel ideal.[6]

To Clare, as to many of those who preceded her, it must have seemed impossible to practice personal poverty in so comprehensively rich a structure. For her it was not enough simply to have humbled herself, to have assumed a lowly condition, to have chosen to become a servant; she felt that for her it was essential that her whole life, including her home and the church in which she was to pray to the Lord, should all be poor as well.[7] From this point of view, the second place where Clare chose to stay is particularly interesting. The sources, and outstandingly the *Life*, which is usually very accurate about this sort of thing, speak of *ecclesia S. Angeli de Panso*, 'the church of Sant'Angelo in Panzo'.[8] The fact that the *Life* uses the term *ecclesia*, church, instead of *monasterium*, a monastery, is not just chance: there is no evidence to make us think that in 1212 Sant'Angelo in Panzo was a monastic community. The documents of the commune only speak of a monastery there from about 1232–33 when it was inserted into the list of institutions supported by public alms, but less than five years later Sant'Angelo appears in a bull of Gregory IX as a monastery of the Order of San Damiano.[9] Some years later again, Sant'Angelo had become a monastery of considerable importance with possessions and a fixed income[10] but when Clare went to that little church on the slopes of Subasio, what did she find there? It is impossible to give an exact answer. Certainly it was by no means unknown for a woman who wanted to live an intense life of prayer and penance to choose to retire near a church, generally in the city although sometimes in the country nearby. There she would be supported by alms from the passers-by. In central Italy in those years, and especially in Umbria, this was a widespread phenomenon.[11] The first half of the thirteenth century saw a great demand for religious life on the part of women who did not find sufficient outlets through the traditional monastic channels. As a result, they fostered a whole series of new experiments.[12] There was a similar phenomenon at the same time in other parts of Europe, especially in Brabant and around the Rhine. Here there was an upsurging of experiences of prayer, of love and the life of penance which were to come to their full flowering in the great Beguinages of northern Europe.[13]

Probably when Clare arrived at Sant'Angelo in Panzo she found there a small group of women, living a life of penance together but without professing any officially recognised Rule (as it is thought that the group did who later lived there).[14] In any case, her stay at Sant'Angelo in Panzo was, for Clare, a period of making contact with the new forms of religious life which other women than herself were also striving to realise at that time.

FLIGHT OF HER SISTER AGNES

The new element which changed Clare's whole perspective was the arrival of her sister. While Clare was at Sant'Angelo in Panzo, Caterina (as she was probably called)[15] wanted to copy her example and, leaving the family, joined her sister.[16] The story of this second flight from the house of Favarone is only told in the *Life* and in all probability Thomas of Celano was told the details by Clare's sister herself. Her testimony would have been very valuable, all the more so because Thomas, as was his way, was well aware of the importance of this episode in the development of events. He did not place it so that it followed in his narrative as swiftly as it had in reality, which would inevitably have underlined the way in which the conflict with the family had built up to a crescendo. Instead, he chose to place it in the heart of the *Life* where he speaks of the power of Clare's prayer. So the *Life* tells us:

Sixteen days after the conversion of Clare, Agnes [this name is the only one given her in the *Life* and is the one by which she was known in religion] inspired by the divine spirit, ran to her sister, revealed the secret of her will, and told her that she wished to serve God completely. Embracing her with joy, [Clare] said: I thank God, most sweet sister, that He has heard my concern for you.[17]

Clare, then, right from the start had not thought she would remain alone. Her dream, her 'care', which she dared confess only to God, had been to have companions and particularly to be followed by her sisters and other relatives.

This possibility, of course, opened the way to any number of problems. All the difficulties which she had encountered in defending her own choice, would be multiplied, beginning with the reactions of the family:

For while the joyous sisters were clinging to the footprints of Christ in the church of San'Angelo in Panzo and she who had heard more from the Lord was teaching her novice sister, new attacks by relatives were quickly flaring up against the young girls. The next day, hearing that Agnes had gone off to Clare, twelve men, burning with anger and hiding outwardly their evil intent, ran to the place.[18]

Monaldo, Clare's uncle, led the family reaction; he was probably the head of the family and would have been responsible for the young girls' marriages. Twelve armed men tried to seize Agnes, to drag her violently away from her new life, without sparing kicks and blows. The account in the *Life* says that they had managed to carry her away, up the hill, when at Clare's intercession Catherine's body became so heavy that even all those men were not able to lift it. Then the uncle, murderous with rage, tried to hit her, but his arm remained in mid air, assailed with an unexpected pain. If, as is most likely, this account in the *Life* originated with Catherine-Agnes, then such a telling of a miracle, which made it impossible for the men of the family to snatch this young girl away, would have been a sister's act of gratitude towards Clare. Even after the passage of a number of years, she knew very well that if on that day she had resisted the pressure and pleading of her family, then it was all due to the power of the prayers of Clare.

At the end of the battle, Catherine received the tonsure at the hands of Francis and it was probably then that she was also given the name Agnes which was to be hers for life. Perhaps it was due to these vicissitudes that Francis was drawn to take a more direct interest in the struggles of Clare and her first companion. The *Life* is very clear: 'In fact, blessed Francis cut off her hair with his own hand and directed her together with her sister in the way of the Lord.'[19] So it was Francis himself who cut off Catherine's hair, repeating the extraordinary gesture which he had made to Clare, and it was he and always he who undertook their spiritual formation, even though he was a simple layman who said of himself that he was uneducated.

THE DEFINITIVE CHOICE OF SAN DAMIANO

Clare's purpose, and Francis' too, was becoming clearer; also Sant'Angelo in Panzo was not to be her home. Having experienced Benedictine monasticism at San Paolo delle Abbadesse, Clare now wanted to move beyond even the new form of penitential life that was probably being realised at Sant'Angelo in Panzo. Clare and Agnes were the start of a new family of religious life, one which was closely bound to the Franciscan experience. In order to achieve this, and on Francis' advice, they left the church on the slopes of Subasio.

Once again, the reasons for this change of direction were not external; that is, they are not to be sought in family pressures. Both Clare and Agnes had shown themselves well able to deal with these and, if indeed they had been the reason, Clare would have needed to go much further afield than she did. Instead, she did exactly the opposite and moved nearer to the city and prepared to live in a tiny semi-abandoned church where she would have been an easy prey to the family. This was the church of San Damiano. So if the family played any part in this threefold move, it was only an indirect one and, as it were, unintentional. The more her relations tried to insist that she give up her choice, and the more Clare felt confirmed in it, so much more did she find life impossible in the monasteries and communities where she found refuge, and so much more radical became her adherence to the ideals of Franciscan living.[20]

San Damiano is one of the key places[21] in the beginning of the Franciscan movement. Here Francis had heard the invitation to repair the church of the Lord which was in ruins, here he had hidden when he fled from his father's anger and here he had gathered with his first companions. When Clare moved there from Sant'Angelo in Panzo, San Damiano took on its central role in the Franciscan community.

This time, however long it was, which Clare spent as a servant at San Paolo and Sant'Angelo was a time of testing for her, a sort of novitiate imposed by Francis himself before he received her definitively into the *franternitas*, the company. This novitiate, which until then (that is, from the beginning of the Franciscan movement)[22] had not been seen as a precondition for joining the brethren, must have tested her strength of purpose.

It was only 'after that he [Francis] wrote us a Form of Life saying above all that we should persevere in holy poverty'.[23] With this spare sentence, Clare records in her Testament the first and simplest Rule, the *forma vitae* or 'form of life', which Francis himself gave to the sisters at San Damiano. In fact, this Rule could not have been a true and proper Rule, but only some words of exhortation which the holy father gave in a solemn form to the sisters[24] and is probably the one to which Clare was referring when she wrote in her Rule of 1253:

Because it is by Divine inspiration that you have made yourselves daughters and handmaids of the Most High King, the heavenly Father, and have made yourselves the Beloved of the Holy Spirit in choosing to live according to Gospel perfection, therefore I want, and I promise, both for myself and for my brothers, always to give the same loving attention and the same special care to you as I do to them.[25]

With this *forma* Francis solemnly gathered the sisters into his fraternity and established a perfect correspondence between the attention and care which he showed to them and that which he showed to his own brothers. It was probably these same words which later became the central core of the formula by which sisters who later joined the community[26] were received to obedience.

Writing her Rule more than forty years later when the outlines of the San Damiano community were more clearly defined, Clare foresaw that anyone wanting to join themselves to the community would do so with the consent of all the sisters, that she would renounce her property, receive the tonsure and make a period of novitiate. After that, 'when the year of probation has finished, let her be received to obedience, promising always to observe our life and the form of our poverty'.[27]

WORK

In the chapter of her Rule following the one in which she inserts Francis' *forma vitae*, Clare speaks about work, taking up again the instructions which Francis had given to his brethren on a number of occasions:

Let those sisters to whom the Lord has given the grace of working, do so from the hour of Terce. Let them work faithfully and with devotion and let it be at a work which builds their integrity and the common good so that, leaving aside all idleness (the enemy of the soul) they may not extinguish the spirit of prayer and devotion to which all other temporal things must come second.[28]

Work, then, according to Clare, serves to banish idleness, the enemy of the soul. In this she is perfectly in line with the monastic tradition. Francis, too, in his Rule of 1223, uses the same expression:

Those brothers to whom the Lord has given the grace of working should do their work faithfully and devotedly so that, avoiding idleness, the enemy of the soul, they do not extinguish the spirit of holy prayer and devotion.[29]

Clare does however makes an addition to the text of the *Regula bullata* and adds a second paragraph in order to establish the way in which the different works were to be distributed among the sisters. Thus, the Rule of Clare:

At Chapter and in front of everyone, the Abbess, or her vicar, is bound to assign the work of her hands which each is to do.[30]

Id quod manibus suis operantur, 'the work of her hands', is an expression which constantly recurs in the New Testament and especially in St Paul. It was also the phrase which during the twelfth and first half of the thirteenth centuries became almost a slogan, or, better, a technical term, used by all those who were working out a new spirituality and seeking to encourage a new attitude to work within the Church.[31]

For Clare, manual work was one of the fundamental characteristics of her own experience. Right up to the last days of her life when she was so ill that she could not lift herself up in the bed, she still wanted to keep on working.[32] This was not simply to avoid the dangers of idleness; Clare wanted to give an example to those sisters who would come after her.

With such an attitude towards work, Clare had placed herself right in the mainstream with Francis, who had made manual work a distinguishing mark of *minoritas* or 'lesserness'. In his Testament the saint records the early days of the fraternity:

And we were simple [unlettered] and subject to all. And I used to work with my hands and I still desire to work; and I firmly wish that all my brothers give themselves to honest work. Let those who do not know how to work, learn, not from desire of receiving wages for their work but as an example and in order to avoid idleness.[33]

Here the monastic concept is definitively and finally transcended, even though the words still echo those of the struggle against idleness. Francis worked in order to 'give an example'; he wanted to indicate that for him work had an intrinsic positive value as long as, naturally, one was talking about honest and suitable work. In the *Regula non bullata*, this positive value given to work allied to the idea of *minoritas* is underlined:

None of the brothers should be administrators or managers in whatever places they are staying among the others to serve or to work, nor should they be supervisors in the houses in which they serve; nor should they accept any office which might generate scandal or be harmful to their souls, instead they should be the lesser ones and subject to all who are in the same house.[34]

Clare worked with her own hands and wished her sisters to do the same, but what work are we talking about? All the sources give us information about this, particularly the canonisation process in which Sister Pacifica di Guelfuccio testifies that Clare:

When she was so sick that she could not get up from bed, she had herself raised to a sitting position, supported with some cushions behind her back. She spun thread and from her work corporals and altar linen were made for almost all the churches of the plain and hills around Assisi.[35]

So the work of Clare was spinning. One gathers from the evidence of Sister Pacifica that the community of San Damiano was organised so that it was Clare who spun and then there were other sisters who wove the thread into cloth. Others again then sewed the cloth and made it into corporals for the churches. Putting the testimonies together, we can conclude that the sisters had gained a certain technical expertise and that they worked with woven wool as well as several other kinds of cloth. In the bull of canonisation it says that Clare 'worked with her own hands not to be idle even in her sickness. Then out of the linen made by her skill and labour, she had many corporals made'.[36] We know that the thread woven by Clare was linen, but the process also speaks of silk, 'lazzo' and precious cloth.[37]

A young woman such as Clare would probably have learnt

to work with cloth right from her childhood[38] but the work which she developed at San Damiano would have been something quite different. Spinning, and above all weaving, were crafts requiring considerable skill and a technical expertise such as would certainly not have been required of a young lady from an aristocratic family.[39] Francis, child of a merchant family, would have been no stranger to this type of work. According to the *Legend of Perugia*, he rejoiced when he saw the brethren from noble families working at humble tasks and going out to beg[40] and he would probably have wished the noble young ladies of San Damiano to do the same.

Working with wool was linked with working on the land to which, according to Clare's Rule, the sisters must devote themselves. Here we are probably not talking about heavy work but about the care of the garden from which would have come the bulk of the community's food.[41] Neither the wool nor the agricultural work were conducted according to strict commercial criteria, and if, in the case of wool, the resulting cloth went outside the monastery, then it would always have been as a gift.[42] The fruits of work were not for trade. Sometimes, perhaps, gifts were given in exchange for alms but never for payment in money. It was in this last characteristic that the community of San Damiano differed from all the other forms of religious life, for men or women, which were flourishing throughout Europe at that time. For example, in Milan and right across central Italy, there were many groups of Humiliati, living either in mixed communities or in communities of men or women, who conducted a flourishing trade based primarily on cloth.[43] Indeed, in Flanders, the communities of women who were becoming known as 'Beguines' were flourishing, and they too gave themselves to manual work, particularly the cloth trade.[44]

The role played by the mendicant Orders in thirteenth-century European society is often underlined, with reference to the development both of a new spirituality and of a new concept of work, but here, as in many other fields, this changing role is always set against the well-studied male Orders. Yet what should really be taken into account are the multitudinous forms of women's religious life which were coming into being at that time.

One of the most painstaking witnesses to thirteenth-century religious life was Jacques de Vitry, that great patron of the cause of women religious in northern Europe. He was also the biographer of Mary d'Oignies who had founded groups of women in Brabant. Jacques found himself in Perugia in 1216 and wrote a letter that same year which is the first description to come down to us of the brothers of Francis and the sisters who gathered around him. In this letter Jacques heavily underlines the matter of work: 'The women live together in some hospices near the city. They do not accept any alms but live by the work of their hands.'[45] These women supported themselves by the work of their own hands. Earlier in the same letter, speaking of the Humiliati, he uses the same expression and, to his mind, he was discussing a characteristic common to the new religious experiments he met in Italy. It was also a characteristic which he thought it good to describe to his Flemish correspondents with a view to introducing something similar there too.

However, when compared with other contemporary experiments, the community at San Damiano appeared to be unique. The attitude of Clare and her companions towards work, however much it might seem to have in common with the Beguines and the Humiliati, does look quite original.

At San Damiano they wove the cloth, they probably dyed it, they certainly sewed and embroidered it. In other words, they had developed all aspects of that most important industry of the thirteenth century, namely the cloth trade. Yet, all this did not generate any form of commerce. The Humiliati had quickly become an economic force, cloth worked by the Flemish Beguines contributed to the fame of the cloth of that region, but in the case of San Damiano, none of this happened. Clare and her sisters made things in order to give them away; they worked so that they could give in alms. Thus their economic activity sprang from anti-economic criteria. At San Damiano, work was important, very much so, but not in order to maintain the community. To do this, it was enough simply to trust in alms, which meant that they lived in a permanent state of dependence upon those outside the community.

Work, for Clare, was fundamental. The evidence of Sister Pacifica, quoted above, shows the measure of this when she relates how even when ill and obliged to stay in bed, Clare still wanted to give the sisters the example of working with her hands, making corporals to give away to all the churches on the plain around Assisi. Pacifica was well aware that she was talking about an important activity involving all the sisters:

Asked how she knew these things, she replied that she saw her spinning. When the cloth was made and the sisters had sewn it, it was hand-delivered by the brothers to those churches and given to the priests who came there.[46]

It would seem that Thomas of Celano did not grasp the real meaning of this, since he places his account of it in the chapter dedicated to 'Her Wonderful Devotion to the Sacrament of the Altar'.[47] In fact, Clare was making a statement about the value of work. In this she was profoundly modern, alert to the reality of a world in transformation where work would assume more and more importance. Even in the preceding century, women had no longer worked only in the house or fields but in the spinning and dye-shops as well, and work was ceasing to be something done by one person alone but was becoming a social activity.[48]

Probably as a child, Clare would have heard that famous lament of the silk-workers which Chrétien de Troyes had inserted into his *Yvain* (around 1180).

> We weave the finest silks, and yet
> we wear the roughest clothes ourselves.
> Half-clad, forever poor, we get
> too little food and drink, and yet
> we never learn the skills that get
> the food we need to eat.
>
> We never gain our daily bread
> unless the day to night we spread
> and even then from all our sweat
> for every lira, all we get

is four denarii, and yet
our food and clothes we cannot get
from that alone, and yet
not even twenty soldi get
us food enough to live. And yet
those we work for, they can get
richer and richer . . .

We stay awake all day
we toil half the night
so they can make away
with what is ours by right.
And when we seek to rest, we get
the treadmill threatened and so yet
again, we dare not rest.[49]

The work the sisters did in common at San Damiano seems to have been the exact opposite of this description by Chrétien de Troyes. The sisters, too, lived by the work of their own hands but their produce was not stolen away by a master who lived off their toil. Quite the contrary, they took what they earned and turned it into gifts, as if it were something superfluous. The 'Poor Sisters' of San Damiano, as Clare loved to call her companions, were poor as well as being workers. Their salary, however, was not the bread of toil but a gift of mercy.

If Clare, even while she was ill, still held fast to her manual work, it was not (as Thomas of Celano seemed to believe) solely out of devotion to the Blessed Sacrament, but rather because such work formed an intrinsic part of the way of life, the state of servitude, she had chosen. This is shown in another part of the *Life*, when it says that Clare never shirked any of the tasks of a servant.[50] In a community, even a poor one of humble means, there is never any lack of work. At San Damiano this work was evenly divided each day among the sisters, with no exceptions. The Rule in fact ordains that the sisters should love and care for each other with even more affection than a mother nourishes and loves the daughter of her own flesh.[51] In the great women's monasteries of that time, above all in the Cistercian houses, there were two categories of nun. There were the so-called 'choir nuns' who gave themselves primarily to prayer and

were generally well educated and from aristocratic back-
grounds. Then there were the 'lay sisters', or those who served,
who dedicated themselves to all the practical necessities of a
life in common.[52] At San Damiano, too, there were sisters who
were called 'those who served'; these were the sisters who went
outside the monastery as occasion required. At San Damiano,
however, 'those who served' were not a category apart, for all
the sisters were obliged to work[53] and the work itself was not
divided into more or less servile work.[54] Right from the start,
Clare herself gave an example by working with her hands herself
and by personally concerning herself with all the more humble
tasks.

THE *PRIVILEGE OF POVERTY*

Jacques de Vitry had come to Perugia in order to plead the
cause of those religious women whom he had seen begin and
rapidly develop in Flanders. In the life of Mary of Oignies which
he had written, he had presented this new model of female
holiness (he had called her the *sancta nova*, the new saint) as
the most effective response to the heretical movements of the
day.[55]

At first glance, the broad outlines of the biographies of Clare
and Mary of Oignies look very different. Mary, born into a
well-to-do family around 1177–78, was married at the age of
fourteen to a devout young man. Soon after their marriage she
decided, with her husband's agreement, that they would live
together as brother and sister in a leprosarium. Here they served
gladly for fifteen years, probably until her husband's death.
Then she chose a life of prayer as a Beguine recluse near the
little priory of the Canons Regular of Oignies where she stayed
until she died. However, although the two women lived so far
apart, they had some aspects of their lives in common. Each of
them refused to live the life which their families had expected
of them. In Clare's case, this refusal included a renunciation of
marriage, while for Mary it meant a transformation of her
marriage itself into a partnership of charitable activity. Each of
them chose a life of prayer as the final context of their human

and religious search, even though Clare surrounded herself with companions with whom she brought a new community to birth, while Mary chose the solitary life, although she too was surrounded by the affection and attention of a number of 'spiritual friends'. These would often visit her in order to receive advice and spiritual assistance.[56]

Jacques de Vitry was certainly one of these 'spiritual friends' of Mary of Oignies, and this is why he was so well informed about the new forms of women's religious life. In the letter already mentioned, he draws attention both to the prayers of the new communities and to the problems they encountered. These women, who lived together in various places (and even as early as 1216 we are talking about quite a large number of communities) were in fact very disturbed because they were held in far greater honour by both clergy and laity than they wished.[57]

With this new kind of community, the problem of external influence, clerical or lay, more powerful or less, was particularly relevant as the communities were not protected either by custom or by precise juridical guidelines. Above all, there was the attitude of the families of those sisters who gradually came to join the new communities. When one thinks of the violent reaction of Clare's family to her and her sister Agnes' choice of life, it is not difficult to imagine a parallel reaction on the part of the families of other sisters.

Jacques de Vitry wrote some four years after Clare had made her choice of life. It is clear from his writings that the tension had by no means evaporated from the situation, either at San Damiano or in the other communities which had sprung up in that short time. For a woman's community which was different from the established monastic institutions, it was far from easy to gain acceptance and respect.[58] Jacques knew all this very well. The community of religious women in Flanders, which he knew best, had met similar problems[59] and he had come to Italy for the express purpose of obtaining some juridical recognition for them from the Holy See.

The beginning of the thirteenth century saw a real explosion of small women's communities right across Europe. In particular, Flanders, Brabant and the Rhineland, on the one hand, and northern and central Italy, on the other, were cradles to this welling up of religious fervour. Until 1215, when they gathered at the Fourth Lateran Council, religious authorities had tended to take a cautious, if not actually a suspicious, attitude towards these communities, and at the Council all forms of religious life which did not follow one of the traditional Rules were solemnly forbidden.[60] These conciliar decrees have been read as if they were some sort of brake on all the new, popular religious movements, especially those which were suspected of heresy, but in fact they were primarily aimed at the new communities of religious women. It was these groups of women, living without any precise Rule and establishing themselves without any authorisation from their bishops, who were the major concern of the religious authorities.

As a result, many communities of religious women had to adopt one or other of the traditional Rules. In practice this meant either the Rule of St Benedict or that of St Augustine. At the same time these communities would seek some kind of *privilegium* which would both define and guarantee their autonomy. Their choice of Rule in fact meant that they placed themselves in a very precise arena of spirituality; if they chose the Benedictine Rule, it meant monasticism; if they chose the Augustinian, it meant the canonical life. In choosing which Rule to follow (whichever choice they made) each community of women would in addition be choosing a man's Order that would assume their spiritual care and be their spiritual guide. More often than not, this choice would, in practice, be made for them.[61]

The men's Orders were often very reluctant to assume the *cura animarum*, the 'spiritual care', of the women who chose to live this form of religious life. It was a heavy task and one that threatened to absorb all the energies of their Order. At the start of the thirteenth century, first the Cistercians and Premonstratentians and later the Dominicans and Franciscans all tried to find ways of avoiding this burden. On the other hand, there were some churchmen who gave particular attention to these new forms of religious life and wanted to encourage them and therefore they made themselves their spokesmen. One such ecclesiastic was Jacques de Vitry; another was someone of major importance in the history of religion and indeed of politics in the thirteenth century, namely the Cardinal Ugolino dei Conti di Segni.[62]

Cardinal Ugolino, countryman and relative of Pope Innocent III, was papal legate in Tuscany when, barely two years after the decrees of the Lateran Council, some local communities of women came to him asking for his protection. This was about the same time as Ugolino's first meeting with Francis of Assisi to whom he was to become both friend and counsellor. Ugolino did his best for the new communities with Pope Honorius (who had succeeded Innocent in 1216) and, because of Ugolino's knowledge of the communities, Honorius authorised him to bring them under the protection of the Holy See. Having received this mandate, Ugolino made it his business to see that the new communities each had some land on which they could build their own house and that they had some guarantee of daily food.[63]

Naturally the new Tuscan communities also had to submit to the decrees of the Council and so to choose an approved Rule. Ugolino chose the Benedictine Rule for them but, using this as a basis, he also wrote 'Constitutions' which formed their own, true second Rule. Although this did not subject them to the Benedictines, it did affiliate them to that Order, thereby defining the character of the new foundations and, above all, their choice of enclosure.[64]

Even at San Damiano, some changes had become necessary. The passage of time had posed the double problem of juridical recognition of their experiment and also a new, internal organisation for the community. In the beginning, Francis' personal direction had been enough, for it was to him that Clare had promised obedience. The little group had lived a spirit of community according to the guidelines given them by Francis in the *forma vitae* which he had drawn up for them.[65] However, from 1214–16, Francis had often been absent from Assisi for longer or shorter periods, and at the same time the San Damiano community was growing with more and more sisters joining the original little group. For all these reasons, various changes became necessary.

Who would be able to assume command of the community, seeing that Francis himself certainly could not do it personally? Francis had no doubts; as Pacifica di Guelfuccio tells us, the person whom he wanted to take responsibility for San Damiano was Clare herself:

The witness also said three years after St Clare had been in the Order, at the prayers and insistence of St Francis, who almost forced her, she accepted the direction and government of the sisters.[66]

The choice was far from obvious. Dominic Guzman, for example, had founded a number of women's communities during those same years, and he had confided the responsibility to certain priests charged with the cure of souls. The most important woman in the community was called the prioress, but she had to acquiesce in the decisions made by the priest who was in charge.[67] Francis made a different choice: he gave the responsibility for San Damiano directly to Clare and in order to do this he chose for her a title which he took from the old monastic tradition, that of 'abbess'. The *Life* makes it quite clear that this is the title he meant:

Three years after her conversion, she declined the name and office of Abbess, wishing in her humility to be placed under others rather than over them and, among the servants of Christ, she was more willing to serve than to be served. However, she was constrained by blessed Francis and in the end she accepted the government of the Ladies. As a result, fear and not arrogance was brought forth from her heart while independence did not increase but rather the spirit and practice of service.[68]

Francis' choice of the title abbess is highly significant. The Benedictine abbesses had always enjoyed the fullest autonomy, so much so that in the end they had acquired privileges and prerogatives normally reserved for bishops.[69] The originality of Francis' idea lay in applying such a title to someone in charge of so poor a community, particularly as the title conferred a kind of power and autonomy which were by no means consonant with the social condition and economic resources of San Damiano.

Both the canonisation process and the *Life* agree that this happened only three years after Clare's conversion, which probably brings us to 1215. This date is too much of a coincidence to be chance. Among the concerns which caused Francis to give Clare this title of abbess was certainly that of bringing the community into line with the directives of the Fourth Lateran Council, for San Damiano, too, had to follow an approved Rule. By calling Clare the abbess, Francis placed the community in the mainstream of the Benedictine tradition and it was possibly he himself who decided that the sisters should follow the Rule of St Benedict.

All this would explain Clare's vehement reaction, for there was no way that she wanted the title of abbess. A number of years later, when the debate about the institutional position of San Damiano was like water long gone under a bridge, Clare's reaction to Francis' proposal is simply attributed, in the *Life*, to her spirit of humility. Celano actually places this event in the chapter dedicated to 'her holy humility'. In all probability, though, it was obvious to Clare that the position in question had nothing to do with personal virtue but with the good ordering of her community. If she chose the Rule of St Benedict and accepted the title of abbess, would this not make San Damiano into a monastery like San Paolo delle Abbadesse which she had not long left?

On the other hand, Clare realised that her community needed juridical recognition from the ecclesiastical authorities. At that time some of the other communities which had spontaneously arisen in and around Assisi had sought the protection of the local bishop, but in the end even that was found to be inadequate.[70] Others, especially in Tuscany, had, as we have seen, sought Cardinal Ugolino's protection. With regard to San Damiano, even though Bishop Guido had almost certainly adopted an attitude of indulgent benevolence towards the community, the fact remained that the diocese had never given it any official document of recognition.

All these were reasons for Clare to accept the title of abbess.

However, anxious lest such a title and such a Rule would end by radically changing the community, she also petitioned Pope Innocent III for recognition of something very specific: the so-called *Privilege of Poverty*.[71] For a long time this document had been lost and its very existence doubted by many, but today we see it as a clear indication of the immense originality of San Damiano. It is a text of such importance that we reproduce it here in its entirety:

Innocent, Bishop, Servant of the servants of God, to his beloved daughters in Christ, Clare and the other servants of Christ of the Church of San Damiano in Assisi, professing the regular life, both those in the present, as well as those in the future for ever:

As is evident, you have renounced the desire for all temporal things, desiring to dedicate yourselves to the Lord alone. Because of this, since you have sold all things and given them to the poor, you propose not to have any possessions whatsoever, clinging in all things to the footprints of Him, the Way, the Truth and the Life, Who, for your sake, was made poor. Nor does a lack of possessions frighten you from a proposal of this sort; for the left hand of the heavenly Spouse is under your head to support the weakness of your body, which you have placed under the law of your soul through an ordered charity. Finally, He who feeds the birds of the heavens and clothes the lilies of the field will not fail you in either food or clothing, until He ministers to you in heaven, when His right hand especially will more happily embrace you in the fullness of His [beatific] vision. Therefore, we confirm with our apostolic authority, as you requested, your proposal of most high poverty granting you by the authority of this letter that no one can compel you to receive possessions.

And if any woman does not wish to, or cannot observe a proposal of this sort, let her not have a dwelling place among you, but let her be transferred to another place.

Therefore, we decree that it may not be permitted to anyone to disturb you and your church rashly or to burden you with any kind of vexation. If, therefore, any one, either an ecclesiastic or a secular, knowing this document of our confirmation and constitution, rashly attempt to oppose it, after the second or third warning – unless he has corrected his fault through an appropriate act of satisfaction – let him lose the dignity of his power and honour, know that he is subject to the divine judgement for the iniquity perpetrated, excluded from the most sacred Body and Blood of God and the Lord Jesus Christ, our Redeemer, and be subject to a severe punishment at the last judgement.

May the peace of our Lord Jesus Christ, however, be with all of you and with those who, in the same place, preserve a love in Christ, so that they may both receive the fruit of their good work here and, before the demanding Judge, discover the rewards of eternal peace. Amen.[72]

This document is the oldest text to speak of the Franciscan *fraternitas* or community. Francis, too, of course, had gone to Rome to seek approval for his small group of penitents, but on that occasion Innocent III had confined himself to verbal approval only.[73] This recognition sought by Clare (certainly on the advice of Francis himself) is, therefore, the oldest papal document about the new *fraternitas*. It is an extraordinary document, wholly focussed on the point which must have been at the heart of the San Damiano experience: the choice of poverty.

The *Privilege* recalls the beginnings of the community when several young women, who ardently desired to dedicate their entire lives to the Lord, chose to sell their goods and to distribute the proceeds to the poor. They proposed to live with no possessions, following in the footprints of the poor Christ.[74] All this corresponds perfectly with what we learn from the *Life* and was taken up and repeated almost word for word by Clare in her Testament[75] so that the *Privilege of Poverty* is also the first biographical profile of Clare herself. The really remarkable aspect of the document arises from the fact that it considers poverty as a juridical value. What we have here is a short juridical *monstrum* which must have been a considerable surprise to the thirteenth-century experts in canon law. The *Privilege of Poverty* (*Privilegium paupertatis*) is in fact the *privilege of living without any privileges*. It is a privilege which guarantees a life with no guarantees. It is a privilege given directly by the pope, the highest authority in the Church, to a young laywoman who had made her profession of religious life into the hands of an uneducated layman. The *Life*, too, shows amazement at such a recognition:

She asked the privilege of poverty of Innocent III of happy memory, desiring that her Order be known by the title of poverty. This magnificent man, congratulating such great fervour in the virgin, spoke of the uniqueness of her proposal since such a privilege had never been made by the Apostolic See. The Pope himself with great joy wrote with his own hand the first draft of the privilege [that was] sought after, so that an unusual favour might smile upon an unusual request.[76]

Reference is made in the papal document to the sisters 'professing the regular life', a sign that at that time the Rule of St Benedict had already been accepted at San Damiano. In the end, however, this Rule had only a relative value for, by obtaining the privilege, the originality of San Damiano was being most solemnly sanctioned, with or without the Rule of St Benedict, with or without the title of abbess. This privilege was the true heart of the community and the treasured secret of the whole of Clare's life. In her Testament, she records how anxious she had been to gain it:

[Those] who will succeed me in office should be bound always to observe [the holy poverty] and have it observed by the other sisters. And, for even greater security, I took care to have our profession of most holy poverty, which we promised to the Lord and to our most blessed Father [Francis] strengthened with privileges by the Lord Pope Innocent, during whose pontificate we had our beginnings, and by his other successors, so that we would never nor in any way, depart from it.'[77]

Even physically, the privilege was jealously guarded by Clare. During the canonisation process a number of sisters testify: 'The Privilege of Poverty granted to her was honoured with great reverence and kept well and with great diligence since she feared to lose it.'[78] All this care demonstrates how much importance Clare attributed to the document. For her, it was not just a privilege, but the very secret of her community, that which defined her uniqueness and her vocation.

After the first three years of life 'in religion' one could say that the experiment conducted by Clare and her companions had taken on those characteristics which were to remain with it for the rest of her life. Having renounced the monastic life as it was lived at San Paolo delle Abbadesse and also after leaving the new form of religious life being lived at Sant'Angelo in

Panzo, Clare, in communion with Francis and his brethren, brought a new experiment into being, one which could be lived by young women such as herself. It had three salient characteristics: life in common, work with their own hands and, above all, the choice of poverty.

The choice of a life in common was not forced upon her; Clare could have chosen the road of the hermit or solitary recluse, but her interest always lay in the direction of building a community where the personal life of each could develop in the context of their life together. To work with her own hands represented her wish not to create a community of prayer that would be distanced from the weariness and problems of the most poor, at a time when more than anything else poverty meant work. The fundamental option of Clare, the choice which gave value and substance to the other two, was her choice of poverty. This meant poverty seen as the choice of a life absolutely shorn of all security, at the mercy of the generosity of her fellow-citizens and the passers-by. This choice of absolute poverty led to what could be called the economic paradox of San Damiano: working in order to give away and begging in order to live. From such a perspective, work was not an economic factor, but instead it became the hallmark of the choice of poverty.

In the light of this choice, one can better understand the need Clare felt to have some juridical guarantee for her community. Had it been a question of a solitary hermit who wanted to live in absolute poverty there would have been no need for a papal privilege of poverty. The folly of Clare's ambition (and of Francis') is revealed in this: that she sought to bring into being an entire community of totally poor women. To realise this ambition it was necessary to devise the *Privilege of Poverty*.

FOUR

The Space of Sanctity: Enclosed and Open to the World

O rtolana's generation lived with a tension between long pilgrimages and daily life. Clare's generation chose a life which was completely religious but attached to one single city. This development echoed a shift in the balance of power between city and country which took place in central and northern Italy around the end of the twelfth and the start of the thirteenth centuries. Ever since the time of the struggle against Barbarossa, the Italian city-communes had been cautiously trying to assert their control over the countryside. During the first decades of the thirteenth century, we find the commune-centred economy dominating that of farming in a way which suggests that this had been decisively achieved.[1]

NEW FORMS OF RELIGIOUS LIFE

The city became the all-enclosing horizon within which the life of the individual was measured.[2] The new forms of religious life also had to adjust to this new horizon, while to the Church it was a huge challenge to change direction. In order to respond, the Church had to make a leap, as it were, from monasticism (even a reformed monasticism such as that of the Cistercians) to the mendicant Orders.[3]

It is obvious that during those years the way in which the ideal of Gospel perfection was proposed to the people also underwent a marked transformation. This ideal ceased to be that of a community closed in upon itself, dedicated to prayer and the cultured life in splendid feudal isolation. Instead, it became a group of itinerant men who were wholly concerned with preaching to and communicating with the people of the city. The transformation in the ideal proposed to women is

76

less obvious, but new forms of urban piety were developing, particularly in Italy, which were neither in opposition to city life nor an alternative to it but instead wholly a part of it.

In the documents of the time, women who lived a religious life without having made a true and proper monastic profession were called *mulieres religiosae*, 'religious women'. Often these *mulieres religiosae* chose to live a life in common, remaining in their own houses while living in chastity, doing manual labour and devoting themselves to works of mercy. In this way they touched on two specific needs of urban life: work and assistance to the poor and sick. These were both areas of major concern to the administrators of the new communes.[4]

This new women's piety, however, was not confined to the discovery of new forms of the active life; it also allowed the women to develop a new spirituality through which they found new ways of prayer. This was the origin of the solitary life lived in the towns.[5] Ever since monastic life began there had been anchoresses, that is women who chose to live in solitude and prayer[6] near a monastery. The sources often prefer to call them 'recluses' (women who live in reclusion, in a *reclusorio* or a hermitage or cave), but from the thirteenth century they generally lived within the city instead. Even if they were living in the more isolated places at least they were always near to some centre of habitation.[7]

Often alone, or living with just one or two companions, these women developed a close network of relationships with their neighbourhood. They received spiritual assistance from local clerics, usually appointed by the bishop, and material assistance from neighbours and passers-by. Some of the women reached heights of extraordinary heroism, choosing to live, sometimes for years on end, as recluses or 'anchoresses', only able to communicate with the outside world through a tiny window.[8] This heroism helped to spread their fame even further and increased the numbers who went to them for spiritual advice or to ask for their prayers.[9] The new city – or anyway the new civic awareness – needed new saints and new heavenly protection in order to legitimate not only their social, but also their spiritual, identity.[10]

Just as many of the old patron saints had been bishops who during their life had defended and protected their citizens, now these new saintly figures were usually women whose prayer had obtained God's protection for their fellow-citizens. We can see that here in these women we have a new kind of relationship between the recluses and the city, for it was precisely their seclusion or isolation from the world which made their intercession for, and their witness to, their fellow-citizens so very effective.[11] We can also see here the paradox by which their very apartness is an essential factor in establishing greater openness and a stronger ascendancy over the collective consciousness of the citizens.[12]

Across the spectrum of this new religious experience of women which developed in the thirteenth century, we can see – as so often in Church history – two main strands. One strand was more strongly focussed on prayer and contemplation while the other sought out new forms of apostolic activity. It is the choice of Martha and Mary again, the one traditionally seen as the representative of the active life and the other of the contemplative life. Sometimes, in the actual experience of religious women, these two strands would unite. Living near the recluse there would often be servants who were committed to the active life, or else women would undertake to live in seclusion for a certain period only, or choose it at the end of a life which was already rich in experience.[13]

We can certainly link these religious stirrings to those of the other Tuscan women we have mentioned who, wanting to live a new form of religious life, had approached Cardinal Ugolino.[14] Their desire, at least so it would seem from Ugolino's letter to Pope Honorius III, was to live in common, 'fleeing from the temptations and riches of the world, and to build themselves a dwelling place'.[15] They were women who chose to be poor because they wanted to renounce all personal possessions; they came from families of good social standing, if not actually the nobility. The women would be 'ladies' from the gentry, hence the significance of the name by which, much later, they were called: *pauperes dominae reclusae* or *pauperes dominae inclusae* – 'poor, enclosed ladies'. Seclusion was a mark of their chosen way of life,[16] and enclosure of an urban character woven into the social and spiritual fabric of thirteenth-century Tuscan life. They lived together and their apartness, which they defended, made possible their mutuality with those around them. On their side, they offered intercession and prayers and, in return, they received material and spiritual support.[17]

This interaction between the religious community and the city must not blind us to the strong opposition the communities would have encountered from the very beginning. We are talking about a large number of women who had chosen to live a life which was not recognised by any authority, civil or religious, and often in opposition to their families' plans for them. This religious movement of women grew steadily right through the thirteenth century and as it grew it acquired all the usual characteristics of a mass movement. It has been estimated that by the year 1300 as many as 7000 women were involved in Dominican or Franciscan communities alone.[18] If we add to these the women who had chosen to live in the small, spontaneous groups which were often on the fringes of heretical movements, then we gain some idea of the social influence which such a way of life must have had.

THE CONSTITUTIONS OF CARDINAL UGOLINO

Cardinal Ugolino was the first to take note of the problem created by women who wanted to live this new form of religious life. Honorius III made him responsible for these communities and Ugolino drew up a way of life for them.[19]

Ugolino's idea was simple and effective. Because the women wanted to stay in or near the city, it was necessary for them to be shut in. Their seclusion thus ceased to be just one element in the women's new religious life (and, at that, one which was not always present); instead it became the main pivot in their option for religious and community life. In short, Ugolino imposed the enclosure on them. In the history of the Church, Ugolino's Constitutions are one of the most explicit and thorough affirmations of the need for enclosure in religious life:

79

They must remain enclosed the whole time of their life. After they have entered the enclosure of this religious life [*claustrum huius religionis*] they should never be given any leave or faculty to go out of it unless it should happen that she be invited to go to another place to plant or build up the same religious life.[20]

In Ugolino's Constitutions, the image describing the community is that of the medieval city itself. Just as the city was enclosed by a wall which protected it from attack by outsiders, so the religious community took on the physical characteristics of an enclosed and inaccessible place (the *claustrum* or 'cloister'). Enclosure was seen as a definite option: from the moment she entered religious life, the enclosure bounded the whole existence of the nun, the *moniales*, in space as in time. She could only go out of the enclosure to found another monastery, in other words only to stay enclosed. Even death did not allow her to leave the monastery: 'Those who die, ladies as well as servants, and who had made profession, shall fittingly be buried within the enclosure [*intra claustrum*].'[21] This was certainly not the first time that enclosure had been so strict. For example, a century earlier Robert d'Arbrissel had founded some communities where the enclosure required grilles everywhere and the women covered their faces with veils lest they be seen. In those cases, however, the community was part of a double monastery, that is, a community of men with a community of women near by. A highly original formula had been worked out by Robert d'Arbrissel of which the prototype was Fontevrault.[22] The French preacher had wanted the major responsibility in his Order to belong to the abbess. Perhaps it was only chance, but the fact remains that the first western statement of enclosure was expressed in a manner characterised by the degree of space granted to women.[23] The same observation could also be made about the monasteries of women attached to the Cistercian Order. In this case, the obligation of enclosure was introduced in 1213, although for some time their abbesses continued to take part in the men's chapters. They also claimed the ancient right to preach in their own monasteries.[24]

Ugolino was attached to the Order of Bernard of Clairvaux and knew its spirituality. It was probably that tradition which inspired him when he had to draw up some Constitutions for communities of women. However, on reading his Constitutions, we do find a particular insistence on enclosure. He does not treat it as only a penitential choice, albeit an heroic one; nor does he see it as only an ascetical means. For Ugolino, enclosure had a value in itself. In his mind it was strongly linked with virginity. He behaved exactly as a good head of a household would have behaved towards his daughters, keeping them in retirement and safeguarding their virginity as a prerequisite for later giving them in marriage to the man of his choice. When the women entrusted to him were taken by the cardinal under the protection of the Apostolic See, he saw himself as in duty bound to protect their virginity with a view to their making the most advantageous marriage of all – with the Lord Jesus himself. This is the origin of Ugolino's constant preoccupation with enclosure.

He did not confine himself to regulating the nuns' dealings with the outside world, but actually gave them a whole new style of life. In fact, he proposed an enclosure which included a double prohibition, for the eye and for the tongue. On the women entrusted to him, Ugolino imposed total silence: 'Let a continuous silence be kept by everyone everywhere because they may not speak without permission neither among themselves nor with others.'[25] This prohibition worked both ways: they were neither to speak nor hear. This was mortification of the senses and death to the world as an exercise of penance, and the link with enclosure is obvious. Just as the physical space may not be violated by anyone coming or anyone going out, so the silence may not be violated by any words.

Ugolino has now travelled some way from the Rule of St Benedict on which, strictly speaking, he was only writing a commentary. In the Rule, a great importance is attached to *taciturnitas*, which is something other than silence and being dumb. Benedict's concern is that we should avoid sin when speaking: 'Let us do as the prophet said: I will set a guard over my ways that I may not sin with my tongue.'[26] The Rule prescribes that the monk should have a disciple's attitude, choosing to listen rather than to talk in an empty way, and that the monks should as the apostle advises, take care that their words 'be such as build others up'.[27] It is only in the chapter concerned with what they are to do after Compline that the Rule uses the word *silentium*, 'silence'. Surely this is an indispensable regulation in view of the custom of sleeping in a common dormitory! In this same chapter, however, Benedict also foresees that one might need to break the silence if a guest turned up or if the abbot gave some other order.[28] However we look at it, it was clearly Ugolino's attitude which made silence into a major preoccupation. So much was this so, that he recommended the visitator of the *moniales*, the 'nuns', to make it one of the points on which he especially checked when making his visitation.

The second prohibition imposed by the Constitutions concerned seeing, being seen. It was not enough that in every place where the monastery touched the outside world (doors, parlours, the interface between the monastery and the chapel) there should be an iron grille. The Constitutions also required that behind the grille should hang a black curtain: 'A black cloth should be placed on the inside of this iron grille so that no one is able to see anything in the chapel outside.'[29]

This fear of being seen cannot but lead us back to the practice of courtly culture in which the glance was part of a highly expressive code used in the language of love. From her girlhood in her father's house, Clare had lived apart, not showing herself at the window for the passers-by to see. In the choice of life which Cardinal Ugolino put before the Tuscan women, this same attitude of withdrawal became a radical renunciation of every form of looking and, therefore, of all contacts with the world around them.[30]

Cardinal Ugolino met Clare very early on. By 1217 the prelate had already come to know Francis, when they were both in Florence, and had persuaded Francis to stay in Italy and postpone his trip to France. From then on, the links between the cardinal and the minorite movement had become stronger and stronger.[31]

A LETTER FROM UGOLINO TO CLARE

Between 1219 and 1220, Francis was in the Holy Land. During this time, the relationship between Ugolino and Clare had developed and, in 1220, the cardinal stayed at San Damiano for Holy Week. As a result, he wrote to Clare and her sisters from Viterbo just a few days after his visit to San Damiano. We only have a copy of this letter, preserved in the next century in the *Chronicle of the 24 Generals*.[32] In it, Ugolino uses particularly affectionate language:

My very own dear sister in Christ: Since that moment when the need to return here separated me from that holy conversation which I had with you and tore me away from the joy I found in heavenly treasure – since then I have been overwhelmed with such bitterness of heart, with so many tears and such a weight of sorrow. Unless, at the feet of Jesus, I find consolation in his compassion, I fear that I shall always be in such distress that my spirit might even die of it and my soul be quite undone.[33]

Behind the rather pompous, curial style, the message comes through sincerely enough. The cardinal recommends himself to the prayer and intercession of Clare and her companions: 'I confide my soul to you. I recommend my spiritual life to you.'[34]

Ugolino had been much struck by the life and dedication of the women gathered around Clare even while he recognised that this community was not the same as those which he himself had founded in various towns of central Italy. In the first place, the San Damiano community was different simply because it had not been founded by a cardinal. When Clare fled from her home, she certainly did not wait for authorisation or protection from the Apostolic See. Hers had indeed been a choice of radical faith.

San Damiano had come into being with no security, no rule, no ecclesiastical protection, quite unlike the other communities with which Ugolino was concerned and which had all been founded on the basis of clear juridical guarantees.[35] This difference in origin was the inner secret which stamped itself on every aspect of the community which Clare, and Francis with her, wanted. When Clare saw that it had become necessary to obtain a privilege, she asked for herself and her companions no other privilege than that of poverty, that is, no privilege except the one of continuing to live without privilege and without security. Did Ugolino understand this difference? Certainly he was struck by the exceptional quality of their life, but in the end he interpreted it in the light of his own understanding which was, again, the enclosed life focussed on mystical marriage with Christ. In fact, several years later when he had become pope, Ugolino wrote to Clare giving exactly this interpretation to her choice of life:

Inspired by the Lord, you have bound yourself by enclosure so that, abandoning the world and everything in it, you can run in the odour of his ointments to embrace your Spouse with a pure love.[36]

There were, of course, several points in common between the communities Ugolino was responsible for and the community at San Damiano, as for instance the choice of a life of poverty, and of a life in common dedicated primarily to prayer. The difference begins to emerge when we consider the place in which the sisters lived.

When Clare first went there, San Damiano was not a *monasterium*, or 'monastery', but simply a small country church. It probably had a house attached to it where the officiating priest lived,[37] in this case Sylvester who, the sources tell us, became one of Francis' first companions.[38] From the architectural point of view, the sisters' house was no different from the other primitive Franciscan places. Like Rivotorto and the Portiuncola, San Damiano was a rural chapel, built of stone, restored by Francis himself, around which modest constructions of wood and straw grew up to allow a life in common. In every aspect, these buildings were the same as the hovels and huts of the Assisi peasants and country folk.[39]

In order to live their mendicant life, Francis and his companions had had no need of large stone buildings, nor would such buildings have been consonant with their choice of poverty or the itinerant character of their way of life.[40] Clare and her sisters, on the other hand, were fixed at San Damiano and this very stability probably brought about a rapid transformation of the various buildings gathered round the little church. The sisters needed a dormitory, an infirmary, a small refectory built of stone; and gradually it all began to resemble a small monastery. However, San Damiano always had an unfinished air, an appearance of being, so to speak, in becoming. Around the buildings for the sisters there were also some mud and straw huts where a small group of brothers usually lived. They were responsible for the material and spiritual welfare of the sisters. These huts were quick and easy to make and one was built especially for Francis when, as a sick man, he spent a winter at San Damiano and, according to the *Legend of Perugia*,[41] composed the Canticle of All Creatures there. Clare always wanted her monastery to retain its temporary character, so much so that she could envisage in her Testament the possibility that her sisters might actually leave it to go and live somewhere else.

THE ORIGINALITY OF THE SAN DAMIANO EXPERIENCE

The originality of the San Damiano experience is shown above all by the way in which Clare handles enclosure. There is no need to underline the fact that life at San Damiano was eremitical. In her writings, Clare chooses to say very little about enclosure, yet she herself lived at San Damiano for a full forty-two years.[42] To an observer, her life was not greatly different from that of the other *pauperes dominae reclusae*, 'enclosed and poor women'. However, enclosure and the eremitical life are not necessarily the same, which is why Clare's life could appear to be similar to that of her contemporaries and yet be so profoundly different, both in the ideals which motivated her and in the way in which she daily lived out those ideals.

The community of San Damiano was an eremitical community right from the start, composed of women who followed to the letter the Gospel precept to 'seek first the kingdom of God and his justice'. They sought to live their life of prayer in isolation and separation from the world.[43] Enclosure was not added later, but was there from the very beginning. However, it is no contradiction that right from the beginning Francis and Clare also thought of San Damiano as being an open com-

munity. It was a community so open as to be without boundaries, with a horizon as wide as the whole world. In this sense,
one can say that the spirituality of enclosure (at least as it
emerges from Ugolino's Constitutions) was never introduced at
San Damiano.

In her Testament, Clare records the beginnings of her community:

In fact, the saint himself, in a great transport of joy and illumination
of the Spirit, made a prophecy in our regard which the Lord has
brought about. This was not long after his conversion, when he had
neither brothers nor companions. While he was repairing the Church
of San Damiano, he received a visit from the Lord which left him
drunk with divine consolation and which gave him the decisive thrust
to abandon the world entirely.

It was at this time that he climbed onto the wall of the same Church
and cried out (in French) to some poor people who lived near by:
Come and help me in this task of building a monastery here at San
Damiano, for soon some ladies will come here to live and through the
renown and the holiness of their lives, they will give glory to our
heavenly father in all his holy Church.[44]

This prophecy by Francis spoke of a fame to be shed over the
whole Church. Many years later Clare was not afraid to say
that she had given reality to what Francis had prophesied. This
universal prophecy was preserved at San Damiano as a relic
might be, for it was their founding prophecy. Not only did
Clare want it inserted in her Testament, but very probably Clare
herself, or at least the San Damiano community, told the story
to Thomas of Celano and he put it into his *Second Life* of
Francis.[45]

The community of San Damiano, therefore, was an enclosed
community but their enclosure was unconfined, without limits.
This is the apparent contradiction of the eremitical apostolate:
by hiding, the example of a life shows forth; by withdrawing,
many children and spiritual disciples are begotten. The bull of
the canonisation of Clare throws this contradiction into high
relief:

How brilliant is the power of this light, how strong is the bright shining
of this luminous source! This light was enclosed in the hiddenness of

the cloister and yet outside [the cloister] she shone with dazzling shining; she contained herself within a small monastery yet she was spread as far as the world is wide; she kept herself within yet she was diffused far and wide. Clare hid herself but her life was known to everyone. Clare was silent but her fame cried aloud. She kept herself hidden in her cell and the whole city knew about her.[46]

The eremitical life is not in contradiction with fame and reputation, in fact in a certain sense the one is a precondition of the other.[47] For Clare, her *conversatio*, that is, the way she lived at San Damiano, had to have value as an example. In giving such a high profile to example, Clare was particularly close to Francis.[48] As Raoul Manselli has written so perceptively:

The brotherhood was not shaped by its function or by its following of a law, but by its copying of an example: Francis himself. Bernard, Peter Cattani, Sylvester and then little by little all the others, joined together to follow this one man who in turn followed his own model, Christ and the life he lived among us as set out in the Gospel. The idyllic scenes of the first brethren at Rivotorto or the Portiuncola could, if isolated from their historical context, give the impression of edifying tales, but they look very different if we see them as they in fact were: contests in good example around Francis, the exemplar, and all in an atmosphere of joyous happiness and an exceptional degree of interior liberty.[49]

It is more than likely that even at San Damiano Clare wanted to live in this same climate of good example. In her Testament, she hammered home the power of example:

The Lord himself has placed us like a model for others, as an example and a mirror, not only for other people but also for our own sisters whom the Lord has called to our vocation, so that they too can be mirrors and examples to all who live in the world.[50]

She transcended the limits of the hermitage in two directions: from the inside towards the outside, by accepting that she was an example, a model, one who had something to say to the whole Church; and from the outside towards the inside, by the way in which she and her sisters welcomed whoever and whatever came from the outside, so that everything became their concern. This widening of interests and preoccupations was not just an inner attitude of Clare and her companions, nor was it limited simply to the intercessory prayer which forms part of any cloistered experience. For Clare and her companions it was the result of a transformation in the primitive Franciscan places brought about by the rapid and tumultuous development of the Order. It is important not to forget the central position which Assisi came to hold as a result of this extraordinary development of the minorite movement.[51] Little by little, as numbers grew and spread among different peoples and nationalities, the brothers saw that the very roots of their movement were nourished from San Damiano[52] and the Portiuncola[53] as well as from the basilica where the body of the saint lay buried.[54] This phenomenon had already begun during the last years of the Poverello's life when the general chapter of the brothers was held at Assisi. It was at this chapter that the movement, which had unexpectedly become so huge and so widespread, was finally able to generate some sort of unity.[55]

After the death of Francis, all the Franciscan places became sanctuaries, holy places. The Portiuncola was granted the privilege of indulgence so that a pilgrimage to the little church on the Assisi plain became a kind of alternative to the crusades, allowing the pilgrims to gain the same spiritual benefits. San Damiano was always intimately connected with the life of Francis, and here was kept the crucifix before which the Poverello made his choice and decision to serve the Church. Clare's community found itself a part of this transformation. From being a small group of women hermits who lived in an isolated little country church, they became a community living next to one of the most important places of Franciscan pilgrimage. Clare and her companions always wanted to maintain the eremitical character of their chosen way of life and yet, without any contradiction, they maintained an intense spiritual dialogue with everyone who came to San Damiano.

AN OPEN COMMUNITY

One of the most consistent and telling differences between San Damiano and the communities living by Cardinal Ugolino's Constitutions was that Clare never dreamt of imposing a total ban on speech. In fact she made spiritual dialogue and preaching one of the focal points of her community's life.

By means of holy preachers, she always provided her daughters with the food of the Word of God, taking a large portion of this food for herself, for she found that great joy was hidden in listening to holy preaching.[56]

A large number of the brethren came on pilgrimage to San Damiano and, therefore, visited the sisters. If one thinks of how far-flung the minorite movement became, with brothers in every part of Europe as well as Africa, the Middle East and, with John da Pian del Carpine, even in China, then one begins to grasp the richness of interests which flooded into the little community at San Damiano. At the same time, as has been said, the current ran in two directions, from the outside to the inside and back again. Thus, all the news of far-off lands which came into San Damiano was complemented by the concern, the letters, the sense of mission which came out of San Damiano. There was even a moment when Clare herself thought about leaving her community and the hermitage at San Damiano. This had been a dramatic moment, testified to in the canonisation process by Sister Cecilia di Gualtieri Cacciaguerra:

The Lady Clare had such a fervent spirit that she willingly wanted to endure martyrdom for the love of the Lord. She showed this when she had heard that certain brothers had been martyred in Morocco and she said that she too wanted to go there. The witness wept because of this.[57]

This was supported by the evidence of Sister Balvina:

For the love of God, she would gladly have borne martyrdom in defence of the Faith and her Order. Before she became ill, she wanted to go to that part of Morocco where, it was said, the Brothers had been martyred.[58]

On 16 January 1220, five brothers, Berardo, Pietro, Accursio, Adiuto and Ottone, had been martyred in Morocco.[59] Their mission had been the direct result of an initiative of Francis himself who had met the sultan of Egypt, Al-Malik al-Kamil, in Damietta and had unarmed proclaimed the Gospel to him, thus embarking on a counter-crusade which only failed because of the intransigence of the crusaders themselves.[60]

The Moroccan mission had been carefully prepared and its leader, Berardo, was an Arabic speaker. The brothers travelled through Spain and Portugal until they reached Seville where they began to preach the Gospel in the mosques. When, however, the five brothers openly criticised Muhammed, declaring that he was an impostor and a servant of Satan, they were no longer trusted. They were arrested and finally transported to Morocco and, since they kept on reviling the name of the prophet of Islam, beheaded at Marrakesh.[61]

Francis had just come back from the East when the news reached Assisi and one source tells us that when he heard about the martyrdom he cried out: 'Now I can safely say that I have five friars minor!'[62] The news made a great impression on Francis.[63] Just at that time, he was busy writing the Rule of the Order that we now call the *Regula non bullata*, and towards the end of it he put in a whole chapter on 'Those who are going among the Saracens and other non-believers'. In this chapter he lays down that the brethren in Islamic countries should conduct themselves in one of two ways, the first of which is simply to be subject to everyone (what a scandal – Christians agreeing to submit to infidels!); the second is explicitly to proclaim the Gospel, but only when circumstances permit. At the beginning of the chapter, Francis reminds the brothers that they must be 'as simple as doves and as wise as serpents'. It is an invitation to prudence which we can probably interpret as the fruit of reflection on the news about the five martyrs in Morocco.[64]

Clare, too, heard the news. We have no information about whether the martyred brothers were personally known to her, but certainly her reaction was powerful: she, too, wanted to go to Morocco and be martyred. It cannot just have been something she said for the sake of it, because Sister Cecilia took it seriously enough to burst into tears. Even as late as 1253, thirty-three years after the event, both Sister Cecilia and Sister Balvina remembered exactly how Clare had intended to go to Morocco. At this time, Clare had been enclosed at San Damiano for about eight years, she was responsible for the community, she held the title of abbess and, yet, confronted by this news of the martyrdom of these five brothers, she thought of leaving all this in order to share their life and death. Sister Balvina relates that Clare wanted to do all this 'in defence of the faith and her Order'. She means by 'her Order' that Clare considered the whole movement of minors, both the male and the female branches, as being one Order. Sister Balvina then goes on to record that all this took place 'before she was ill'. This is a fairly precise chronological reference, because Clare became ill in the early 1220s, but more than that, it is a completely understandable explanation of why she did not go to Morocco. In other words, she did not give up the idea because of the advice of other people, nor because it seemed better to stay with her community, but simply through force of circumstances: she became ill.

In the second half of the thirteenth century, when the *Life* of Clare was written, the ideal of the crusade was much less strong than it had been.[65] Frederick II, who died in 1250, had been excommunicated for making an agreement similar to the one which Al-Malik al-Kamil had offered the Christians at Damietta. After 1250,[66] and after all the polemics about how the crusades had been betrayed, the matter of the Holy Land seemed to become one of indifference and distrust. In such a climate, even the witness of Francis' unarmed dialogue was forgotten, even among his own brethren. The *Life* of Clare bears this out, for its author, although a Franciscan, says nothing about Clare's failed pilgrimage to Morocco, even though his readers were themselves close to the minorite movement.

So San Damiano was a place both closed and open at the same time. Clare lived there for forty-two consecutive years. Yet, confronted by the death of some of her brothers, she had been ready to leave everything and travel to a distant country in order to bear witness with her life.

CLARE AND ENCLOSURE

In order to resolve the apparent contradiction in Clare's attitude to enclosure, we need to try and share her innermost thoughts about her choice of the eremitic life. What *was* Clare's personal attitude towards enclosure? We can reconstruct this fairly accurately by starting with her writings, even though she actually says very little there on enclosure.[67] The very absence of the term speaks volumes about her approach; enclosure, for Clare, was not a value in itself and by itself; above all, she did not link it with virginity and chastity, as we have seen was the case in the Constitutions of Ugolino. Even when she speaks at some length about virginity, as she does in her letters to Agnes of Bohemia, she still does not link it with the theme of enclosure. What is more, this same Agnes lived in a monastery in Prague with a hospital next to it where the sisters worked, so they were, in fact, leading an active life. Clare certainly knew all about the life-style of the sisters in Prague and it must have seemed to her perfectly acceptable, for she never thought she should intervene or criticise.[68]

Of the four letters which we have from the correspondence of Clare and Agnes, only one makes any allusion to enclosure and this talks about an enclosure which is wholly interior in imitation of the Mother of God 'who gave birth to a son, such that even Heaven could not contain him, yet she received him into the little enclosed space of her womb and carried him on her virginal lap'.[69] The 'home', the cloister, which according to Clare must house the Lord Jesus, is not a house of stone but the actual body of each sister. Here we also find the meaning of virginity for Clare. She did not equate virginity with solitude but saw it rather as opening wide her whole being, her whole life, in order to contain the Lord 'whom the Heavens could not contain'. In this, Clare was perfectly responding to Francis' invitation: 'Let us build within ourselves a house, a permanent dwelling place for him, that is for the Lord Almighty, Father, Son and Holy Spirit.'[70]

The fact that the only statement Clare has to make about enclosure is contained in this third letter to Agnes does not mean that her life apart was in no way reflected in her writings, but rather that she preferred to express it in other words such as integrity (*honestas*) and privacy (*remotio*). These are less technical expressions, less bound to monastic religious language, so to speak more 'lay' in their meaning.[71] *Honestas*, as we find it used of the childhood of Clare and the work which she chose to undertake, implies one's good name, one's good repute, the reputation required for a lady of that period and even more so for a consecrated one. So in her Testament Clare places integrity among the fundamental virtues of her community:

I admonish and beg in the Lord Jesus Christ, that all my sisters, present and to come, should always strive to imitate the life of holy simplicity, of humility and of poverty and also the integrity of that holy life which we were taught by our blessed Father Francis right from the beginning of our conversion to Christ.[72]

Just as for a young woman, *honestas* was simultaneously the evidence and the guarantee that she had kept herself apart, so for the ladies at San Damiano this integrity was linked to their isolation, their *remotio*. This was why, in her Testament, when Clare speculates that after her death the sisters might move to another monastery, her main preoccupation was that this new monastery should not contravene the characteristics of her ideal of life. She was particularly anxious that they should not have land within the enclosure 'except as much as is necessary to cultivate their vegetables'. After having said that, however, Clare was probably concerned lest a vegetable garden would not be sufficient guarantee of this remoteness, and so she adds:

But if at any time it becomes necessary for the fitting privacy of the monastery to have a little land beyond the amount of the vegetable garden, they may not acquire more than is absolutely necessary. Then, too, this land must not be worked or sown but should always remain unploughed and uncultivated.[73]

Isolation and good repute were such fundamental characteristics of the community of San Damiano that for their sake Clare makes her one and only exception to the ideal of absolute poverty for which she had fought all her life.[74] What is more, the eremitic apartness envisioned by Clare in her Testament was quite other than the ideal of enclosure as set out in the Constitutions of Ugolino.

It does seem, however, that for a while the Constitutions which Ugolino had drawn up for other women religious in central Italy had been accepted at San Damiano.[75] There is a hint to this effect in a letter to Agnes of Bohemia from the cardinal himself, written after he had become Pope Gregory IX.[76] All the same, the Constitutions of Ugolino must have been applied at San Damiano in a unique way, given that the community had a document which, juridically speaking, guaranteed its originality, namely the *Privilege of Poverty*. This gives us grounds to conclude that daily life at San Damiano actually went on according to the dispositions which Francis made in the first years of the community. Ugolino's Constitutions were not well suited to life at San Damiano as is proved by the fact that they were dropped so quickly.

There had been a number of attempts to devise a new Rule for all the women's communities of central Italy, but Clare was not satisfied with any of them and in the end she decided that she herself would write a Rule for her community. This was an unprecedented decision in the life of the Church, since it had never been known for a woman to write a Rule for other women. This decision alone would have been enough to make Clare one of the most significant women in the history of Christianity.[77]

Obviously, this Rule of Clare looked back to those Rules which had gone before, not only the Rule of Benedict and Ugolino's Constitutions but also – and above all – the Rule of Francis in its two revisions, that is the so-called *Regula non bullata* and the *Regula bullata*. In Clare's Rule, the problem of enclosure was systematically dealt with and she devoted different sections to descriptions of the door, the grilles and the other characteristics typical of a cloistered community.[78] Such details were obviously needed in a legislative document which would have to be submitted for papal approval, yet we may still ask why Clare entered into such minute detail. It is possible that one of the factors which made her decide to write her own Rule, and insert those sections on enclosure, was the appearance of other groups of women who called themselves *minoretae*, 'minoresses'. This was in about 1240. These groups of women, appealing to the spirit of Francis, had no fixed abode but went around preaching as the brethren did. They had been condemned several times by the pope, who did not recognise them as a religious order and did all he could to obstruct them.[79] It could be that Clare wanted to underline her non-involvement with this movement, which was often considered heretical, and she did so by stressing the cloistered character of her own experience.

The Rule which Clare wrote was to supersede all the preceding Rules. If we systematically juxtapose her Rule and the others (particularly the Constitutions) we can reconstruct the directions in which Clare was moving and her reasons for rejecting those Rules which had been imposed on her.

In the chapter which she dedicates to the custody of the enclosure, the doors of the monastery and the visitation, Clare follows Ugolino's Constitutions almost to the letter. The door must have two locks of which the abbess keeps one key and the portress the other; only those permitted by the pope or the cardinal protector may enter the monastery, and so on. The prescriptions are the same in both Rules. What does change is the value which enclosure assumes in the context of each. Clare's Rule does not conceive of perpetual enclosure and settles that a sister who has received the tonsure 'may not go outside the monastery except for a useful, reasonable, obvious and approved motive'.[80] In other words, even after solemn profession, a sister can leave the monastery. There can be reasons for this which are useful, reasonable, obvious and approved (other than the single one of founding another community, which is all Ugolino allows for).

The difference between Clare's Rule and that of Ugolino is highlighted in the arrangements about silence: 'Let the sisters observe silence from the hour of Compline until Terce.'[81] Thus, in Clare's Rule, silence is in fact to be observed for the night and not perpetually as Ugolino expects. This is not just a juggling of how many hours' silence; it is a question of spirituality. Clare saw no intrinsic value in the forbidding of words. Her Rule ordains absolute silence only in the Church, the dormitory and the refectory, and she is concerned that these rules should not be interpreted legalistically. To this end, she adds two guidelines which are entirely her own and which were obviously born out of her long experience of living the common life at San Damiano:

For the comfort and the service of the sick in the infirmary, the sisters may always (in moderation) speak. Anyway they can communicate what is necessary always and everywhere, though briefly and in a low voice.[82]

So it is always permissible to speak 'for the comfort and service of the sick' because, for Clare, the spoken word is always a comfort especially when one is ill. She was concerned about this earlier on:

The sick sisters, when they are visited by anyone coming into the monastery, can in their turn respond briefly with some good words for those who speak to them.[83]

Similarly, in Clare's Rule the prohibition about not seeing or being seen also has no absolute value. It is true that she provides for a grille in parlour and choir, with a curtain to prevent the sisters from seeing or being seen, but she adds:

At this grille, on the inside, shall be hung a curtain which shall not be moved (aside) except when someone is preaching the Word of God, or when any person is speaking with another.[84]

In other words, each day when the moment comes for the Gospel to be read during Mass, the curtain at the grille is to be pulled aside so that the sisters can hear the Word of God better. In addition, whenever they have occasion to speak with someone from outside the monastery (in the manner and with the precautions set out in the Rule), the sisters may peacefully see the face of the one to whom they speak and may themselves be seen in their turn.[85]

All these are not just concessions which Clare wanted to introduce into the harshness of Ugolino's Constitutions, rather they are the expression of a completely different concept of the life of apartness. For Ugolino, the choice of religious life is an option for seclusion, self-mortification, the denial of the very functions of life like seeing and hearing. For Clare, religious life is exactly the opposite; it is the fulfillment of the life of a man or a woman. Seclusion for her is really openness to the world, isolation is the fullness of spiritual communion.

Within this paradoxical Gospel perspective, the little space of San Damiano contains the whole world; the tiny cloister holds, within itself, infinite space.

FIVE

A Woman of Penance

At San Damiano there can have been no lack of things to do and far more manual work than simply that involved in weaving. There was the cleaning, the cooking, the gardening, all the tasks of everyday life that must have required a great deal of time, but the task to which Clare most gave herself was undoubtedly that of prayer.[1]

CLARE'S PERSONAL AND COMMUNITY PRAYER

The canonical hours were said at San Damiano. During the canonisation process the sisters spoke about this prayer of praise as something completely obvious. They talked about Terce, Sext, None, Vespers and Compline, all of which were in common and which set the rhythm of the San Damiano day. Clare went to great trouble to ensure that this prayer was conducted in the best possible way. Now that we have considered her conversion and her choice of poverty, we cannot ignore this aspect of her life if we are fully to evaluate her experience.

At the canonisation process, Sister Balvina said of Clare that 'she was very diligent and solicitous in prayer, contemplation and the exhortation of her sisters. She had given her whole mind to this'.[2] Her whole mind focussed on this life of prayer. It was Clare's major preoccupation and a theme about which the sisters were eloquent. At San Damiano they followed the traditional rhythms of the monastic life:

The said mother Clare was very assiduous, day and night, in prayer. At about midnight she woke the sisters with certain signs in silence to praise God. She lit the lamps in the church and frequently rang the bell for Matins. Those sisters who did not rise at the sound of the bell she called with her signs.[3]

The sisters were concerned above all to show what trouble Clare took over the small gestures necessary to community prayer. For example, Sister Agnes records that

the lady Clare, with an abundance of tears, stayed at prayer for a long time after Compline. At about midnight she likewise arose to pray, while she was still well, and she woke the sisters by touching them in silence. She particularly prayed the hour of Sext because she said the Lord was placed on the cross at that hour.[4]

This loving behaviour corresponds to the guidelines which Clare herself gave in her Testament to those who would follow her in responsibility for the community (notice that Clare never uses the term 'abbess' in her Testament):

I also beg that sister who will hold office in the future that she strive with love to precede all the others more by virtue and the holiness of her behaviour than by her office.[5]

To participate in community prayer was important and in the Rule of Clare there is a disposition which reflects the practice of San Damiano but is not included in the preceding Rules:

The sisters who can read shall celebrate the divine office according to the custom of the Friars Minor; for this they may have breviaries, but they are to read it without singing . . . those who do not know how to read shall say twenty-four Our Fathers for Matins; five for Lauds; for each of the hours of Prime, Terce, Sext and None, seven; for Vespers however twelve.[6]

The biggest surprise here is her veto on singing. The monastic office provided for singing at all the hours and the chant was one of its most precious ornaments. At San Damiano, instead of singing, they chose a poorer way of prayer which, for those sisters who were not educated, was commuted to the recitation of a number of paternosters, just as Francis had prescribed for the brethren who could not read.[7]

This arrangement in the Rule of Clare is all the more striking when we recall that the Rule of Innocent IV provides for singing.[8] What we have here is a radical interpretation of Francis' provision in his Letter to the Entire Order that:

The clerics [shall] say the Office with devotion before God, not concentrating on the melody of the voice but on the harmony of the mind, so that the voice may blend with the mind, and the mind be in harmony with God. Let them do this in such a way that they please God through purity of heart and not charm the ears of the people with sweetness of voice.[9]

The absence of singing in prayer underlines all the more strongly the importance of the spoken word. The psalms would have been recited and the Gospel read aloud. One of the witnesses at the canonisation process spells out the full import of Clare's love for the spoken word:

The witness [Sister Agnes] also said Lady Clare delighted in hearing the Word of God. Although she had never studied letters she nevertheless listened willingly to learned sermons.[10]

In these words there is, perhaps, an echo of Clare's first experience of faith. In the life of San Damiano, the central place taken by preaching parallels the central place taken in Francis' early experience by his service to the lepers. Just as Francis in his Testament says that he began to do penance after he had had his encounter with the leper, so Clare in her Testament says that she began 'to do penance according to the example and teaching of our most blessed Father Francis'.[11] This memory of the moment when Clare had begun her undertaking offers a deeper reason why she settled in her Rule that the black veil, which normally covered the grille, should be drawn aside when anyone was preaching.

Clare's concern for the common prayer does not, however, exhaust the whole of her life of prayer. Even if she could not exactly be defined as a contemplative in the modern sense of the word,[12] yet she was most certainly a woman of intense prayer.

When we try to learn a little more about the personal prayer of Clare we find, once again, that the most interesting source is the canonisation process. This gives us important evidence, born of a familiarity which is open even to the point of indiscretion, as for example when Sister Pacifica responds to the question of the notary about whether Clare watched through the night in prayer. Pacifica says that she 'heard her when she was in prayer'.[13] Clare's personal prayer had grown all the stronger because for many years her illness had prevented her from going to the church for the community prayer:

At that time when she, the witness, entered the monastery, the Lady Clare was sick, yet she nevertheless got out of bed during the night and kept a vigil in prayer with many tears. She did the same thing in the morning at about the hour of Terce.[14]

Above all, the sisters had been struck by Clare's face when she came from prayer:

She was vigilant in prayer and sublime contemplation. At times, when she returned from prayer, her face appeared clearer than usual and a certain sweetness came from her mouth.

She was assiduous in prayer and contemplation. When she returned from prayer, her face appeared clearer and more beautiful than the sun. Her prayers sent forth an indescribable sweetness so her life seemed totally heavenly.[15]

Again we have this description of Clare's face,[16] but this time it is not a young girl ready for marriage who is being described, as when Messer Ranieri de Bernardo had spoken of her beauty. The face of Clare which the sisters saw so resplendent with light was the face of a woman of prayer who had just been speaking with God. The prototype who comes to mind here is Moses, who covered his face after speaking with God in the Tent of Meeting, although the author of the *Life*, usually so free with his scriptural references, simply repeats the words of the sisters:

When she returned with joy from holy prayer, she brought from the altar of the Lord burning words that also inflamed the hearts of her sisters. In fact, they marvelled that such sweetness came from her mouth and that her face shone more brilliantly than usual.[17]

That we are not just talking about a biblical image is reinforced by the fact that the sisters found this phenomenon of light not only on the face of Clare but even in the place where she had prayed:

In that place where the Lady Clare usually prayed, she saw above it a great brilliance so she believed it was the flame from an actual fire. Asked if anyone else had seen it, she replied, at that time she was the only one who saw it. Asked how long ago this had been, she replied it was before the Lady was sick.[18]

What we have here is a new form of religious expression in which the presence of the divine power is, so to speak, material-ised in a human being. These luminous phenomena came to be associated above all with women of prayer such as Clare herself and, after her, others like Clare of Montefalco and Catherine of Siena.[19]

Certainly this description by the sisters was rooted in their love; all their attention focussed on Clare and her prayer. So Sister Pacifica can record with simplicity that 'when she returned from her prayer, the sisters rejoiced as though she had come from heaven'.[20] This must have been all the more so because Clare used then to give the sisters an exhortation:

When she came from her prayer she admonished and comforted her sisters always speaking the words of God who was always in her mouth, so much so that she did not want to speak or hear of vanities.[21]

THE PRACTICE OF PENANCE

The whole of this life of prayer, whether personal or in common, found its external expression in fasting and penance. Through-out the testimonies given at the canonisation process we con-stantly hear these two terms, prayer and penance. However, while the prayer of Clare was a source of consolation to the sisters, her abstinence was often a source of concern:

The blessed mother kept vigil so much of the night in prayer, and kept so many abstinences that the sisters lamented and were alarmed. She [Sister Pacifica] said that because of this she herself had sometimes wept.[22]

There can be no doubt that such penance was a clear sign of holiness, even, for Sister Lucia, the outstanding sign:

She said she always saw the Lady Clare acting in great holiness. Asked in what sort of holiness, she replied in great punishment of her flesh and in great harshness of her life.[23]

This mortification of the flesh sprang directly from that 'culture of penance' so characteristic of the thirteenth century. While in the New Testament, the word 'penance' (which corresponds to the Greek *metanoia*) was used to signify conversion, an interior change,[24] in the course of the centuries, and helped along by the development of public confession, the word acquired another meaning, so that it came more and more to mean those exterior acts which accompanied conversion or reconciliation. This second, more juridical and exterior meaning came to be the one which often prevailed.[25]

The beginning of the thirteenth century was marked by a great resurgence of penance which led, in the end, to the establishment of new Orders of penitents who stayed 'in the world', that is they did not enter monastic life, but lived a religious life, practising continence and engaging in works of mercy.[26]

Through these Orders, the themes of penance and the external practice of mortification entered into the fabric of people's lives, so much so that they became the defining characteristics of what has been called 'the culture of penance'. This culture represented a psychological attitude in people towards life and death, themselves and God. As a result, penance ceased to be a moment of transition or the practice of some mortification, and instead it became a dimension of life itself.[27] Angela of Foligno, although she lived in the century after Clare, still shared in the same penitential culture and expressed this ideal of perpetual penitence very succinctly. 'This is the duration and the end of penance: the whole life of a man; this is when it is great: when a man can sustain it'.[28]

Clare's practice of penance, which she chose and which was described in her canonisation process, is very like that practised by other women of the same period, in other parts of Europe. One example out of many will help us to understand the devotional climate in which we need to place Clare's penitential practices. Let us take Mary of Oignies, whose life was written by Jacques de Vitry. Geographically she was far away from Clare, although it is quite possible that Clare had heard her spoken about, since, as Jacques himself tells us, she was known even in Italy by 1216. Mary well reflects the general climate in which women's spirituality developed at that time, even if some of the overtones of heroism should really be attributed to her biographer. In the *Life of Mary of Oignies* he tells us that:

Embracing the Cross of Christ, she was crucified in her flesh. She denied herself, placing herself under obedience to the will of another. She carried the Cross, chastising her body with abstinence, and imitated Christ by humbling herself . . . She never drank wine, never ate meat, ate fish only rarely and took very little fruit, herbs or vegetables, the minimum with which to keep herself alive. She ate the blackest and coarsest bread such as even a dog would hardly be able to manage, and she did this for a long time. Because of these and similar hardships and harsh treatment, the inside of her throat became lacerated and would bleed, which called to her mind the sweet memory of the Blood of Christ.[29]

These quotations could be multiplied; the pattern of religious piety, above all that of women, at the beginning of the thirteenth century, remains the same. The vision of Christ crucified generated the longing to imitate him and to share his sufferings, even physically. Suffering became a value in itself, so that those who practised this piety very often practised a high degree of violent self-punishment. This was a solitary religiosity; the faithful chastised themselves in solitude, punished their own bodies.[30]

Clare was tempted by this piety, this religiosity. At certain moments it must have seemed sweet to her to punish herself so that her own body felt the sufferings of Jesus on the cross. This is the great temptation, to seize salvation by one's own strength, by a mighty effort of denial, by conquest of one's own passions, even the most natural ones such as eating and sleeping. It is in this sense that we must interpret her decision, made in the early days at San Damiano, to wear under her clothes a small rectangle of coarse material (woven of horsehair) which, like a scourge, was a martyrdom to her flesh.[31]

So Clare was a typical 'woman of penance';[32] that is, she was an exponent of that form of devotion and spirituality which linked the following of the Crucified with a stern regimen of personal mortification. Francis, too, was a 'man of penance', so much so that he was almost the exemplar of this spiritual and cultural attitude.[33] However, it is precisely on this point that we see the contrast with Clare most clearly, for right at the heart of the spirituality of San Damiano we find Clare's greatest temptation – to follow an ideal of penance which was a long way from that of Francis.[34]

FRANCIS IN CONTRAST TO CLARE?

On two separate occasions Francis himself had to intervene decisively with Clare in order to correct what he considered to be grave errors. In both cases he took a different view of the life of penance from Clare. His interventions were extremely positive and as a result were recorded in the canonisation process by the sisters. The first problem concerned the place where Clare slept, usually a bed of vine-branches, but sometimes the bare floor, her head resting on a stone. This privation nearly made her ill and so Francis had to intervene:

[Sister Agnes] had heard before she, the witness, had entered the monastery, that Lady Clare had a bed made of twigs, but after she was ill, she had a sack of straw because of a command of St Francis.[35]

We can see clearly that Francis did not approve of mortifications that Clare had voluntarily undertaken, for the Poverello's spirituality gave no room to the kind of self-punishment which ended by making one ill.

The second episode is even more eloquent.

The portions of food she consumed were so small it seemed she was fed by angels. She certainly afflicted her body: three days a week, Monday, Wednesday and Friday, she did not eat anything. On other days, she fasted on bread and water, until St Francis commanded her to eat something on those days when she had not been eating at all. Then, to practice obedience, she ate a little bread and drank a little water.[36]

Francis put a lot of effort into making Clare see reason. Sister Pacifica's evidence reveals some particularly interesting details:

She said she was so very strict in her food that the sisters marvelled at how her body survived. She also said blessed Clare fasted much of the time. Three days of the week, Monday, Wednesday and Friday, she did not eat anything. She said on other days she kept such abstinences she developed a certain illness so St Francis together with the bishop of Assisi commanded her to eat on those three days at least half a roll of bread, about one and a half ounces.[37]

We are first struck by what Sister Pacifica says about Clare's illness, especially when she says that it was the illness itself which made Francis decide to intervene. The second striking point is Pacifica's own conviction that it was Clare's privations which made her so ill. The information that the bishop also intervened makes one think that Francis had sought the support of someone in authority. We might well ask ourselves how Clare had become so attached to the practice of mortification and fasting that she even resisted the advice of Francis.[38]

These different conceptions of penance arose because Francis and Clare had differing attitudes towards the body or – to put it better – the two saints each had a different concept of their own body.[39] It has been remarked that in all Francis' great love for every created being, the single exception was his own body[40] and this is at least partly true. In his Second Letter to all the Faithful Francis had certainly written, 'We must hate our bodies with their vices and sins', and immediately explains why, 'because the Lord says in the Gospel: All evils, vices and sins proceed from the heart'.[41] In the Admonitions he had taken up the same theme:

Many people, when they sin or receive an injury, often blame the Enemy or a neighbour, but this is not right for each one has the real enemy in his own power; that is, the body through which he sins.[42]

Francis' thought is quite clear here: we must consider the body an enemy in the same sense as we consider ourselves to be enemies of the grace of God.[43] So we cannot say that Francis believed the body, considered as a created reality, to be despised, rather the contrary, for in the Admonitions he recalls that '[God] had created you and formed you to the image of his beloved Son according to the body, and to his likeness according to the spirit'.[44] The body is made in the image of God or, more specifically, in the image of his Son Jesus Christ. It is *this* body which interests Francis, not our body of flesh but the body of Christ, the one in whose image everyone is made. The whole of this Letter to all the Faithful is an invitation not to trust in the strength of one's own body, in oneself that is, but in the love of God who has given his body for all. Francis does not disguise our radical guilt:

All the creatures under heaven, each according to its nature, serve, know and obey their Creator better than you. Even the demons did not crucify him, but you together with them have crucified him and crucify him even now by delighting in vices and sins.[45]

Under this affirmation of each person's radical guilt there is also hidden, as Francis saw it, the mystery of each person's radical freedom. It is useless to accuse others of our own weaknesses and sins, just as in the end it is useless to blame the devil, because the only person responsible for our own good or bad deeds is ourself. The enemy is within, not without.

When Francis speaks of his body he does not seem to be speaking about himself; he seems to be looking in on himself from outside, or as if he were speaking of someone else. If his body is ill and in need of treatment, he speaks of it gently and calls it 'Brother Body',[46] as on the occasion when, seriously ill, he sent a brother to find a zither or a lute 'to give the comfort of some beautiful poetry to Brother Body who is so full of pain'.[47] On the other hand, if he was aware that his body manifested a desire, to possess perhaps, to dominate or to act violently, then Francis would call it 'Brother Ass' and subject it to severe disciplines.[48] This was not just a manner of speaking, for we see in Francis a detachment from his body which was a detachment from himself. It was as if he had overcome the limits of his physical existence and widened his life beyond his biological boundaries. Francis never sought after suffering, illness or even death, but he was led to grapple with a concept of life which superseded all these limitations. We do not find in Francis the ideal of the ascetic man conquering illness and sin by his own strength. Rather we find a man who grows weaker and weaker but who progressively identifies with Christ crucified and sees his own life more and more transfigured into that of Christ.[49] In the light of that observation, we can better understand the reason for the different attitudes of Francis and Clare towards food and sleep.

In the beginning Clare probably had held some kind of ascetic heroism as an ideal, subjecting herself to increasingly heavy tests, even to the point of endangering her health. Francis' correction was timely: sufferings which come must be accepted but they may not be sought out, still less created for oneself. For this reason, the penitential practices of Clare, even though they look so severe, were actually always held in balance, as we can see if we compare them with those of other women of her time. For instance, in the spirituality of Clare there is a complete absence of that contempt for all material things which lay at the root of the piety of Margaret of Cortona who prayed: 'Lord Jesus, who alone I desire with a simple and pure mind, who alone I love, for whom I would lose my body and wholly despise the things of this world'.[50]

Such rejection of physical beauty is quite absent in Clare while it led Margaret right to the edge of self-multilation:

At times she would cut the clothes she had on and even her own face, at times she would strike her cheeks or scourge herself across the shoulders with knotted rope . . . The Servant of God would use ever new remedies, greater austerities, harsh flagellations and corporal afflictions which with supreme eagerness she would constantly increase . . . she would invent ever new and untried tortures in order to obtain the desired ruin of her lovely face.[51]

Thanks to Francis, Clare was opened to a new concept of penance and, as a result, towards a new rapport with her own body. More than likely she would have stopped wearing a hair shirt at the same time as she agreed to eat daily and sleep on a sack of straw. This would have been about the time when she first became ill.[52]

What happened to Clare's relationship with her body was analagous to what had happened to her relationship with space. Just as through the very restrictions of the cloister her life had been opened to the whole world, so through the restrictions imposed on her body, it was as if her life was now widened until it assumed a new body, no longer solitary but collective, the body of the community of San Damiano in which the body of Clare was also contained.

In those early days, life at San Damiano was a very hard school of privation and penury.[53] Clare slept on the bare ground with only a stone for a pillow, dressed in a tunic of rough wool like those worn by the peasants, and she went barefoot. There was no assurance of even the most basic necessities for survival and sometimes the sisters would lack even the bread which formed their staple food.[54] In these circumstances Clare made her first, painful discovery of just how frail her body was. Tiredness from work in the garden, hunger, exhaustion resulting from undernourishment – any and all these could have caused Clare to desist from the most high poverty she intended for herself.

At first, Clare seemed to take the difficulties to heart, so much so that she increased her fasting and tested herself even beyond that which necessity demanded. Afterwards, however, perhaps advised by Francis, she underwent a change. Clare was less and less preoccupied with her own body as something to be subjected to ever increasing discipline and focussed her attention more and more on the body of sisters which she had made her own. As Sister Benvenuta da Perugia said at the canonisation process:

She was so severe to her body that she was content with only one tunic of 'lazzo' and one mantle. If she ever saw that the tunic of another of the sisters was worse than what she was wearing, she took it from her for herself and gave the better one to that sister.[55]

Clare seemed always concerned to make the sisters' lives less hard and to this end she was as anxious about their bodies as about their souls. It was she who nursed the sick, caring for them with all the means at her disposal.[56] In her Rule, and in the light of her own experience, she provides that the abbess should inform herself about the needs of the sick sisters, taking advice about what will help them best.[57] Nor should she confine herself to doing all she can to cure their illnesses. Clare concerned herself with the whole of the sick sisters' lives, knowing very well that sickness of body can also wear out the spirit. This was why she did not shirk even the less attractive tasks such as washing the mattresses and serving at table.[58] If one of the sisters were distressed, she would comfort her tenderly, and at night was concerned to replace the covers any of the sisters might toss off.[59] In the same spirit she would often wash the feet of the *sorores servientes*, 'the sisters who served', probably when they returned from begging alms outside the monastery.

From the time the mother St Clare entered religion, she was so humble she washed the feet of the sisters. One time, while washing the feet of one of the serving sisters, she bent over, wishing to kiss the feet. That serving sister, pulling her foot away, accidentally hit the mouth of the blessed mother with her foot.[60]

Nearly all the miracles recorded in the life of Clare were cures of her sick sisters. This is just one more expression of her extreme preoccupation with the health and lives of her companions. As the *Life* says: 'This venerable Abbess loved not only the souls of her sisters, she also took care of their bodies with wonderful zeal of charity.'[61]

This awareness of having a 'wider body' definitively drew Clare away from certain forms of penance which figured in the lives of other religious women of her time, so much so that she would oppose any such extreme attitude initiated by the sisters at San Damiano. Sister Agnes bears witness to one example of this:

She also said that at one time the aforesaid holy mother Clare was washing the feet of the witness who insisted on drinking the water which she [Clare] had used. It seemed to the witness so sweet and delicious that she could hardly drink it. Asked if any other sister had tasted that water, she replied no, because the aforesaid holy mother Clare had instantly thrown it away so that there was none left to drink.[62]

Sister Agnes evidently wanted to imitate Clare, who washed the feet of the servants, by adding another act, that of drinking the water, an act which had precise parallels in the penitential practices of her contemporaries. For example, there is the famous episode, in the life of Angela of Foligno, of washing the feet of lepers:

We gave everything to the poor, we washed the feet of the women and the hands of the men, and especially those of a certain leper whose limbs had putrefied and were so infected that the flesh was falling to pieces. Then we drank the water which we had used. This time it had so great a sweetness . . . almost as if we had been to communion.[63]

Clare threw away the rest of the water which Sister Agnes had drunk, making it quite clear that she would have no part in this kind of penance. She never had any sympathy with humiliating the body, just as she never had any morbid seeking for illness or suffering.

A further reason for this may have been that for more than twenty-eight years Clare did experience bodily suffering through illness.[64] For the whole of that time, she was nearly always confined to her bed, unable even to raise herself up without help. She was not ashamed of this condition of need and dependence on others, but confided herself with great simplicity to the care of her sisters.[65] Quite simply, she never stopped thinking about the others. Even when she was ill, her attention and concern were not concentrated on herself and her pain, but remained open to her 'wider body'. This was why she continued to work with her hands, spinning and weaving, right up to the last days of her life. She wanted to give an example in this way to the other sisters, and the work she produced went as gifts to the churches of the plain of Assisi.[66] Clare was not just continuing to work at all costs in order to prove right to the end that she could, nor even to demonstrate her spirit of self-abnegation. Far more simply, she continued to work because she thought that the churches of the plain of Assisi had need of the corporals which she helped to make. One could even say that Clare kept on working in order not to miss the pleasure of being able, right to the end, to give to those in need.

Clare's life had been spent in a hard school of penance, but in this school her understanding matured into something much closer to the mind of Francis. For him, there is no need to seek out penances for oneself, it is enough to confront them with the poverty of heart of a person who is not concerned with self, but who suffers with the Crucified and in solidarity with the needy.

THE HEART OF PERFECT JOY

At the end of this school of penance, Clare graduated with a heart of joy.[67] As for Francis, so for Clare too, joy was not a condition of unthinking gladness; on the contrary, it was only attained through much material difficulty and spiritual discomfort.

For Francis, joy had been one of the elements in his knightly education. The *Legend of the Three Companions*, which gives us the best idea of the cultural climate in which Francis grew up, tells us that he was 'naturally cheerful'.[68] Joy and generosity were the two qualities most typical of the knightly courtesy that the young Francis had wanted to imitate. The moment of conversion was, for him, a reversal of values: 'that which seemed bitter to me was changed into sweetness of soul and body'.[69] The meeting with the leper and his suffering transformed the whole idea of joy for Francis: 'and those who came to receive life gave to the poor everything which they were capable of possessing and they were content with one tunic, patched inside and out.'[70]

It was not the patched tunic in itself that contented the brothers, that is, they did not delight in misery in itself but were content with such a tunic because by its means they had renounced all possessions in favour of the poor.[71] This was no smug impoverishment, for Francis did not love sacrifice and renunciation in themselves, and he never abandoned the search for joy. It was rather that, after his conversion, his search changed its character: 'Blessed are those who weep for they will be comforted.'[72] There is a greater joy in a suffering which finds consolation or companionship and solidarity for its sorrow, than in one young wandering scholar who goes forth in search of glory. It is only just that joy be kept for those who suffer, either in the great or little things of every day. Francis applied this general rule to himself as well: we have seen how, when he was ill, he asked a brother to find him a lute with which he could rejoice and sing the praises of the Lord. The brother refused, thinking it a little undignified, but during the night Francis heard the sound of a music so marvellous as to show that God approved of his reasonable request.[73]

The joy of Francis did not just happen but was the hard won and blessed result of long spiritual and personal discipline. The joy of Francis was a religious conquest. The most famous episode is that of 'perfect joy', the best-known story in the *Fioretti*. Just as St James says, 'Consider it perfect joy, my brothers, when you undergo all sorts of tests'[74], so New Testament joy as it was rediscovered by Francis passes all the tests and is a victory over sorrow and sin, a sign of the resurrection.[75]

However, according to Francis, precisely because joy is hard won, it must also be manifested externally:

It is not becoming for a servant of God to show himself sad or upset before men, but always he should show himself to be serene. Examine your offences in your own room and groan and weep before God, but when you come back to your brethren, leave off your sorrow and conform with the rest.[76]

The same recommendation is made in the *Regula non bullata*:

The brothers must beware not to appear outwardly sad and like gloomy hypocrites; but let them show that they are joyful in the Lord and cheerful and truly gracious.[77]

It is easy to see here how far Francis was, not only from the

Cathars' pessimistic vision of humanity and the world, but also from the strongly moralistic attitude which at that time was a characteristic of the concept of *fuga mundi*, 'flight from the world'.[78]

Clare was an attentive pupil of Francis' teaching; right at the end of her life, writing her Testament and wanting to record the beginnings of her community at San Damiano, she recalls how Francis 'in great joy and illumination of the Holy Spirit, made a prophecy about us which the Lord later fulfilled'.[79] In this way, joy was installed in the foundations of the community which was to be born at San Damiano. It is significant that, at the end of her life, it was this detail that Clare recorded, as if, having explored various ways and tried different forms of devotion, she then wanted to return to the very roots of her own vocation and to those qualities which she so loved to remember about Francis. We know that Clare was not present at that moment when Francis, filled with the Holy Spirit, made his prophecy about a community of women at San Damiano, so how was she able to say that he was in a transport of joy? More than likely because Francis himself had told her, and in her Testament she in her turn wanted to set on record the feelings she had had when she heard from Francis about this episode.

Joy, however, was not only a characteristic of the early and then later days for the community at San Damiano: instead it was a constant attitude of mind which Clare wanted to share with all her sisters, near and far. For this reason she says, for instance, in a letter to Agnes of Bohemia:

The Lord, coming into the womb of the Virgin, wanted to appear in the world as a man who was despised, in need and poor, so that people might become rich in him by possessing the kingdom of heaven – for they were extremely poor and needy, starved by this great lack of heavenly nourishment. Therefore, rejoice greatly and be glad, be filled with tremendous joy and spiritual happiness, for certainly you who have preferred the scorn of the world to its honours, poverty to temporal riches and have preferred to place your treasure in heaven rather than on earth – certainly you know (I am sure of it) that the Lord both promises and gives the Kingdom of heaven only to the poor.[80]

Here Clare is filled with Franciscan spirituality. The lady of Assisi writes to Agnes, who had just begun a poor and evangelical life in which she had renounced the honours of her own royal family, and speaks to her about joy, linking it with poverty. For Clare, as for Francis, true joy exactly corresponds to true and perfect poverty chosen in imitation of the Lord Jesus who himself chose to live in poverty in order to make everyone rich in his love. In the eyes of Francis, and therefore of Clare, penance, like poverty, was never the fruit of renunciation and sacrifice. The two qualities were nothing but aspects of the imitation of Christ which come to their fulfilment in happiness and spiritual joy.

Clare's conformity to the Franciscan ideal was not instantaneous, all done in the moment of her conversion; rather the opposite, even the renunciation of extreme forms of penance as a means to spiritual joy was the result of a wearisome journey, both culturally and experientially. What enabled her to travel along this road, and justified her in leaving the path of more extreme penance and mortification, was her 'wider body' made up of the community of sisters who were all united around her. Once again the testimony of Sister Benvenuta is significant. At the canonisation process she told how when 'from the time the Lady was ill, the sisters took the [hair] shirt, rough as it was, away from her'.[81] The sisters' intervention in taking away the hair shirt with which Clare martyred her flesh, an intervention similar to Francis' in the matter of Clare's bed and food, is evidence that the Franciscan ideal of penance had become part of the culture and spirituality of everyone in that little group of sisters. It is also worth noting that Clare, even though she was the abbess, still thought it right to allow the sisters to act in this way, to make herself obedient to their filial but firm injunction. On the other hand, Clare herself had given the first example here:

She herself used such rough hair cloths and shirts for herself but was very merciful to the sisters who could not endure such harshness and willingly gave them consoltion.[82]

It was through such mutual encouragement, and this saving

victory over any temptation to excessive harshness, that Clare and her companions made their human and personal journey towards the Franciscan ideal of penitence.

SIX

The Theology of Clare

It is practically impossible to speak of the theology of Clare. We have so few of her writings and what we have are so occasional in character that we cannot reconstruct a theology out of them in any scientific meaning of the word. On the other hand we have exactly the same difficulty when we come to try and describe the theology of Francis, even though his writings are six times the volume of Clare's.[1] It was Francis who coined the phrase 'an understanding faith': that is, a faith which, out of a life in process, generates original reflection on the truth contemplated, yet without becoming a systematic theology.[2] One could offer an analogous definition for Clare, for to speak of her theology is, in a smiliar way, to speak about her reflections on faith as they emerge from her writings.

This kind of awareness of faith best emerges from Clare's Testament where she reflects, for the benefit of her sisters present and to come, on the vocation of the community at San Damiano:

The Lord himself, in fact, has placed us in the shape of an example and a mirror, not only for others but also for our sisters whom the Lord himself has called to follow our vocation, so that they in turn might be like a mirror and an example for all those who lived in the world.[3]

CHRIST, CLARE'S MIRROR AND EXAMPLE

In the thinking of Clare, the word 'mirror' is a keyword.[4] Francis had underlined the importance of being an example, a mirror, for the others[5] but Clare applied the mirror metaphor directly to Christ. She does this in one of the most significant passages of her last letter to Agnes of Bohemia:

In so far as this vision of him is the splendour of eternal glory, the brightness of everlasting light and an unspotted mirror, look into this mirror every day, O Queen, beloved of Jesus Christ. There, continually ponder on your own face so that you may adorn your whole being, within and without, in robes of wonderful variety, adorn your whole being with virtues like flowers and with garments every bit as ornate as those of the daughter and beloved bride of the Most High King, for this is only fitting. And then in this shining mirror . . .[6]

To reflect on and to reflect Jesus was an attitude of life for Clare.[7] If she were to overcome the fundamental traits of her culture and of her own human and religious awareness, it was essential that she reconstruct the image of Jesus so that he became more and more familiar to her. Once again we can turn to the sources and follow them: the evidence of the canonisation process first, because although what the sisters said obviously tells us more about their own awareness than that of Clare, yet it also shows how her awareness was reflected in the whole group. After the canonisation process come the other sources, above all the letters to Agnes because these were the writings in which Clare gave fullest expression to her theological thought.

'Most Holy and Beloved Child'

The first image to surface from the sisters' testimonies is that of Jesus as a child. The one who speaks most about this is Massariola di Capitanio di Coldimezzo, a young aristocratic woman who entered San Damiano in May 1232 and took the name of Sister Francesca. She says:

Once on Calendamaggio, she, the witness, saw in the lap of Saint Clare, before her breast, a young boy who was so beautiful that he could not be described. The same witness, because she saw that young boy, felt an indescribable sweetness and believed without a doubt that he was the Son of God. She also said she then saw about Lady Clare's head two wings, brilliant as the sun, which at times were raised on high and at other times covered the head of the Lady. Asked who else had seen this, she replied that she alone saw it and had never revealed it to another and would not have revealed it then except to praise so holy a mother.[8]

It is impossible to tell from this evidence whether or not we are talking about the first May which Sister Francesca spent at San Damiano; we can only be certain that this vision of a child in the arms of Clare was repeated right at the end of Clare's life:

She also said that once, when the sisters believed the blessed mother was at the moment of death and the priest had given her the Holy Communion of the Body of our Lord Jesus Christ, she, the witness, saw a very great splendour about the head of mother St Clare. It seemed to her the Lord's Body was a very small and beautiful young boy. After the holy mother had received with great devotion and tears, as was her custom, she said these words: God has given me such a gift today, that heaven and earth could not equal it.[9]

Sister Francesca linked this vision of the 'very beautiful young boy' to the Eucharist, thus uniting the two devotions of the Eucharist and the Incarnation of Jesus, both of which were hallmarks of popular piety at the start of the thirteenth century. However, the next testimony, that of Sister Agnes, takes the same kind of vision but unites it with preaching:

The witness also said Lady Clare delighted in hearing the Word of God. Although she had never studied letters, she nevertheless listened willingly to learned sermons. One day when Brother Filippo d'Atri of the Order of Friars Minor was preaching, the witness saw a very handsome young boy, who seemed to be about three years old, appear to St Clare. While she, the witness, was praying in her heart that God would not let her be deceived, He answered her in her heart in these words: 'I am in their midst', signifying through these words the young boy Jesus Christ who stood in the midst of the preachers and listeners when they were preaching and listening as they should.[10]

The vision must have set up some ripples in the little community of sisters who would have talked about it among themselves. When the notary, in accordance with protocol, asked Sister Agnes to specify the date of this vision, she was very precise:

Asked how long ago this was, she replied: about twenty-one years ago. Asked what time, she replied it was during the week after Easter when 'I am the Good Shepherd' is sung. Asked who was present, she replied: the sisters. Asked if some of them saw the young boy, she replied that one sister told the witness: 'I know you have seen something.[11]

The reference to the antiphon, 'I am the Good Shepherd', enables us to date the vision very accurately on the second Sunday after Easter in 1232, twenty-one years before the death of Clare and the process at which the vision was recorded. This date makes it likely that the episode in question coincided with the first of the two spoken about by Sister Francesca. This must have been a specific experience, involving the whole San Damiano community.

The same Sister Agnes spoke about Pentecost:

Asked about the length of time the young boy stood there, she replied: for the great part of the sermon. She said it seemed, then, as if there was a great brilliance around holy mother Clare, not like anything material, but like the brilliance of the stars. She also said she, the witness, smelled an indescribable sweetness because of the apparition. After this she saw another brilliance, not the colour of the first, but all red in a way that seemed to emit certain sparks of fire. It thoroughly surrounded the holy Lady and covered her entire head. The witness, doubting this, received a reply, not with a voice but in her mind: The Holy Spirit will come upon you.[12]

These testimonies give us some idea of the way in which devotion to and feeling about Jesus as a 'young boy' came to life at San Damiano.[13] The link between the Eucharist and preaching is also no chance, rather it is an example of the way in which the sisters' spiritual reflections sprang from the quality of their prayer. Without doubt, it was the particular concentration of Clare herself which focussed the sisters' attention on the child Jesus. Sister Filippa, talking about this, recalled an episode, also mentioned in the *Life*, which has become one of the best known events in the life of Clare:

The Lady Clare also narrated how on the most recent night of the Lord's Nativity because of her serious illness she could not get up from her bed to go to the chapel. All the sisters went as usual to Matins and left her alone. The Lady then said with a sigh: Lord God, look, I have been left here alone with you. She immediately began to her the organ, responsories and the entire Office of the brothers in the Church of St Francis, as if she were present there.[14]

Sister Balvina confirms this same vision of Clare, adding a little reproach which Clare gently made to the sisters on their return:

Then she said to her sisters: You left me here alone after going to the chapel to hear Matins, but the Lord has taken good care of me because I was not able to get up from my bed.[15]

Thomas of Celano quotes both these testimonies verbatim and inserts in the middle a detail which only served to accentuate the extraordinary character of the event:

She heard the jubilant psalmody of the brothers, listened to the harmonies of their songs and even perceived the very sounds of the instruments. The nearness of the place was in no way such that a human being could have heard this unless either that solemnity had been divinely amplified for her or her hearing had been strengthened beyond human means. But what totally surpasses this event: she was worthy to see the very crib of the Lord![16]

While Thomas stresses this episode, the famous account in the *Fioretti* develops it even further:

When the Solemnity of the Birth of Christ came round, all the other sisters went to Matins and she was left in bed, sad that she was not able to go with the others and to have that spiritual consolation. But Jesus Christ her Beloved, not wishing her to remain sad, had her miraculously carried to the Church of St Francis and to be present at all the Office of Matins and the Mass of Midnight and even to receive Communion, and then to be carried back to her bed.[17]

It was probably this passage that in 1958 gave Pius XII the idea of proclaiming Clare the patroness of television.

In reality, however, the evidence as it was given at the canonisation process was much more reserved than in the *Life* or the *Fioretti*, nor did it embark on any description of consolations given to Clare that night. During the process the sisters only recounted the episode in order to underline Clare's particular devotion to the birth of Christ, as it is quite clear from the evidence of Sister Amata:

She said the same as Sister Philippa about all these things and about the miracle of the night of the Lord's Nativity. But she added she had heard from the Lady Clare that, on the night of the Lord's Nativity, she also saw the manger of our Lord Jesus Christ.[18]

There is also a trace in the Rule:

And out of love for the most holy and most beloved Child, wrapped in poor little covers, laid in a manger, and for love of his most holy Mother, I admonish, plead and encourage my sisters that they always wear the poorest of garments.[19]

This passage is unique to Clare and we find no parallel in any other Rule observed by the Poor Sisters. It is significant that she uses the phrase, 'most holy and most beloved Child', because this is an expression used by Francis in the hymn which he wrote for Vespers of the Nativity in his Office of the Passion, and Clare used to pray this Office.[20]

Christ Crucified

In speaking of the Office of the Passion we touch the very heart of Clare's spirituality, her focus on Christ crucified.[21] The sisters reiterated this several times during the canonisation process, as when Sister Benvenuta di madonna Diambra stated quite simply that Clare 'instructed her always to have the Lord's passion in her memory',[22] or when Sister Agnes recalls: 'She particularly prayed the hours of Sext because she said the Lord was placed on the cross at that hour.'[23] This concentration on the Crucified expressed itself in gestures of penitence, often involving the whole community, as Sister Angeluccia di Angeleio da Spoleto testified:

The witness also said once, when holy mother Lady Clare heard the *Vidi Aquam* being sung after Easter, she was so overjoyed and kept it in her mind. After eating and after Compline she had the blessed water given to her and her sisters and would say to the sisters: My sisters and daughters, you must always remember and recall this blessed water that came from the right side of our Lord Jesus Christ as He hung upon the cross.[24]

Thomas of Celano did not choose to insert a description of this paraliturgical practice in his *Life*, but he does confirm that the verbal similarities between the Rule of Clare and the words of Francis' Office of the Passion were no chance. He says that she 'learned the Office of the Cross as Francis, a lover of the Cross, had established it and recited it with similar affection'.[25]

Francis had a special devotion to Christ crucified and composed an Office of the Passion.[26] The long monastic tradition had produced a great many liturgical books for the recital of the Hours, some long, some short, and Francis could easily have found something among them to suit his needs, but instead he chose to compose an Office of his own because he wanted to express the whole of his devotion to the Passion of the Lord.[27] How would he have set about such a composition? Attempts to answer this question have not produced complete agreement, but what we can say with certainty is that, in his Office, Francis tried to imagine the thoughts and state of mind of Christ in his sufferings. To do this, he only used words from the psalms, composing short prayers which are simply a collage of psalm verses. These can be read as the prayers which Jesus himself would have been saying at various moments of his Passion.[28] By making these prayers his own, Francis (like anyone else who prays his Office) was drawn deeper and deeper into identification with Christ; praying the very prayers which Christ prayed, feeling the same feelings, suffering the same pain as Christ on the cross.[29]

Francis did not give this Office of the Passion to the Franciscan movement as a whole; it was for personal prayer. The passage in the *Life* envisages a spiritual chain, binding Francis and Clare, and yet here, right at the heart of Franciscan spirituality, we perceive a distance, a gap between the ideas of Francis and those of Clare. This time it was not a gap in their actual practice of penance, it was on the deeper level of personal religious awareness.

Clare, while she did indeed pray using Francis' Office of the Passion, was more accustomed to pray the Prayer of the Five Wounds.[30] Nothing now remains of this prayer, except a fifteenth-century redaction. Undoubtedly this has been considerably added to in comparison with the one which Clare would have known, but it still allows us to clarify the difference between the spirituality of Francis and that of the contemporary penitential movements. While the Office of the Passion seeks a purely spiritual identification with Christ on the cross,[31] the Prayer of the Five wounds describes far more of the physical sufferings of the Crucified.[32] Francis' concern was to relive the feelings which Christ would have had in the Garden of Olives or on the Way of the Cross, or to pray with the very words which would have been on his lips or in his heart, that is, the words of the psalms. In the Prayer of the Five Wounds, the desire seems rather to get in touch with the intensity of grief which Christ would have suffered.

Clare seemed to oscillate between the two spiritualities. On the one hand, she said the Office of the Passion daily, and felt particular sorrow at the times of Sext and None (the moments in the Office when the crucifixion and death of Christ are recalled). On the other hand, as her biographer tells us: 'In order to nourish her soul on the unutterable joys of the Crucified, she frequently prayed the Prayer of the Five Wounds of the Lord.'[33] Again, the distinction between the two spiritualities seems very subtle, so much so that Clare could have considered them perfectly compatible one with the other. Each, in fact, underlines the humanity of Jesus in his sufferings and in this way assists in renewing the life of devotion. The difference is simply that one, the Prayer, stresses the physical sharing in the sufferings of the Crucified and the other, the Office of Francis, stresses an interior and spiritual sharing.

In his life of Clare Thomas of Celano paid no more attention than anyone else to the differences between the spirituality of penance and the Franciscan spirituality. He was quite satisfied: for him, Clare was a heroine whose every act, including her devotions, had that extra something which made her exceptional, inimitable. This is why he underlines 'Admire, O Reader, what you cannot imitate'.

In this context, to meet the crucified becomes a joy and a delight:

Crying over the Lord's Passion was well known to her. At times, she poured out feelings of bitter myrrh at the sacred wounds. At times she imbibed sweeter joys. The tears of the suffering Christ made her quite inebriated and her memory continually pictures him whom love had imprinted upon her heart.[34]

Francis would never have spoken about the sufferings of Christ with words like 'made her quite inebriated' or 'to suck sweetness from the sacred wounds'; yet these were both expressions in common use in contemporary Christological devotion. For Francis there was never satisfaction simply in suffering, whether his own or Christ's on the cross.

Here we have not only a difference between Francis and Thomas of Celano, but also, as we have seen, between Francis and Clare herself. In fact, the theology of Clare seems to be more original than that of Francis, at least at first glance. She accepted everything that Francis gave her, and then she reworked it using her own insights.[35]

The Theme of the Mystical Marriage

The source in which we best see the originality of Clare is, without question, her letters to Agnes of Bohemia. These were written on various occasions and in a style which it was customary to use at that time when addressing a royal lady, and yet in these letters there constantly recurs one theme which almost formed a leitmotiv in the friendship between Agnes and Clare, and that is the theme of the mystical marriage.[36] Here, too we can see, in spite of superficial resemblances, a profound difference between the spirituality of Clare and that of her contemporaries in the Church.[37]

Cardinal Ugolino, as we know, tightly bound the idea of virginity to that of enclosure, in effect saying that women were to remain enclosed and to preserve their virtue in view of the celestial marriage. In this concept, there are echoes of a secular mistrust of women,[38] and yet the cardinal was certainly not alone in his thinking. Thomas of Celano himself, even while he was writing a life in which he exalts a woman, has no hesitation about inserting expressions of his instinctive anti-feminism into his prologue:

It was not fitting that help be lacking for the more fragile sex, caught in the maelstrom of passion, which no less a desire drew to sin and no greater frailty impelled.[39]

These were the ideas current at that time. The female sex, precisely because it was weaker, was seen as the more easily drawn into sin, hence the need for enclosure and the exaltation of the choice of virginity.[40] The cardinal's preoccupations, however, suggest a second line of thought which centred on women's religious life. St Augustine had already said that 'the true virgin is enamoured of the most beautiful of the sons of men'.[41]

For centuries the idea of virginity had been tied in with the idea of a mystical marriage with Christ. This was a concept rich in spiritual reflection, so much so that during the Middle Ages the book of the Bible on which the greatest number of commentaries were made was the Song of Songs. The mystical marrige of the soul with God became a theme of spiritual devotion and at the same time, for many women, an ideological basis for their choice in life.[42]

Clare's main development of this theme of mystical marriage comes in her first letter to Agnes of Bohemia.[43] The occasion for it was this: Agnes had in fact been promised as a bride to various imperial personages, but she had always refused to contract a marriage with them, and then, in 1236, at the age of thirty-one (which was mature for a woman of that period), she entered the monastery of San Salvatore in Prague which she had herself founded. In her letter Clare goes right to the heart of her argument:

You, more than many others, could have rejoiced in the pomp, the honour and the dignities of this world, you could quite legitimately have married the illustrious Caesar with outstanding glory, as would have been fitting to both your and his most high condition. Casting all that aside, with all your soul and with the love of your whole heart you have preferred the most high poverty and chosen physical penury. You have taken the noblest of husbands, the Lord Jesus Christ, who will keep your virginity forever intact and unmarked.[44]

The classical summons to the mystical marriage is here given a unique interpretation by Clare in this balancing of Christ against the emperor. It is as if she said: in view of the fact that the greatest dream of a young girl is to marry the most powerful man on earth, I am showing you someone even more powerful still – the Lord Jesus Christ. This has a completely Franciscan slant; just as Francis had wanted to become the knight of some lord and in the end became the knight of the Lord of lords, so Clare issues this invitation to marry this same Lord of lords.

This is by no means the end of the individuality of Clare's interpretation on this theme, however. Taking her inspiration from the Office for St Agnes and using this as a pattern,[45] she elaborates what the embrace of the Lord meant for Agnes. The letter ends with a description of the mystical marrige in these words:

Therefore, beloved sister – or better: lady who is worthy of great honour because you are the beloved and the mother and the sister of my Lord Jesus Christ – you have been wonderfully distinguished by the standard of inviolable virginity and most holy poverty, that you may be strengthened in the holy service which you have begun with ardent love for the poor Christ.[46]

In her fourth letter to Agnes, Clare returns to this mystical marriage theme, with a different interpretation, a sure sign of her own continuing reflection on the matter. This time she takes the Roman martyr St Agnes as her model;[47] we are now considering the only saint to be mentioned in all the writings of Clare. (It is worth noting that Francis, too, loved St Agnes and that, when Clare's blood-sister Catherine joined Clare at Sant'Angelo in Panzo and he received her to obedience, he changed her name to Agnes.)[48]

In this letter Clare draws freely on the Office of St Agnes of 21 January, quoting the antiphons and the responsories of the three nocturns. She could hardly avoid doing this: writing to one Agnes about the other, how could she not quote and offer the example of the very saint whose name the other bore? Yet there was more to it than this, because for Clare the Roman martyr was exactly the human model to be followed.

And now, writing to you who are so beloved, I rejoice and delight with you in the joy of the Spirit, O bride of Christ, because, just like the other most holy virgin, saint Agnes, you have been most marvellously wedded to the Lamb without blemish who takes away the sins of the world, for you have lain aside all the emptiness of this world.[49]

By offering a martyr in this way, offering her as the perfect model of the bride of Christ, Clare adds a note, a colour, all her own to this mystical marriage theme. The whole of the fourth letter to Agnes of Bohemia is based upon the theme of the ultimate witness of faith. It was probably written during the last year of Clare's life and so reflects the focus of her own attention on death and martyrdom. Martyrdom had indeed been a constant theme in Clare's reflections throughout her life. During the canonisation process, many of the sisters spoke in their evidence about Clare's plan to go to Morocco and become a martyr.[50] For Clare martyrdom represented the fulfilment of holiness, the naked testimony of faith right up to shedding one's own blood. This is probably why the martyr St Agnes is the only saint to be cited in her writings.

MARIAN SPIRITUALITY AND SPIRITUAL MOTHERHOOD

The theme of mystical marriage is not fully undertsood unless we also consider the Marian spirituality of Clare.

In the Office of the Passion, which Clare used to pray, Francis had inserted an antiphon to the Virgin in which he greets Mary as:

Daughter and servant of the most high and supreme King, and Father of heaven, you are the mother of our Lord Jesus Christ, you are the Beloved of the Holy Spirit.[51]

When Clare, as we have seen, called Agnes of Bohemia 'the beloved and the mother and the sister of my Lord',[52] she probably had this antiphon to the Virgin in her mind. The link between the concept of mystical marriage and the figure of Mary very well explains why Clare so particularly underlines the concept of spiritual motherhood.[53] She saw virginity as the precondition for a much richer human and spiritual fecundity.

Hold fast to his most sweet Mother who begot such a Son as the heavens could not contain, and who received him into the tiny room of her holy womb and held him on her young girl's lap.[54]

This sums up the subtle yet profound difference between the ecclesiastical concept of virginity and that known and valued by Clare. In Ugolino, as in Thomas of Celano himself and in almost all the men of that time, the period spent in the cloister was seen as analogous to the period of engagement or – to use the imagery of the Song of Songs – of the confusions of love, while the goal of the heavenly espousals will only take place after death. For Clare, on the other hand, the time spent in religious life is itself the time of fruitfulness, that is, the time for the marriage to bear fruit. Like Mary, without renouncing her own virginity, she lived the mystery of the birth of the Lord, both in her own body and in her life.

Clare's spiritual maternity was also a real human experience, for she brought so many sisters to life as they chose to share her experience with her. She had a maternal love for each one of them. Their personal growth as well as their numerical growth (and Clare felt no embarrassment about revealing her desire for this) represented the fullest human and personal fulfilment for Clare herself. This emerges from the Blessing which she wrote for all her sisters, present and to come:

May the Lord bless you and keep you. May he show his face to you and be merciful to you. May he turn his countenance to you and give you peace; to you my Sisters and daughters, and to all those who will come after you and be part of this community . . .

I, Clare, a handmaid of Christ, a little plant of our holy father Francis, a sister and mother of you and the other Poor Sisters, although unworthy, ask our Lord Jesus Christ through his mercy . . . that the heavenly Father give you and confirm for you this most holy blessing in heaven and on earth. On earth, may he increase his grace and virtues among his servants and handmaids of the Church militant. In heaven, may he exalt and glorify you in his Church triumphant among all his men and women saints . . .

I bless you . . . with all the blessings with which a spiritual father and mother could bless and will ever bless their spiritual sons and daughters. Amen.[55]

Clare's reflections on Mary are immensely rich in imagery and overtones. In order to understand the originality of Clare's religious awareness, it is of fundamental importance to specify exactly what images we are dealing with. Each age and each school of spirituality has chosen its own image of Mary. For example, it has recently been demonstrated that Bernard of Clairveaux invented, so to speak, devotion to Mary as Queen and Mother. Before him, many had spoken about Mary's role as Queen and Bride, but her new characterisation only comes to the fore with Bernard, although this too is a reflection of the prestige in which queen mothers were held in the twelfth century.[56]

The suggestion has been put forward that the spirituality of Clare was, in many respects, more influenced by Bernard than by Francis, but here, in this central theme of the image of Mary, we can see quite clearly how very 'Franciscan' Clare was. In all her writings, the name of Mary is always associated with the idea of poverty. Mary is seen as the poor woman, mother of the poor Jesus. In one of just two writings which have come down to us addressed by him to the sisters of San Damiano, Francis himself links Mary with poverty:

I, brother Francis, the little one, wish to follow the life and poverty of our most high Lord Jesus Christ and of his most holy Mother and to persevere in this until the end; and I ask and counsel you, my ladies, to live always in this most holy life and poverty. And keep most careful watch that you never depart from this by reason of the teaching or advice of anyone.[57]

In her Rule, Clare looks at Mary, wrapping her son in swaddling clothes, and offers her as a model for the sisters:

For love of the most holy and most beloved Babe who was wrapped in poor little clothes, laid in a manger, and for love of his most holy Mother, I advise, plead and encourage my sisters always to clothe themselves with really poor garments.[58]

Mary chose poverty as her portion and inheritance. The sisters must do likewise:

Let this be your portion which leads you to the land of the living. Beloved sisters, being totally committed to nothing else, for love of our Lord Jesus Christ and of his most holy Mother, do not ever want to have anything else under heaven.[59]

The same Rule concludes with the invitation always to observe the holy Gospel, as they have firmly promised to do, to remain steadfast in the Catholic faith, and in the poverty and humility of our Lord Jesus Christ and his most holy Mother.[60]

So we return to the themes with which these reflections on Clare's theology began: the poverty and humility of Christ, the poor child born on a journey. These are the same themes as those which Francis had first pointed out to her. Clare reworked the images which he had already used, but she did so in an original way, as we can see in those writings of hers which are still preserved. She reflects primarily on the themes of mystical marriage (on which Francis himself did not have all that much to say) and spiritual motherhood, but it is the latter which she develops most of all. This theme exactly corresponds to the reality of the 'wider body' which, as we have already seen,[61] represented the community structure at San Damiano. It is precisely on this point and for these reasons that the 'theology' of Clare stands forth in all its profound originality.

SEVEN

Clare as Another Francis

Clare's 'task' of knowing, loving and imitating Francis, leads us to understand and respect her Franciscan witness even better. The more the years passed, the more she became a witness to Francis. This process of identification with the Poverello came slowly into focus for her so that, within and without, she increasingly became an *alter Franciscus*, 'another Francis'.[1]

That span of twenty-seven years after the death of Francis was the larger part of Clare's life and during those years her witness became clearer and more intentional until, right at the end, when she wrote her Testament, she wanted to bless her sisters not only in her own name but also in the name of Francis:

So that it may be observed better, I leave this writing for you, my dearest and most beloved sisters, those present and those to come, as a sign of the blessing of the Lord and of our most blessed Father Francis and of my blessing – I who am your mother and servant.[2]

At this point, her identification with Francis was complete, she was at the end of a long, interior labour.

There was a second 'task', too, which was severely to test her Franciscan witness. This was neither a personal problem nor a matter of differing ideas about penance. It arose from the difficulties and obstacles created for this woman of Assisi by the incomprehension of the world outside her community.

CLARE, GREGORY IX AND
THE *PRIVILEGIUM PAUPERTATIS*

At first glance, what is surprising is that these difficulties came from that very Cardinal Ugolino dei Conti di Segni (later Gregory IX) who had not only written letters full of such esteem for

Clare and her community, but who had also been the intimate friend of Francis himself.[3]

The first and most famous episode took place in 1228, less than two years after the death of the Poverello. Gregory IX was in Assisi with all his retinue for the canonisation of Francis and he paid a visit to Clare at San Damiano. Here he took part in quite a lively exchange: the pope proposed that the young woman (Clare was little more than thirty) should consent to have enough possessions to guarantee the support of her community. The episode was reported by Sister Benvenuta of Perugia during the canonisation process:

She also said she specially had a great love of poverty. Neither Pope Gregory nor the Bishop of Ostia could ever make her consent to receive any possessions. Moreover blessed Clare sold her inheritance and gave it to the poor. Asked how she knew these things, she replied that she was present and heard the Lord Pope tell her that he wanted her to receive possessions. This Pope personally came to the monastery of San Damiano.[4]

Thomas of Celano, in his *Life*, enriches the account:

Pope Gregory of happy memory, a man most worthy of the papal throne as he was venerable in his deeds, loved this holy woman intensely with a fatherly affection. When he was attempting to persuade her that because of the events of the times and the dangers of the world, she should consent to have some possessions which he himself willingly offered, she resisted with a very strong spirit and would in no way acquiesce. To this the Pope replied: 'If you fear for your vow, we absolve you from it.' 'Holy Father', she replied, 'I will never in any way wish to be absolved from the following of Christ.'[5]

So Clare felt bound to the choice of poverty by a solemn promise made before God, in other words, by a vow, and the pope proposed to dispense her from such a vow. This suggestion arose from what the biographer calls his 'fatherly affection', something Clare knew well. She had had great and numerous examples of the pope's affection for her, the latest of which had been a letter written only a few months earlier in which the pope had confidently committed himself to her prayers. Yet the response of Clare was still this very firm: *Nequaquam a Christi sequela in perpetuum absolvi desidero*, 'I never want to be absolved from following Christ'.

To the pope, who was keenly aware that he held the power of binding and loosing given by Christ to his disciples, the woman of Assisi replied that if he did so for her, she would hold it as a denial of her very following of that same Christ! The daring of this response is obvious, not only because it implied that Clare had a reading and interpretation of the Gospel which were different from that of the vicar of Christ himself, not only because it was a woman who was saying these things, but above all because Gregory was not simply the pope but also the Cardinal Ugolino who had been the personal friend of Francis and, for the last years of the Poverello's life, protector of the Order.[6] So less than two years after Francis' death, Clare was being constrained to defend the Franciscan ideal of life as it was practised at San Damiano, and to do so against the person who had been nearest of all to Francis himself.

It was certainly no chance that, immediately after this episode, Clare sought written confirmation from the pope of the *Privilegium paupertatis* which Innocent had already granted her. In fact she was given this on 17 September of that same year. In the text of the *Privilegium paupertatis* which he approved, Gregory follows to the letter the *Privilegium* approved by Innocent, but after the months of dialogue at San Damiano the pontiff's words sound like a recognition on his part that he had made a mistake:

Therefore, we confirm with our apostolic authority, as you requested, your proposal *of most high poverty*, granting you by the authority of these present that no one can compel you to receive possessions.[7]

The *Privilegium* of Gregory IX is the final document to bear witness to the friendship between these two old friends of Francis. From then on, the rapport betwen Gregory IX and Clare seemed to cool and soon further problems would come between them.[8]

Clare was too important a figure in the primitive Franciscan movement for her to be able to stay on the fringes of the disputes which were presently to disturb the life of Francis' disciples, all the more so because initially these disputes involved the city of Assisi. Here Brother Elias, who had been made vicar of the Order while Francis was still alive, was presiding over the construction of a huge basilica in honour of the saint.[9] In 1230, scarcely four years after the death of Francis and two years after his canonisation, two solemn events had taken place in the life of the movement: the translation of the body of Francis into the new church-sanctuary dedicated to him, and the convocation of a general chapter to ratify the enormous increase in the number of the friars and to put order into a movement which had so far developed haphazardly.[10] Both events were fraught with incidents. The Minister General John of Parenti had settled that only the ministers provincial were to take part in the chapter, not all the friars as had been the case in the early days of the movement. However, it seems that Brother Elias – at least, according to the chronicle of Thomas of Eccleston, a fierce adversary of Elias – had brought forward the translation of the body of Francis specifically to prevent the provincials from being present.[11].

Without a detailed reconstruction of what happened, which by now is probably impossible, it does seem as if 1230 was the year which could have signalled the triumph of the Franciscan movement and instead became one of the most difficult moments in the life of this new spiritual movement. The friars themselves, gathered in chapter, were unable to reach agreement on a number of points of difference and so they decided to place everything in the hands of the pope.

CONFRONTED WITH THE BULL *QUO ELONGATI*

Gregory IX responded at once, with the bull *Quo elongati* on 28 September,[12] in which he answered all the questions which the general chapter had submitted to him. These concerned the obligation to observe at least the Testament of Francis, obedience to the Gospel, the use of money, poverty, houses, confession, preaching, the training of novices, the election of the Minister General, dealings with the monasteries of women. To all these questions, each of which was of vital

importance for the future of the Order, the pope freely replied
out of his familiarity with the Poverello.[13].

Gregory IX did not acknowledge any juridical value in the
Testament of Francis because, as he recalled, it had been written
when Francis no longer held office in the Order. With regard
to obedience to the Gospel, the pope said that the friars were
only obliged to observe literally the passages of the Gospel
expressly quoted in the Rule, thus lending strength to those
brethren who were claiming that all the evangelical precepts
could never be observed to the letter.[14] As for other questions,
the pope widened the powers of the ministers general and provincial, committed to the latter the election of the General, and
allowed the brethren to possess goods, not in their own person
but through a mediator. This mediator was to be a lay person
whom the community trusted and who would undertake the
task of dealing with their affairs.

The final question was one close to the pontiff's heart: the
relationship between the Friars Minor and the new forms of
women's religious life.

Finally, as it is written in the Rule: The brethren shall not enter the
monasteries of nuns except when they have been granted a special
permission to do so by the Apostolic See. However, until now the
brothers have believed that theirs was this permission as regards the
monasteries of the Poor Ladies Enclosed because the Apostlic See has
a particular care for them and they have held that this disposition has
been made by the Ministers Provincial in a General Chapter by means
of a particular ruling at the same time as the Rule. This was while the
Blessed Francis was still alive. None the less, you have sought a clearer
understanding as to whether this ruling referred in general to all the
monasteries, seeing that the Rule excludes none of them, or only to
the monasteries of the aforesaid nuns. We reply that the prohibition
holds with respect to all the convents of nuns.[15]

Here, as with the preceding problems, the pope's interpretation
was restrictive: the brothers were forbidden to have any dealings
with the women's communities without the direct authorisation
of the Apostolic See.

The whole encyclical represents the first comprehensive
attempt to place the new needs arising in the Order within the

framework of a juridical structure.[16] It was no chance that only ten years later the Franciscan spirituals were to consider that *Quo elongati* had been the first triumph of those who, even while Francis was still alive, had wanted to dilute and devalue the primitive Franciscan spirit.

Confronted by so decisive and authoritative a papal intervention, and one which could not possibly have gained the consent of all the brothers, how did the first companions of Francis conduct themselves? How did they receive it, Angelo, Leo, Rufino, Giles and all the others? The silence of the sources is almost complete. Only one of the earliest companions of Francis, so we are told, reacted strongly and explicitly to the bull: this was Clare.

When news of the dispositions contained in the bull reached San Damiano, and especialy when the sisters heard the last part which forbade the brethren to go to the monasteries of nuns without papal permission, Clare opposed it totally. Four or five of the brethren were living near San Damiano, some of whom were responsible for obtaining the necessary provisions for the monastery, others for the spiritual needs of the sisters. At the news that the pope had reserved to himself the choice of the brothers charged with the sisters' spiritual care, Clare sent away those responsible for their alms saying: 'Let him now take away all the brothers since he has taken those who give us the food of life.'[17] In effect, this was a hunger strike. The pope had deprived them of the spiritual alms represented by the brothers' visits and so Clare renounced the material alms; by so doing she ran the risk of finding that she and her sisters had no food to eat. The pope, learning of this, hastily handed the matter over to the Minister General.

One could see this episode as marginal to the application of such a bull as *Quo elongati* which touched on all the major problems of the young Franciscan Order, except that given the stature of the two protagonists, Clare and Gregory, one cannot overestimate the importance of such an encounter. In general, Clare only took part in the controversies of the Order when they concerned her specific pastoral responsibility for her sisters, and she never involved herself in this kind of Franciscan dispute.

The two fundamental issues for which she fought all her life were: total poverty according to the Gospel and the spirit of Francis, and the spiritual friendship of all the Minors.[18] Just as in 1228 she had had to defend her choice of poverty, so in 1230 she had to fight for the free and fruitful spiritual union which bound San Damiano to the whole minorite movement.

With the passage of time the arguments about the various interpretations of the Rule included the figure of Francis himself. The memory of the Poverello was too much alive, his words were too recent and too much quoted from one friar to another, to allow him to be contained simply by the official *Life* which Thomas of Celano had written just after his death. In 1244 the Minister General Crescentius of Jesi, at the general chapter held in Genoa on the occasion of the feast of St Francis, 4 October, had sent an invitation to all the brethren that they should collect, write down and send to him all the memories of Francis they possibly could.

Among those who responded to this invitation was one particular group of Francis' companions, and their testimony, that of Leo, Angelo and Rufino, was sent to the Minister General together with a famous letter from Greccio, dated 11 August 1246.[19] This account went under the name of the *Florilegium* or the *Legend of the Three Companions*, or the *Florilegium* of Greccio, but how it was used is very unclear. It formed the basis for various compilations and biographies, one of which was certainly the *Second Life* of Thomas of Celano. This was written at the instigation of Crescentius of Jesi in order to fill in the gaps and inaccuracies of what we still call the *First Life*.[20]

CLARE IN CELANO'S *SECOND LIFE*

In the *Second Life*, Thomas of Celano gives plenty of space to Clare and her sisters, dedicating part II, chapters 155-157, to them. He particularly devotes the conclusion of chapter 155 to the theme of the unity of the brothers and sisters:

For when the saint (Francis) recognised by many signs of highest perfection that they [the sisters] had been proved and were ready to make every sacrifice for Christ and endure every difficulty without ever wanting to depart from Christ's holy commandments, he firmly promised them and the others who would profess poverty in a similar way of life, that he would always give them his help and counsel and the help and counsel of his brothers. This he always diligently carried out as long as he lived and when he was close to death, he emphatically commanded that it should always be so, saying that one and the same spirit had led the brothers and the poor ladies out of the world.[21]

Who gave Thomas of Celano this detail about the rapport between Francis and the sisters? Who told him about Francis' promise always to have the same care for them as for the brothers? Who, finally, cherished the memory of those beautiful words of Francis in which he reiterated on his death-bed that the brothers and sisters were united by the same spirit? Thomas of Celano's source was undoubtedly Clare. A swift philological comparison with the writings of the woman of Assisi reveals the exact correspondence betwen these and the passage from the *Second Life* already cited. In her Rule Clare actually says:

When the blessed Father realised that we had no fear of any poverty, work, trouble, shame or contempt by the world but that we rather held all such things as great delights, he was moved by respect to write us a form of life in these words:

Because, by Divine inspiration, you have made yourselves the daughters and handmaids of the Most High King, the heavenly Father, and by electing to live according to the perfection of the holy Gospel you have espoused yourselves to the Holy Spirit, therefore I wish and promise both for myself and for my brothers, always to have the same loving care and special concern for you as for them.

As long as he lived he did this most lovingly and always wanted his brothers to do the same.[22]

The *Second Life* was composed about 1246–47, while the Rule of Clare was not written until 1253; but it is clear that as he wrote Thomas had before him the text of the *forma vitae* which Francis had written for the sisters of San Damiano. This text must have been most jealously preserved in Clare's monastery and later she wanted to insert it directly into her own Rule.[23] It seems more than likely that Thomas, or any other biographer of Francis, would have been unable to write about the relationship between Clare and Francis while Clare was alive without consulting her. This likelihood is made almost a certainty by his exact citation of a document preserved at San Damiano.

Clare accepted that she was an explicit witness for Francis and that by her personal memories she was contributing to the work of reconstructing a true image of the Poverello some twenty years after his death. One episode of Francis' life, remembered by Clare and inserted by Thomas of Celano into the *Second Life*, deserves to be considered in detail:

Repeatedly asked by his vicar to preach the word of God to his daughters when he stopped off for a short time at San Damiano, Francis was finally overcome by his insistence and consented. But when the nuns had come together, according to their custom, to hear the word of God, Francis raised his eyes to heaven, where his heart always was, and began to pray to Christ. He then commanded ashes to be brought to him and he made a circle with them around himself on the pavement and sprinkled the rest of them on his head. But when they waited for him to begin and the blessed father remained standing in the circle in silence, no small astonishment arose in their hearts. The saint then suddenly arose and to the amazement of the nuns, recited the *Miserere mei Deus* in place of a sermon. When he had finished he quickly left.[24]

This can only have been told by Clare. The place, San Damiano, the use of the term 'daughters' to mean the sisters, the originality of Francis' behaviour, so laden with references not only to a penitential mind-set but also to popular culture, all make us see this as a faithful eye-witness account. It is an account which can only have come from Clare.[25]

Memories of Francis, of his deeds and his words, must always have filled the atmosphere of San Damiano. It was Clare herself who became their interpreter through her continuing effort to link the present moment with what she remembered of the times she lived through with Francis.[26] For example, in the life of Blessed Giles it is related that once when Clare saw Blessed Giles interrupt the preaching of a learned English brother in order to exchange a few words with one who was uneducated, she exclaimed: 'It is as if I saw Francis himself!'[27]

Clare's testimony is steadfast: one single spirit had led both the brothers and the sisters out of an evil world. They were not two different Orders, one of men and one of women; rather, through the diversity of their life-styles, they formed one single spiritual family. Throughout this intense fidelity to the spirit of Francis, did Clare herself realise the importance of her witness, or of the authority which she held within the Order? To what extent was the woman of Assisi aware of her relationship with the blessed father?

Surprisingly enough, we find very little by way of an answer to these questions in the official biography. In the whole *Life of St Clare the Virgin* hardly anything is said about the relationship of Clare and Francis and, after the account of his initial conversations with Clare, the name of Francis itself only occurs three times.[28] This silence is partly explained by an anxiety lest memories of a famous figure like Francis should confuse the official account of the life and vocation of a new saint whom the Church wished to honour.

A VISION OF THE BREAST OF ST FRANCIS

Clare fully understood the weight and the spiritual authority which she gained from the friendship and affection binding her to Francis. This meant that she continued his work, guaranteeing that the primitive spirit which the Poverello had passed on to her should not be betrayed as time went on. There is one piece of evidence which more than any other throws light on the deep awareness Clare had of the bond between herself and Francis and of the value of her own witness. We are referring to a deposition made during Clare's canonisation process by Filippa di Leonardo de Gliserio, one of the very first sisters at San Damiano, in which she refers to a vision that Clare had told to the sisters:

Lady Clare also related how once, in a vision, it seemed to her she brought a bowl of hot water to St Francis along with a towel for drying his hands. She was climbing a very high stairway, but was going very quickly, almost as though she were going on level ground. When she reached St Francis, the saint bared his breast and said to

Lady Clare: Come, take and drink. After she had sucked it, the saint admonished her to imbibe once again. After she did so what she tasted was so sweet and delightful she could in no way describe it.

After she had imbibed, that nipple or opening of the breast from which the milk came remained between the lips of blessed Clare. After she took what remained in her mouth into her hands, it seemed to her it was gold so clear and bright that everything was seen in it as in a mirror.[29]

With this vision we touch one of the most intimate and personal aspects of Clare's personality. The language in which she describes the vision is for her, as for all her contemporaries, the language best suited to indicate deep truths, the language of religious experience itself, the very language of feeling and of desire.[30] This was one of the most typical aspects of women's monastic spirituality. Ever since the start of the twelfth century and the great German visionaries, women's mysticism had run parallel to a strong male monastic theology, yet had developed along different lines, so that it became a unique vehicle for the religious experience of women in the thirteenth and fourteenth centuries.[31]

Obviously, mysticism and the language of visions were not the exclusive preserve of women, but because of the difficulties women faced in gaining access to the learning of the universities or to theological expertise, vision and prophecy certainly became their chosen means of religious expression.[32]. This expression sometimes assumed an anti-intellectual and anti-cultural tone, but it always retained a character and a language which were cultured in the most profound meaning of that term.[33] In other words, the language of vision was never considered an impoverished language. What is more, the quality of holiness which women gained from being an intermediary with God guaranteed that both they and what they had to say carried an authority which otherwise they might never have held.[34] Even socially, women's holiness gained greatly in dignity through their visions. A case in point was Rose of Viterbo who foretold the death of the emperor: although only of humble birth, she was exiled from her city and when her prophecy was later fulfilled she became the champion of the Guelph party there.[35]

It must be remembered, though, that, visions, dreams and voices were all part of the collective imagination that informed everyone's life.[36] Men and women of every social level used to underline every important happening in their lives, whether birth, death, war or famine, with this sort of extraordinary event.

A woman was absolutely forbidden to preach, to administer the sacraments or to live as an itinerant, but she could not be forbidden to have visions, because these came directly from the Spirit, nor could she be forbidden to speak about them, because they belonged to the common patrimony of popular culture. This is why the language of visions became the language most typical of women's spirituality, particularly of those women who brought the new forms of religious life into being. It is also why visions are one of the most interesting ways by which we can directly touch the hopes and culture of these women, and can do so without the mediation of male culture or writings which in any other type of source are always present as conditioning factors.

Clare was deeply steeped in this culture. For her, vision and prophecy were sure signs of the divine will. We have already recorded how she herself, in her Testament, rooted the origin of her own community at San Damiano in a prophecy of Francis.[37] She had been brought up from earliest childhood to give great importance to these signs. More than that, before her birth her own mother, Ortolana, when she was pregnant, had prayed before the crucifix against the dangers of childbirth and had heard a voice which said: 'You will give birth to a light which will give light more clearly than light itself.'[38] Sister Filippa, who recounted the episode during the canonisation process, specified that it had been Ortolana herself who had told her this 'about the time St Francis passed from this life'.[39] Because of these events, the sisters freely spoke at San Damiano about Clare as someone specially marked for election by God, even while she was still alive.[40]

However, Clare was not a mystic in the technical sense of

the term. She did not make her mystical experiences the core of her religious life, even though she had a number of visions, voices and signs of which some are recorded in the sources. The same Sister Filippa stresses, for example, that:

During the day of Good Friday, while thinking about the Passion of the Lord, she [Clare] was almost insensible throughout that entire day and a large part of the following day.[41]

The biography gives a fuller description and at the end of the ecstasy has Clare saying these words to one of the sisters:

May that vision be blessed, most dear daughter! Because after having desired it for so long, it has been given to me. But be careful not to tell anyone about that vision while I am still in the flesh.[42]

The power of her meditation on the Passion had carried Clare into a state of insensibility, which Thomas of Celano calls a *somnus*, in which she took no notice of the passage of time.[43] For the whole of Good Friday and nearly all the next day, Clare remained as one dead, which was no chance likeness to the day passed by the Lord Jesus in the tomb before his resurrection.

This is the cultural context within which we must interpret the vision of the meeting between Clare and Francis: that vision which other witnesses at the process simply call 'the vision of the breast of St Francis'.

Thomas of Celano chose not to recount this vision in his biography. Its contents must have seemed to him too embarrassing to put into a work destined for the edification of young girls. The silence of the *Life of St Clare the Virgin* on the subject has not caught the attention of scholars until the present day.[44]

We have here a particularly interesting vision, even when we compare it with other contemporary texts. We see at once that it has a certain literary elaboration which distinguishes it from many other modest, medieval visions. The sisters who recounted it at the canonisation process had heard it from the lips of Clare herself. The notary, Martino, had written it down in Latin, probably leaving out the repetitions which are typical of any spoken account, but without omitting any important details. After that, some unknown person translated the Latin text faithfully into the Umbrian-Tuscan dialect. This might seem rather a long journey but, in fact, if we compare the way other medieval texts developed to form the literary genre of vision, we see at once that this one has, by and large, preserved the freshness and immediacy of direct speech.[45]

The vision merits a deeper analysis because, helped by this medieval text, it gives us a rare opportunity to enter into the secrets of Clare's mind and heart.

AN HISTORICAL ANALYSIS AND PSYCHOLOGICAL INTERPRETATION

Before we analyse the vision, however, we must try to put a date to it. We can almost certainly say that it happened after the death of Francis, since one of the witnesses to recall it was Amata di Martino da Coccorano who did not enter the monastery until 1228–29.[46] Or at least we can say that if Clare had had the vision earlier, then she had not felt able to relate it to her companions until after the death of the saint. The immediacy of the account and the richness of the details suggest that the vision must be dated not very long before the canonisation process at which it was recounted. In that case, by means of this vision Clare was telling the story of her struggle for fidelity to Francis at a time when she had attained total identification with him.

The vision can be subdivided into six 'frames' or images, each of which can be studied either from the angle of Clare's personal life or from the angle of what was, in all probability, the cultural and symbolic language most available to her. In the first frame Clare carries a vessel of hot water to Francis; in the second, Francis is at the top of a flight of stairs; thirdly, Clare is suckled at the breast of Francis; in the fourth, she mentions the sweetness of the milk she drinks; in the fifth, Francis' nipple is left between her lips; and in the last, Clare takes it in her hands and looks at it.

The image in which Clare takes a bowl of hot water and a towel to Francis probably records an actual experience she would have had. Towards the end of his life, Francis was very ill and so – according to the *Legend of Perugia*[47] – spent a whole winter at San Damiano. During those days Clare looked after him and it is more than likely she had also attended to any needs arising from his illness. The hot water and the towel were probably a natural part of her caring of him. If the vision should be dated after his death, we can well understand how Clare came to recall her concern for him so strongly, imagining herself hurrying to reach him before the water became cold.[48]

In the second frame we see Francis not ill but high up at the top of a steep stairway. By thus placing Francis high up, even physically, we already gain an insight into Clare's interior attitude towards him; even though just a little while earlier she had been taking care of him, yet Clare knew very well that of the two it was she who was the little one, she who was lower down, she who had so much to learn from him.

The third frame is the one which startles us a little when we see Clare suckling from Francis. The truth is that the language of visions, like the language of dreams, knows no distinction between masculine and feminine.[49] In this language, the image does not express external reality but the meaning the image holds for the one who dreams or has the vision. To suck at the breast is everyone's primitive experience. In her vision, Clare relives, with Francis, that same primitive experience of total rapport and affectivity. When the baby attaches itself to its mother's breast, this in some measure means that it continues to be one person with her in its desire to possess, to join and to own her. The relationship between mother and child is an intense relationship of exchange between one who gives and one who receives. In exactly the same way Francis in the vision takes the nipple of his breast and hands it to Clare so that she can take it and suck milk from it. The repetition of the gesture and Francis' command are simply a strong statement on Clare's part, albeit unconscious, by means of which she indicates what importance this moment of childlike dependence on Francis has for her.

In the fourth picture, Clare said that 'what she had tasted was so sweet and so delightful that she could in no way describe it'. To understand the power of this indescribable sweetness, we must remember how total is the experience of being fed at the breast, both physically and psychologically. We must also recall that in the Middle Ages the child was normally suckled until it was two or three years old, so that the recollection of the experience remained alive in the memory, and this would have been the case for Clare, too. The indescribable quality is her way of expressing what it meant to find herself confronted with something which transcended every human dimension.

The parallels with being suckled are further developed in the fifth frame. Not only did Clare suck from the breast of Francis but 'that nipple, or opening of the breast from which the milk came, remained between the lips of blessed Clare'. Just as a child, while he is being nursed, bites at the mother's breast in his desire to take something from her and make it his own, so Clare was not content that her hunger should be assuaged by Francis but rather she wanted to introject him, to become one with him. In visions, as in all symbolic language, the part stands for the whole. The baby seeks to have his mother's breast because what he really wants is to make his mother entirely his. So in the vision the detail about the 'opening of the breast' stands for the whole person, Francis. In this frame, Clare is expressing her longing to make him hers, to possess him, to become one with him.

In essence, the vision could have stopped here: Francis has been taken into her, made her own, by Clare. Was this not the deepest desire of the woman of Assisi? Yet the vision presents one last picture which reveals further very interesting details.

Clare takes into her hands that which had remained between her lips and this thing seems to be made of gold, in other words, it was transformed into something precious. We need to emphasise that it was gold: Clare had freely renounced her dowry, that is all her property and all her riches, at the word of and – why not – for love of Francis. The vision seems to be saying that in her friendship and love with Francis there is 'gold', there is a treasure, and that treasure is more precious than any jewels she might have renounced.

The vision ends, 'it seemed to her that it was gold so clear and bright that everything was seen in it as in a mirror'. Clare's desire was not simply to make Francis her own, to possess him, but she desired a fuller identification; she wanted to become one with Francis. She had so interiorised Francis that he became a mirror in which she saw herself.

All that we have said helps us to understand the power of the relationship which bound the two saints of Assisi, so that we see how, for Clare's part, her feelings were so deep that we can only call them feelings of love. This is the right name for that fidelity with which Clare, for twenty-five years after Francis' death, strenuously defended the primitive ideal of Franciscan life and by means of which she really and truly became, both to the Order and to the whole Church, *alter Franciscus*, 'another Francis'.

It only remains to explain why Clare used these images, or rather these symbols, and no others to express her relationship with Francis. The water, the stairs, the breast, the milk, the mirror: these are all images which we often find in the literature of visions and, more generally, in the language of mythology and dreams.[50]

THE CULTURE OF CLARE AND SYMBOLIC IMAGES

At this point, we must consider the culture which these visions expressed and therefore also the personal culture of Clare herself. She never went to school; any education she had had been given her at home by her mother[51] and later at San Damiano by Francis and the other sisters and brothers who frequented the place.[52] Nevertheless, Clare was educated and her writings, particularly her letters and the Rule, show that she was a highly cultured woman.

There were two main cultural sources available to Clare: the biblical-liturgical[53] and the monastico-hagiographical.[54] Any philological analysis of the components of the vision throws both into high relief. With these two parallel approaches in mind, we can see that the symbolic images threading the story gain in validity because of Clare's personal culture, even though they cannot actually be identified as part of her heritage.

'It seemed to her that she brought a bowl of water to St

Francis along with a towel for drying his hands.' Water is a universal symbol found in every culture, no matter how primitive. It symbolises life itself and the sources of life; in every cosmology, water is the basic element and it is a symbol of life in the Bible as well. In the New Testament, which was undoubtedly the part of the Bible most easily accessible to Clare, water is primarily associated with the rite of baptism through which the catechumen is purified of sin and in the same moment becomes part of the community of believers. John in his Gospel speaks in this sense of 'living water', a symbol of the Spirit of God himself, leading us from darkness to light, from death to life. The fathers of the Church pursued this symbolism, enriching and developing it. They praised the freshness of water, symbol of diminishing desires; and its clarity, symbol of illumination by the Spirit.

In the farming culture of the Middle Ages, water had immense importance. The abundance or poorness of the harvest depended on it, and the water used in the liturgy was considered to have almost wonder-working properties. Did not Francis say in the Canticle of the Creatures, 'be praised my Lord through Sister Water, who is so useful and humble, precious and chaste'?[55] It is to this 'useful water' that the vision refers; but Clare carries 'a bowl of hot water' to Francis so it cannot be referring directly to the living water of baptism. In order to understand the symbolic meaning of this water aright, we must consider the other thing Clare was carrying: a towel. At once we see that the reference is to a quite different passage of John's Gospel:

[Jesus] got up from table, removed his outer garment and, taking a towel, wrapped it round his waist; he then poured water into a basin and began to wash the disciples feet'.[56]

This is the passage about the washing of the feet, a passage particularly dear to Franciscan tradition. The washing of the feet was a symbol of that poverty and humility freely chosen by Francis and Clare. Just so did Francis wash the feet of the lepers in imitation of this act of the Lord himself.[57] Just so did Clare, with direct reference to Holy Thursday when the washing of the feet is recalled, wash the feet of those who served.[58] This is how Sister Agnes di Messer Oportulo tells it:

She also said that the humility of the Lady was such that she washed the feet of the sisters and the serving sisters. One time, while washing the feet of one of the serving sisters and wanting to kiss them as she usually did, that sister involuntarily hit [Lady Clare's] mouth with her foot. The Lady rejoiced at this and kissed the sole of that foot. Asked how she knew this, she replied that she had seen it. Asked what time, she replied it was during Lent. Asked what day, she replied a Thursday.[59]

The account of the vision then moves on, showing Clare in action: 'She was climbing a very high stairway, but was going very quickly, almost as though she were on level ground.' The vision now presents us with the classical image of a staircase, or an ascent towards heaven, an image dear to myth, legend and ritual, as is borne out in every continent and age, an image whose echoes go far back. Of this there can be no doubt.[60]

The idea of an ascent to heaven arises out of a cosmology which sees the earth as the centre of the universe, surrounded by various 'heavens' arranged hierarchically, like the steps of a cosmic staircase which the soul must climb after death before it can be reunited with God. This idea may well be of Iranian origin and is found in ancient Hebrew extra-biblical literature as well. In classical times it was developed in Judean and Hellenic gnostic thought, and reasserts itself time and again through the centuries, both before and after the Christian era. The primary biblical reference is to the vision of Jacob:

He had a dream: a ladder was there, standing on the ground with its top reaching to heaven; and there were angels of God going up it and coming down. And Yahweh was there, standing over him. (*Genesis* 28: 12–13)

Jacob's ladder was to have a large part to play in all Christian literature, especially since Jesus himself had referred to it: 'You will see heaven laid open and, above the Son of Man, the angels of God ascending and descending' (John 1: 51).

Ever since the martyrdom of Perpetua in Africa in the third century (202–203), there has hardly been a single Christian author who did not have recourse to the image of stairs in one of the many variants of the cosmic staircase: scales of perfection, ladders of virtue, stairs of spiritual love, scale of the martyrs and ladder of contemplatives. In the twelfth century that stairway underwent immense development in the different schools of spirituality. So we find that Bernard of Clairveaux, Richard of St Victor, Eckbert of Schönau developed a true and unique genre of literature which continued to enjoy great success in the centuries that followed. Clare must have heard echoes of this huge bulk of writing. The problem is, how can we discover the direct sources of her inspiration?

One work which Clare certainly knew, and which was to have a decisive importance in making the idea of a spiritual stairway more widely known, was the Rule of St Benedict. The whole of chapter 7 is devoted to this theme:

Wherefore, brethren, if we wish to attain to the summit of humility and desire to arrive speedily at that heavenly exaltation to which we ascend by the humility of the present life, then must we set up a ladder of our ascending actions, like unto that which Jacob saw in his vision, whereon angels appeared to him, descending and ascending. By that descent and ascent we must surely understand nothing else than this, that we descend by self-exaltation and ascend by humility.[61]

The ladder of St Benedict, then, is a ladder of humility. This recalls one of the themes which have already emerged from the ideas of water and the washing of the feet – humility, the real leitmotiv of this vision.[62]

However, Clare also had another work available to her, one much nearer home. In his *Second Life* of Francis, Thomas of Celano tells a story about a vision in which Fra Pacifico realises that the most beautiful of the thrones destined for the blessed was in fact empty. At that moment he hears a voice saying to him: 'This throne belonged to an angel who fell, and now the throne is reserved for the humble Francis.' This vision which, by good luck, Giotto would want to include in the upper basilica at Assisi, again shows us the theme of humility. Lucifer, the most proud of the angels, is thrown down; Francis, the most humble of men, must take his place.[63] From this reference alone we can begin to form a precise notion of the meaning of Clare's vision: Francis, who had preceded Clare on the ladder of humility, is already at the top; Clare, holding in her hands the symbols of the washing of feet, that is of humility, is following him.

The stairway is high, that is, steep, but Clare ascends it lightly, 'almost as if she were going on level ground'. The absence of any struggle comes from Clare's high degree of perfection. This is in line with classical cosmology such as we find, for example, in Dante where the purer the soul, the swifter its ascent towards God.

'When she reached St Francis, the saint bared his breast and said to the Lady Clare "Come and drink".' Benedict, in his Rule, immediately before the passage about the ladder of humility, quotes from Psalm 130:

> O Lord, my heart is not proud
> nor haughty my eyes . . .
> [like] a weaned child on its mother's breast,
> even so my soul. (Grail Version)

The parallels with the vision are too strong not to be underlined: the Rule uses the image of a child denied milk, in order to introduce the image of the ladder of humility; Clare climbs a steep stairway and there finds a mother – Francis – who offers her the breast. There is another detail, too, which emphasises the reference. The psalm is one of a group of fifteen called, in the Vulgate, *Cantica graduum* (from the Hebrew *Ma'aloth* = steps). Thus, even in this title, the concept of a stair or ladder of holiness is brought to mind. In this case the stairway was probably that of the temple in Jerusalem which the pilgrims climbed processionally during the major festivals of pilgrimage.

The words which most attracted the attention of the notary who wrote down the evidence during the canonisation process, however, were those of 'the breast of St Francis'.[64] While the breast constitutes part of that primitive experience so formative for the individual unconscious, it also forms part of the mytho-logical-religious mystery common to the collective unconscious of the most widely differing peoples. The Bible speaks of the breast in reference to Jerusalem, the 'mother' of the people of Israel:

> Rejoice, Jerusalem,
> be glad for her, all you who love her! . . .
>
> That you may be suckled, filled,
> from her consoling breast,
> that you may savour with delight
> her glorious breasts. (Isaiah 66: 10–11)

This is the final prophecy in the book of Isaiah where the prophet speaks of that glory and peace which are destined to surround Israel on her return from exile. The image here refers to Jerusalem, but more often it is God himself who is presented as a mother nourishing her sons:

> I led them with reins of kindness,
> with leading-strings of love.
> I was like someone who lifts an infant close against his cheek;
> stooping down to him I gave him his food. (Hosea 11: 4)

Clare's vision then goes on to tell of the nourishment she received:

After she had sucked from it, the saint admonished her to imbibe once again. After she did so what she had tasted was so sweet and delightful that she could in no way describe it.

Thus Clare was nourished at the breast of Francis. In this feeding were satisfaction and a response, not only to Clare's own unconscious desires but also to something which amounted to an overriding obsession for everyone who lived in the Middle Ages, namely: hunger.

Our attention is then drawn to 'what she had tasted', that is, to the milk which she sucked from Francis' breast. Clare does not explicitly use the word 'milk', even though the substance which she sucked was 'so sweet and delightful' that it could have been no other. It was a milk 'so sweet and delightful that she could in no way describe it', that is, it was spiritual milk of sweetness beyond utterance. It was like the sweetness described by the prophet Ezekiel who, when he had seen the glory of God, was given a scroll filled with lamentations over his people and 'I ate it, and it tasted sweet as honey' (3: 3). More than likely, the choice of the words 'what she had tasted' instead of 'the milk' was far from being casual; they were probably chosen in order to draw out the spiritual meaning of the vision that much better.

Suckling is also a recurring image in religious tales: the hero is suckled by animals or by a goddess. For example, Hercules, through the miraculous intervention of the gods, sucked milk from the breast of Hera and thus attained immortality. Milk, in mythology, is the food of the gods; in eschatology it is the food of Paradise; in magic it is seen as the very medium of life itself.

In the Old Testament, milk represents abundance, that characteristic of the Promised Land (where it is often found together with honey) and thus, more generally, a mark of the last days. In the New Testament, milk is a spiritual drink meaning divine teaching. In the first Letter of St Peter we read: 'You are new born, and, like babies, you should be hungry for nothing but milk – the spiritual honesty which will help you grow up to salvation' (1 Peter 2: 2). The Fathers of the Church, beginning with Irenaeus and Clement of Alexandria, adopted this theme of milk as doctrine, indeed as the Word of God itself.

This is the context from which we can begin to draw out the cultural meaning of this strange vision of Clare's. In addition, there are other indispensable and more direct references which are nearer in time to Clare herself. One of these would seem to be the story of the feeding of St Bernard with milk. In this account, the saint was praying before a statue of the Madonna feeding her child, and at the moment when Bernard said the words *Monstra te esse matrem* ('Show yourself a mother') the statue came to life and the Virgin, compressing her breast, allowed a few drops of milk to fall on the saint's lips. This may well be a pious story, for it is not found in any text earlier than the fourteenth century. It would be interesting to trace the development of such accounts in devotion and popular culture, particularly as similar episodes were attributed to St Augustine, Fulbert of Chartres, St Dominic, Alain de la Roche and St

Catherine de' Ricci. It is impossible, in the present state of research, to say how widespread were (at least) the oral accounts, by the thirteenth century.[65]

Within the Franciscan tradition itself we find further references. In the *Second Life* of Celano, Francis called Christmas the 'feast of feasts' because it was 'the day when God, having become a tiny infant, clung to human breasts'. After his death, popular piety considered Francis as a protector of pregnant and nursing mothers.[66] In the *Treatise on the Miracles* Celano devotes a whole chapter to women who have survived the dangers of childbirth and recounts a miracle which seems particularly relevant for interpreting Clare's vision:

In the diocese of Magliano Sabino there lived an eighty-year-old woman who had had two daughters, one of whom had promised to nurse the remaining child of her dead sister. When she herself conceived a child by her husband, she had no milk and there was no one who could come to the help of the baby orphan who grew weaker and weaker, smaller and smaller, and even the grandmother was almost dying of grief. One night, in order to quieten the whimpering of the child, the old woman put its lips to her own dried up breasts and full of tears begged for the help of blessed Francis. Suddenly he was there beside her, this friend of the innocent, and out of the tenderness he always showed towards those who were unhappy, he was moved by compassion for the old lady. He said: I am that Francis whom you, O Lady, have invoked with so many tears. Place your breast between those young lips – he went on – because the Lord will give you plenty of milk!.[67]

Clare's vision ends with another image which would have been culturally significant in her day:

After she had imbibed, that nipple or opening of the breast from which the milk came remained between the lips of blessed Clare. After she took what remained in her mouth into her hands, it seemed to her it was gold so clear and bright that everything was seen in it as in a mirror.

So the vision ends with the word 'mirror'. This was a keyword in the spirituality and culture of the Middle Ages.[68] More than two hundred and fifty works have come down to us in which the word *speculum* or its translation appears in the title.[69]

Across the whole of Europe from the twelfth century onwards, the image of a mirror seems to have had particular meaning in women's religious circles. Obviously the *Speculum Virginum* stands out, because there can be no doubt of its influence on currents of spirituality throughout succeeding centuries; but it was primarily in German mysticism (and in northern Europe generally) during the twelfth and thirteenth centuries that the image of the mirror takes its definitive form.

In Matilda of Magdeburg, a contemporary of Clare, the mirror metaphor expresses the mystic's union with God: 'You are my mirror on high, the delight of my eyes . . . my greatest help'. Here the 'mirror on high' indicates an ecstatic rapport far beyond ordinary living. The expression 'to look into the mirror of the Godhead' was the expression current in German mysticism to mean mystical union. The mystical and spiritual experiences of Clare were, then, deeply rooted in a culture which, while it may not have influenced her directly, was certainly shared by the other *mulieres religiosae* in the thirteenth century.

Considering this final mirror-image in which, having once reached the top of the stairway and been nursed by Francis, Clare looked and saw her own self reflected – how can we not associate it with the 'mirror on high' of Matilda and recall its meaning of mystical marriage?

In the tide of women's spirituality which preceded and survived Clare, she probably represents a minor expression – in terms, that is, of cultural evaluation. Yet she was an essential point of reference in the movement, and her originality, perhaps never to be repeated, was not without influence. The originality of Clare's spirituality, and thus of the vision, lies in this one unusual element, already spelt out, namely that Francis is the centre towards whom the whole vision converges.

Clare's love for Francis, thrown into relief so well by this vision, was so much a characteristic of her love for God and of her spirituality that she brought about a true and original shift in meaning of the traditional symbols for the love of God. Clare used these symbols to indicate her love for Francis, and yet this love left her love of God no less pure. As for Matilda, so for

Clare, the Lord was her greatest help; Francis was the specific agent through whom she came to know and love God. So much was this so, that in her Testament she could say that Francis was their 'pillar of strength, and after God our one consolation and support'.[70]

It was this human love which enabled Clare to avoid the dangers of an excessive exaltation of religious ecstasy which marked spiritual experiences of others such as the *minnemistik* or – geographically nearer to Clare – Angela of Foligno.[71]

EIGHT

Mother of the Sisters and Defender of the City

HOLINESS AND MIRACLES

Holiness has always had one distinctive sign, one unambiguous characteristic: miracles. The *conversatio*, that is, the way a religious person lived both before and after their entry into religious life, is seen as a relatively less important mark of holiness than his or her miracles. What is a miracle? It is a wonderful event, something extraordinary which cannot be understood simply by human reasoning. This is the classic interpretation given to the word *miraculum* by St Augustine: '*Whatever is difficult or too unlikely to hope for or which appears wonderful.*'[1] In this understanding of the word, not everything which looks miraculous is necessarily holy, that is, coming from God; but certainly all that comes from God is holy and sometimes also miraculous. Gregory the Great imposed a further definition by distinguishing natural from supernatural events, for even ordinary events of nature are miraculous in so far as they are the work of God.[2]

For the whole of the Middle Ages, this concept predominated, that the ordinary and the extraordinary, the everyday and the miraculous, were closely bound together as one. A miracle was part of everyday life, something both extraordinary yet familiar. The boundaries between the marvellous and the ordinary seem to have been extremely subtle,[3] and binding these two worlds in constant dialogue was above all the life of the saint. The saint was seen as the intermediary, the one who opened the world to God and opened the way to God for the world, and miracles were the clearest manifestation of this key function.[4] In this context, holiness is a *virtus*, 'a power', coming from God and revealing itself in the lives of the holy one.[5]

This miraculous force seemed, at least in part, to be independent of faith. The authors of the lives of medieval saints tended not to stress faith, and even accepted that sometimes a miracle could happen without the saint being aware of it.[6] It was as if this miraculous power had a life of its own which transcended the biological limits of the saint's own life and transmitted itself to the relics as well as to any objects brought into contact with those relics.[7]

The tendency to make miracles into the clearest expression of holiness reached its apogee in the eleventh and twelfth centuries. This was the period of saints like Thomas à Becket and Bernard of Clairveaux, each of whose miracles added up to several hundred.[8] A shift of perspective took place during the thirteenth century, for while miracles still continued to be the sign *par excellence* of holiness, moral strength also took its place alongside them and was sometimes substituted for them. Sanctity was still recognised by its power to produce extraordinary events, but was seen even more in the way the saint incarnated the Gospel virtues of that model of all holiness: Jesus Christ.[9] The mendicant Orders played a crucial role in this shift of perspective, which is why the definition of miracles which Thomas Aquinas gives us seems much clearer than the one quoted from Augustine. Aquinas says:

Now a miracle is so called as being full of wonder; as having a cause that is absolutely hidden from all: and this cause is God. Wherefore those things which God does outside those causes which we know about, are called miracles.[10]

THE MIRACLES OF CLARE

The author of the *Life of St Clare the Virgin* shares in this current belief that miracles underlined the virtue of the saint. He spells this out quite clearly in the introduction to the second book of his work, 'The miracles of St Clare after she passed from the world':

These are the marvellous signs of the saints, these are the testimonies of miracles that should be honoured, that rest on their foundation of holiness of character and the perfection of their deeds.[11]

If Thomas of Celano set out to write a whole book on the miracles which Clare worked after her death, then he had a reason. He tells us himself about the devotion of the people and, in fact, this work was an act of homage to that devotion. What is more, not all miracles are equal. Not only do they vary from country to country and person to person, but there is also a great difference according to whether we are speaking about those worked while the saint is alive or those worked after his or her death.[12] In the first group, which the medieval authors call *miracula in vita*, 'miracles in life', the centre of attention is the saint who works the miracle. In the second, *miracula post mortem*, 'miracles after death', the interest centres on the devout person who asks for the miracle.[13] During the canonisation process of Clare, it would seem that there was a problem of continuity from one type of miracle to the other. In the sisters' evidence, the miracles were all put together at the end of their testimony, but in fact the witnesses were mainly talking about miracles worked during her life. As we have already pointed out, the canonisation process was begun very soon after Clare's death, and a true and proper cult near her tomb (which anyway was in the church dedicated to San Giorgio) had certainly not yet developed and could not have produced many miraculous events. Thomas of Celano, on the other hand, wrote some time later. From the accounts of miracles which he had, he could compose a second part for his work, in accordance with the literary tradition of such biographies, and thus complete the first part dealing with the life of Clare.

The miracles worked during life and those worked after death are both interesting for different reasons. The wonderful signs and marvels which Clare wrought when she was alive are very important if we are to understand her thinking and feelings. The miracles worked after her death, on the other hand, are indicative of the rapport which she had built up with those around her and above all with her city.[14] In the end this basic distinction forces us to classify the various works of wonder which the sources have handed down to us. What type of miracles do they speak about? Healings certainly, which were the miracle *par excellence* throughout the Middle Ages, but also visions, extraordinary auditions, the multiplication of food, protection in the face of danger: the list is extremely varied, not to say original.[15]

The first characteristic of Clare's miracles is that they are mainly concerned – obviously – with the happenings within the narrow confines of San Damiano. They are not miracles *in via*, 'on the road'. *In via* was the usual setting for the great and holy wonder workers of the twelfth century who based themselves on the Gospel model,[16] but in Clare's case the road is replaced by the cloister. This helps to explain the relatively low number of healings, which would normally have happened out on the street as the saint passed by. Another distinction we can make about Clare's miracles concerns the people for whom they were worked: some were in the interests of and to the advantage of the sisters of San Damiano (what we might call 'miracles at home') and some were for those outside the monastery ('miracles of the city', given that the recipient was from the Assisi area).

The miracles worked at home, at least those explicitly recorded by the sisters during the process, numbered fourteen: these included healings, multiplication of food, special events. There were nine miracles worked outside the enclosed space of the cloister. Here we have to remember that the part of the canonisation process which has come down to us is almost exclusively composed of evidence from the sisters. This suggests that other witnesses would have made considerable additions to the number of miracles that took place outside the monastery.

Finally, we must remember the visions of Clare, which we spoke about in the preceding chapter. These were signs that she had overcome all limitations of time and space.[17] The process records eight such visions and to these we can add Clare's discernment that a woman sent to San Damiano by Francis lacked a vocation. This last case is what the hagiographers called *spiritum prophetiae*, 'the spirit of prophecy', that is, the saint's capacity to go beyond her own physical and mental limitations. It was no chance that this element of vision developed so strongly in an enclosed community; even the sisters shared in it, so that the presence of the Spirit was perceived as a feeling that their physical and spatial boundaries were being widened and enlarged.

Miracles at Home

Sister Cristiana di Bernardo da Suppo gave evidence during the process that the very first miracle wrought by Clare had been during her flight from her father's house to join Francis at the Portiuncola. This is the episode, already recorded in Chapter 2, of the barricaded door of the house:

Because she did not want to leave through the usual exit, fearing her way would be blocked, she went out by the house's other exit which had been barricaded with heavy wooden beams and an iron bar so it could not be opened even by a large number of men. She alone, with the help of Jesus Christ, removed them and opened the door. On the following morning, when many people saw that door opened, they were somewhat astonished at how a young girl could have done it. Asked how she knew these things, she replied that she, the witness, was in that house at that time because she lived in Assisi.[18]

For Sister Cristiana this was clearly a miracle worked solely with the 'help of Jesus Christ', and she records it as such in the canonisation process in order to demonstrate the special love which the Lord had shown for Clare right from her first steps in religious life. Thomas of Celano is more prudent. He records the event in his *Life* but simply speaks of a 'strength which seemed to them to be extraordinary', leaving the reader with the responsibility of deciding whether or not this was a miracle.

Since she was not content to leave by way of the usual door, marvelling at her strength, she broke open – with her own hands – that other door that is customarily blocked by wood and stone.[19]

Clare's biographer often seemed to be embarrassed at the way the sisters interpreted everyday things in a miraculous light and he says nothing, in consequence, about another episode told at the process by Sister Angeluccia:

The witness also saw when the door of the palace, that is of the monastery, fell upon Lady Clare. The sisters believed the door had killed her and thereupon raised a great moan. But the Lady remained unharmed and said that she had not felt in any way the weight of that door which was so heavy three brothers could barely return it to its place. Asked how she knew this she replied: because she saw it and was present. Asked how long ago this was, she replied: almost seven years ago. Asked about the day, she said during the octave of St Peter, a Sunday evening. At that time, at the cry of the witness, the sisters immediately came and found the door still lying upon her since she, the witness, could not lift it by herself.[20]

The quality of the daily life at San Damiano shows clearly through this testimony, with Clare personally concerning herself that the door of the house be shut (it was Sunday which may be why it was open). This was the house which Sister Angeluccia calls a palace, but quickly corrects herself (or is corrected by the notary) and adds 'that is, the monastery'. The house was in such poor condition that a door could fall off on to the person who tried to close it. This was the door about which so much was to be said in the Rule, how it should be closed and bolted.[21] It also becomes clear how simple the sisters' lives were that such an incident, seven years previously, should be so memorable.

The two miraculous multiplications must be placed in this same context of daily life. The sisters relate these during the canonisation process and Thomas of Celano also includes them in his *Life*. In order to show God's goodness towards the new form of religious life which Clare had begun, he puts them into a special section just after he has spoken about her choice of poverty.[22]

The first of these multiplications was the miracle of the oil, told by Sister Pacifica during the process.[23] The container, which Clare had left for the brother whose turn it was to beg, was miraculously found to be full. When he reported this to Clare, she herself asked who could possibly have filled it. On this occasion, Sister Pacifica leaves it vague as to whether or not this was a divine intervention[24] but Thomas of Celano makes it explicit:

For by the bountiful God alone that jar was replenished with oil, since the prayer of the holy Clare had anticipated the concern of the brother for the welfare of the poor daughters.[25]

The only problem is that there is no trace in the canonisation process (Thomas' source) of any such prayer on Clare's part, and so her biographer has had to invent one in order to give the episode the dignity of the miraculous. The multiplication of oil was not an unusual miracle in lives of the saints up to that time. For instance, in his life of St Benedict, Gregory the Great tells how once, during a time of severe famine, the holy abbot wanted the last drop of oil in the monastery to give away in alms. He overcame the resistance of the cellarer and immediately after he had given the oil away, while all the monks were together at prayer, they found a jar in the church full to over-flowing with fine oil.[26] In that case there was a neat coincidence between the miracle and the prayers of the monks, but the whole context shows quite clearly that Gregory told this story in order to underline Benedict's detachment from the goods of this earth and that this detachment was rewarded by the Lord with a miraculous multiplication of oil.

Thomas of Celano, who certainly knew about the episode recounted by Gregory, found himself a little embarrassed by the very different attitudes of Clare and Benedict. Benedict, for his part, was detached, but this only highlighted Clare's concern and involvement which in themselves seemed somewhat suspect, particularly as it was only a matter of oil, not an absolutely essential item of food. The fact is that these two miracles demonstrate the difference between the poverty of Benedict, which he saw as renunciation and detachment, and the poverty of Clare, which she saw as insecurity of life and dependence on others for alms and mercy.[27]

The second multiplication was that of the half loaf of bread which became fifty slices. The account, as told by Sister Cecilia during the process, is reminiscent of the multiplication of loaves on the shores of the lake at Tiberias and Sister Cecilia herself mentions the Gospel example:

She also said one day when the sisters had only a half loaf of bread, since the other half had been sent to the brothers who were staying outside, the Lady directed the witness to make fifty slices out of the half loaf of bread and to bring them to the sisters who had gone to table. The witness then said to Lady Clare: The Lord's miracle of the five loaves and two fishes would be needed to make fifty slices out of that!

But the Lady told her: Go and do as I have told you. And so the Lord multiplied that bread in such a way that she made fifty large and good slices as St Clare had directed her.[28]

Sister Cecilia had no doubt that she was talking about a major miracle here. When she received Clare's command, had she not underlined that only the Lord himself could do such a thing?

The multiplication of loaves is one of the most frequent miracles in the hagiography of the Middle Ages. The recollection of the multiplication in the Gospel,[29] together with a situation in which scarcity of food often led to famine, go far to explain why this particular miracle should have so caught the imagination and so attracted popular devotion.[30] Because of this, the most interesting aspects of Sister Cecilia's evidence are those which differ from the Gospel account, the less usual details. We do not have a huge and hungry crowd before us but simply a small group of sisters who had gathered one day in the refectory and had nothing to eat. The episode speaks volumes about the uncertainty of the lives of these women at San Damiano. Their poverty was no abstract ideal but a hard condition of life.[31] Somewhere else in the process we are told how Clare, when alms had been collected, was much happier to see only small pieces of bread and not whole loaves. To have a whole loaf was rather like having a small amount of capital: it was a kind of luxury which could only have been offered to them by families who, while not necessarily wealthy, still were not poor.[32]

We should also note that the event did not happen during the very early years at San Damiano because the fifty slices surely indicate that fifty sisters were present and this figure was only reached after some years. So the conditions of indigence and extreme poverty were not just characteristics of the first very difficult years of the community's life, but remained a constant factor of their experience. The growth in the number of sisters might even to some extent have added to the daily needs and difficulties.

Through healings which Clare worked for the sisters,[33] we can see most clearly the aspect of her power which became the interface between their daily lives and her holiness. In the *Life*, the healings are all collected together into a paragraph called, 'Various miracles that she performed by the sign and power of the cross', thus underlining that it was through the sign of the cross that she healed: 'When she traced the sign of the life-giving Cross on the sick, sickness miraculously fled from them.'[34] The sign of the cross was, in fact, the central element of all the healings, as Sister Pacifica testifies:

She also said that the medicine of that witness and of the other sisters when they were sick was that their mother made the sign of the cross over them.[35]

While this is the only factor that the *Life* emphasises, it emerges very clearly from the sisters' evidence at the process that the sign of the cross was not the only gesture used by Clare in such cases. For example, in the case of Sister Benvenuta, the healing gesture was preceded by a vision in which she was told that she would be healed.[36] When Clare cured Sister Amata, she also touched her sick body.[37] In another case, Clare recited the Our Father[38] as she made the sign of the cross. Sister Balvina gave evidence that, when she had had a pain in her thigh, Clare had stretched herself out on the place of the sister's pain.[39] All these accounts reveal the solicitous and attentive nature, even the sacred character, of the healings worked by Clare during her life.

By placing these healings in the context of Clare's devotion to the cross, her biography fails to give us the essence and spirit of them. Instead it gives us a lesson in theology which may well go beyond the theology of Clare herself. It is the Crucified himself, according to Thomas of Celano, who works the miracles by means of Clare:

The beloved Crucified took possession of the lover and she was inflamed with such love of the mystery of the Cross that the power of the Cross is shown by signs and miracles.[40]

In Thomas' view, the important thing is Clare's love for the cross. In his eagerness to underline the value of the interior elements over those which were only external, that is, the spiritual over the wonder-working, he ends up by putting all Clare's careful concern for her sick sisters into second place:

It should be perfectly clear from this that the Tree of the Cross was planted in the breast of the Virgin; while its fruit refreshes the soul, its leaves externally provide medicine.[41]

Miracles in the City

In the canonisation process, only five healings worked by Clare for people outside the community of San Damiano are mentioned, but two other witnesses tell us that there were really many more even though they could remember no names. This becomes understandable when we reflect that the sisters were enclosed at San Damiano and had no chance of further meetings with those people who came there to be healed.[42] During her life, Clare was not, in fact, considered a 'healer'. Even her healings of those outside the San Damiano community had a modest quality about them, an absence of display. Crowds did not gather at the gates of San Damiano and Clare almost seemed reluctant to give relief to those whose paths crossed hers. As Sister Amata tells us:

She said that a young boy from Perugia had a certain film over his eye which covered all of it. Then he was brought to St Clare who touched the eyes of the boy and then made the sign of the cross over him. Then she said: bring him to my mother, Sister Ortolana (who was in the monastery of San Damiano) and let her make the sign of the cross over him. After this had been done, the young boy was cured, so that St Clare said her mother had cured him. On the contrary, though, her mother said Lady Clare, her daughter, had cured him. Thus each one attributed this grace to the other.[43]

The picture of this little argument between mother and daughter, as to who should have the credit (or the blame) for gaining the grace, shows us the atmosphere of familiarity in which these healings took place, as well as demonstrating Clare's reluctance to reveal herself as a wonder-worker, which is a classic trait in a saint.[44]

For the most part we are talking about the healing of ordinary people. One was a baby with a high fever, another a little boy who had pushed a pebble up his nose:

A young boy, the son of the Lord Giovanni di Maestro Giovanni, procurator of the sisters, was seriously ill with a fever. This was mentioned to mother St Clare. When he received the sign of the cross from her, he was cured.[45]

A young boy of the city of Spoleto, Mattiolo, three or four years old, had put a pebble up one of the nostrils of his nose, so it could in no way be extricated. The young boy seemed to be in danger. After he was brought to St Clare and she made the sign of the cross over him, that pebble immediately fell from his nose. The young boy was cured.[46]

Over half Clare's healings were worked for children. During her life she specially loved the young, and she continued to show this predilection after she died. We find that many of the miracles worked after her death concern children.[47]

Clare's love of children also echoes a characteristic of the spirituality of the San Damiano community. The sisters gave evidence at the canonisation process that in a vision they had several times seen the child Jesus come close to Clare.[48] Devotion to the child Jesus was an integral part of the cult of Christ made man and is found throughout the whole of the thirteenth century. In particular it was an aspect of the new women's spirituality and there are exact parallels between the experience of Clare and her companions[49] and the experience of, for instance, Mary of Oignies and the whole Beguine movement.[50]

This same interest in children shows through in one of the very few miracles recounted in the canonisation process by someone other than the sisters. This is the evidence of the Lord Ugolino de Pietro Girardone, one of the most illustrious men of Assisi.

He also said that he, the witness, had left his wife, Lady Guiduccia, sent her back to the house of her father and mother, had been without her for a period of more than twenty-two years, and had never been able to be persuaded by anyone to want to send for her and receive her back, even though he had been admonished many times even by religious persons. Finally he was told, on the part of Lady St Clare, that she had learned in a vision that he, Lord Ugolino, had to receive her back immediately and, by her, produce a son from whom he would have great joy and consolation. When the witness heard this, he was somewhat distressed.

But after a few days, he was impelled by great desire, so he sent for and received the woman, who such a long time before had left him. Then, as it had been seen in a vision of Lady St Clare, he begot by her a son still living and from whom he is very much overjoyed and has great consolation.[51]

Ugolino was one of the *maiores* of Assisi. To repudiate a wife was without question a political act, an expression of the clan hostility which was tearing Italian cities apart at that time. Clare intervened in order to make the will of God known, a will, that is, to reconciliation and peace. It was in this same spirit that Francis had reconciled the bishop and the mayor.[52] So this miracle, too, served to underline the bond between Clare and her city.

Clare remained near Assisi all her life. This bond with her city gave her a permanent framework, in marked contrast to the itinerancy of the Minors, and is one of the ways in which Clare most resembles the other religious women of her generation. Like Umiliana de' Cerchi in Florence or St Rose in Viterbo (to choose those who were spiritually and geographically close to Clare), for Clare, too, holiness was closely bound up with the political life of her city.[53] This notion of a religious life which was local and 'residential', given to prayer and in direct contact with the civic community from which it sprang, was a development of the expressions of women's religious life in preceding generations. Clare's mother, Ortolana, had travelled to the Holy Land and taken part in pilgrimages to Rome and St Michael at Monte Gargano,[54] but Clare always stayed near Assisi. Her generation was no longer the generation of great pilgrimages to Jerusalem.

The spiritual climate had profoundly changed and the greatest of the changes must surely be the weakening of the crusading ideal. The crusades, at least until the tragic ending to Louis IX's expedition, had continued to nourish a certain spiritual and emotional energy, but there is no doubt that the first half of the thirteenth century was marked by the Christian people's progressive loss of interest in the *bellum iustum*, 'the just war'. Or, perhaps, it was rather that popular devotion veered towards other objects of veneration, other points of reference, and so slowly slid away from Jerusalem and the Holy Sepulchre.[55] The very possibility of gaining indulgences without travelling far from one's own land, or by going to much more accessible places, increased as the century went on. In the end this cancelled out any interest which had previously existed in the source of all indulgences, namely Jerusalem and the Holy Sepulchre.[56]

From such a perspective, devotion to the Holy Eucharist was the ineradicable mark of thirteenth-century spirituality, and was itself a turning-point. Devotion shifted from reverence for the place where the body of the Saviour had been laid to reverence for the consecrated Eucharist, and it was no chance that, at the Fourth Lateran Council of 1215, reception of the Eucharist at least once a year became obligatory. The major centres from which eucharistic devotion was to spread and be sustained were the new religious houses of women right across Europe.[57]

It is in this context that we can best understand Clare's miracle of expelling the Saracens. Face to face with danger from Frederick II's troops who had already entered the monastery cloister, Clare

made them [the sisters] bring her to the entrance of the refectory and bring a small box where there was the Blessed Sacrament of the Body of our Lord Jesus Christ. Throwing herself prostrate on the ground in prayer, she begged with tears, saying among other things: Lord, look upon these servants of yours because I cannot protect them.[58]

This event can quite definitely be dated 1240. In that year, the emperor Frederick II, by now excommunicated for the second time, tried to impose his authority on the whole Italian peninsula. In the vale of Umbria, he was particularly anxious to gain Assisi, once a bulwark for his imperial army but now independent and pursuing a pro-papal policy. Frederick sent his troops against the city. Like all the small buildings of the countryside, San Damiano was unprotected; the little church was a long way from the city walls and there were not many houses nearby. Clare, who was ill, gathered the sisters together in prayer. Hers was a struggle without weapons, like that of Francis at Damietta. There the Poverello had had himself led to the sultan without any protection; here Clare presented herself to the Saracen forces, armed only with the Most Holy Sacrament. All her strength was in her intercession and that intercession not only saved San Damiano but the whole city.

There are many such episodes in which saints, and above all bishops, become protectors of their cities.[59] What distinguishes this story is the fact that we have the idea of the crusades (the invaders were Saracens) woven into the demonstration of devotion to the Blessed Sacrament.

While in the account given during the canonisation process we are struck by the weakness out of which Clare confronted the soldiery all alone, in the *Life* of Thomas of Celano there is a racist note, giving the impression of Clare as a powerful saint, far stronger than the hated enemy:

The Saracens, the worst of people, who thirsted for the blood of Christians and attempted imprudently every outrage, rushed upon San Damiano . . .

Without delay the boldness of those dogs began immediately to be alarmed. They were driven away by the power of the one who was praying, departing in haste over those walls which they had scaled.[60]

The link between the Blessed Sacrament and Clare the powerful saint was even more strongly accented in the iconography which followed her death:[61] the Saracens were seen as blind men put to flight by the blinding light coming from the Host in Clare's hands.[62] Put like this, the miracle instantly becomes an anti-imperial text and there are plenty of hints which reinforce that interpretation. Frederick, the true antichrist, had not only come to an agreement with the sultan of Egypt (or so papal propaganda maintained) to avoid fulfilling his solemn imperial coronation promise to set out on a crusade, but he had also used his Arab-Sicilian army to promote what was in effect a Saracen counter-crusade in Italy. While the sisters' account during the canonisation process is rather confused (so much so that at one point they call the Saracens 'Tartars') the *Life*, on the other hand, is extremely precise. For Thomas of Celano, Clare is the last bulwark of the Catholic faith against a heretical emperor and his Saracen allies.

The Spoleto valley more often drank of the chalice of wrath because of that scourge the Church had to endure in various parts of the world under Frederick the Emperor. In it there was a battle array of soldiers and Saracen archers swarming like bees at the imperial command to depopulate its villages and to spoil its cities.[63]

Clare, then, came to be seen as a champion of the faith who, like the first martyrs and indeed like the crusaders, confronted God's enemies as they thirsted for the blood of Christians. She is seen above all, however, as *defensor civitatis*, 'the defender of the city'. The miracle seemed almost like the fruit of some parley between Clare and God, as a result of which Clare could obtain her sisters' safety and at the same time guarantee the salvation of her city.[64] During this negotiation Clare spoke in the name of the whole city, and the result was a double obligation: on God's part, 'the city will endure many dangers but it will be defended'; on the side of the sisters and the people of Assisi, 'as long as you wish to obey God's commandments'.[65] In quite a formal manner, Clare took on that role of defender of the city which in preceding centuries had largely belonged to the bishops. The bond between the woman and the city assumed an official quality. This was strengthened twelve months later when a similar episode occurred in which the protagonists were again the imperial troops.

In 1241, Vitalis di Aversa, commander of Frederick II's army, again tried to take Assisi. This time it was not a question of an assault with intent to sack, but of a full-scale siege. The city was to be 'taken', that is, made to surrender. On this occasion, Clare was under no pressure through immediate danger to herself or her companions; she was moved to intervene for no other reason that that of her bond with the city:

After the Lady Clare had been told by someone that the city of Assisi must be handed over, the Lady called her sisters and said to them: we have received many benefits from this city and I know we should pray that God will protect it.[66]

In the words of Clare, prayer was a fitting recompense for all the help, even (and why not?) the material help, which the city had given to the monastery. Here she shows us just how concrete was her awareness of prayer, and that she had no doubt of its effectiveness.

In this episode we have a most expressive example of the mutual solidarity which united women religious (and especially recluses) to citizens living nearby. These women who chose a life of prayer, alone or in a group, often took up their abode near a bridge or gates or other exposed place, or else they would live where people constantly passed by and in this way would receive their food from the very people who were protected by their prayers.[67]

Throughout the thirteenth century, a great many new local cults flourished in the cities of central and northern Italy.[68] Just when the pope was pruning and refining the canonisation procedure, personality cults were growing up which, in one way or another, typified the new social and religious life. Often these cults were never officially recognised by the Roman curia and were utilised by protagonists in the struggle for political predominance in the communes.[69]

In this sense, the holiness of Clare was another example of this new wave of 'urban saints'. The date of the miracle of liberation from the troops of Vitalis di Aversa became an official feast for the commune of Assisi and the cult of Clare became (perhaps even more than that of Francis) a symbol of the unity and concord of the whole city.

However, seen in the spectrum of other urban cults in the second half of the thirteenth century, Clare was also a bit of an anomaly. The very fact that her *cultus* was not promoted and adopted by any specific group or confraternity or congregation of lay people, but was rather an official cult of the whole city, meant that it did not give rise to any particular devotional enthusiasm. As a result, it met with considerable difficulties after her rapid canonisation.[70] The delays and uncertainties which surrounded the transformation of the church of San Giorgio and the erection of a new basilica dedicated to the saint bear witness to these difficulties.[71]

Miracles during Clare's Life

AT HOME

Healings
1 Five sisters, of whom Pacifica was one
2 Sister Bonaventura da Perugia lost her voice
3 Sister Bonaventura di Madonna Diambra (sores)
4 Sister Amata (dropsy)
5 Sister Andrea (scrofula in the throat)
6 Sister Cristiana (deafness)
7 Sister Cecilia (cough)
8 Sister Balvina (pain in the thigh)
9 Sister Balvina (abcess on the breast)
10 Sister Francesca (pain in the head)

Multiplications
1 Of oil
2 Of bread

Extraordinary events
1 Dialogue with the cat
2 Unhurt after the door fell on her

Visions and extraordinary perceptions
1 Vision of St Francis
2 Vision on Christmas night
3 Vision of Ortolana
4–6 Light seen around Clare
7 Vision of Sister Francesca
8 Vision of Sister Agnes
9 Discernment about a false vocation

IN THE CITY

Healings
1 Brother Stefano
2 Child from Spoleto (Mattiolo)
3 Child from Assisi
4 Child from Perugia
5 Woman from Pisa (possessed)
6 Others unnamed

Defence of the city
1 From the Saracens
2 From the army of Vitalis di Aversa

Extraordinary event
Strange flight from her father's house

Promise of motherhood
Reconciliation between Ugolino and Guiduccia di Assisi
and promise of a son

NINE

The Liturgy of the 'Transitus'

CLARE'S LAST YEARS

Clare was ill for more than twenty-eight years. During the course of this long illness, she was on the point of death several times. When this happened, the anxious sisters would gather around her bed in prayer. There were a few dramatic moments during which some unusual mystical events took place. Death is a passage and, to some extent, the dying person already lives in the world towards which she is hurrying. Those who were close to Clare, praying with her and for her, became caught up into this spiritual atmosphere. This is what happened to Sister Francesca:

She also said once, when the sisters believed the blessed mother was at the moment of death and the priest had given her the Holy Communion of the Body of our Lord Jesus Christ, she, the witness, saw a very great splendour about the head of mother St Clare. It seemed to her the Lord's Body was a very small and beautiful young boy. After the holy Mother had received with great devotion and tears, as was her custom, she said these words: God has given me such a gift today that heaven and earth could not equal it.[1]

It was probably during one of these crises which took her close to death that Clare wrote her Testament,[2] just as Francis had done;[3] and perhaps on another such occasion she wrote her Blessing for her sisters present and to come. What is certain is that, for Clare, her illness was a long preparation for her final *transitus* or passage from life.

Clare's biographer dedicates the last chapter of the first book specifically to this *transitus*.[4] He relates the events according to the received ideas of the thirteenth century about a 'good death', that is, the long agony, the sisters standing round, the last rites of religion and at the centre the one who was dying: Clare.[5] Death was not seen as something shameful, it was not something to be hidden from those who were to live on, to be forgotten as soon as possible. Rather the contrary, death was seen as a constant everyday presence, the necessary crown of daily life. This is how Clare is presented as she prepares for death through those long twenty-eight years of illness:

Since the strength of her flesh had succumbed to the austerity of the penance she had practised in the early years, a harsh sickness took hold of her last years, so that she who had been enriched with the merits of good deeds when well, might be enriched with the merits of suffering when sick. For virtue is brought to perfection in sickness. How her marvellous virtue had been perfected in her sickness will be hereafter told at length: because during the twenty-eight years of her prolonged sickness, she did not murmur or utter a complaint but holy comments and thanksgiving always came from her mouth.[6]

During the canonisation process the sisters gave evidence about Clare's death in the tones of people who were both loving and involved. It was her biographer who made it into an exemplary death. To the testimonies given at the process he added the evidence of Clare's blood-sister, Agnes, and that of the nuns in the nearby monastery of San Paolo delle Abbadesse (where Clare had gone at the start of her religious life). Putting all this material together, Thomas of Celano fused it into so vibrant a rendering as might have come from an eye-witness, and out of it he draws an account of a 'holy death', a death which would serve as an example to anyone who read the *Life*.

It will, perhaps, be useful to recapitulate the order of events as the *Life* sets them out. The author seemed well-informed and his account is supplemented by that of the *Rhyming Life* which offers exactly the same development of the facts.[7]

In the autumn of 1251 Clare had a graver crisis than usual, but it was still not time for her to die. There remained one unresolved question which preoccupied Clare and her sisters and this was the defence of the *Privilege of Poverty*. In 1247 Pope Innocent IV had drawn up his own Constitutions[8] for the Poor Ladies which were, for the first time, not based on the

Rule of Benedict but on that of Francis. In this way the community was firmly bound to the movement of Minors. On the other hand, the Rule of Innocent stressed the necessity for the community to hold goods in common in order to support themselves. This was a great danger, because it called into question the choice of poverty, that specific quality of life at San Damiano which Clare had not hesitated to defend to Innocent's predecessor, Gregory IX.

As a result, Clare set herself to write a Rule of her own in which the option of poverty would be solemnly confirmed.[9] This was her final anxiety before she could die. By now, however, the pope was at Lyons: how was she to contact him and persuade him to set aside a rule which he had himself promulgated, in favour of a new form of life? As Clare's condition got worse, the sisters' remaining hope seemed to vanish:

While the Pope and cardinals took their time in Lyons, a sword of enormous sorrow was afflicting the minds of her children since Clare began to be afflicted more than usual by her illness.[10]

At this point a kind of sisterly solidarity intervened: a nun of San Paolo delle Abbadessa received a vision to console the sisters of San Damiano:

It seemed to her that she was together with her sisters in San Damiano assisting at the sickness of the Lady Clare, and that Clare was lying on a precious bed. However, while they were grieving at the passing of the blessed Clare, crying and eyes filled with tears, a certain beautiful woman appeared at the head of the bed and said: Do not weep, children, for her who is about to be victorious, she said, she will not be able to die until the Lord comes with his disciples.[11]

The monastery of San Paolo had declined to defend Clare from the attack of her family, but we see them now thoroughly caught up in the spiritual orbit around the woman of Assisi. This bond between women of the same city, centred around one of particular spiritual quality, was a phenomenon characteristic of the religious panorama of central Italy in those years.[12]

The sisters of San Damiano could keep calm: Clare would not die before she had seen Christ's successor on earth and had manifested all her wishes to him. The one who confirmed this revelation for them was none other than the first of all women, their own immediate patron: Mary, the *mulier formosa*, 'the most beautiful of women'. The confirmation was sent by another woman. This spiritual solidarity was also a feminine solidarity leaping over the boundaries which, at that time, were clearly drawn between the different religious Orders.

The prediction of the nun of San Paolo was punctually realised. The pope left Lyons on 5 November 1251 and came with all his curia to Perugia. Cardinal Rainaldo, protector of the Order, hurried to Assisi. Clare was constantly on the point of death, and his visit is presented by the biographer as the first part of a 'liturgy of dying' in which Clare was the central figure:

[The Cardinal] nourished the sick woman with the Sacrament of the Body of the Lord and fed those remaining with the encouragement of his salutary word. Then she begged so great a father to take care of her soul and those of other Ladies, for the name of Christ. But, above all, she asked him to petition to have the Privilege of Poverty confirmed by the Lord Pope and the cardinals. Because he was a faithful helper of the Order, just as he promised by his word, so he fulfilled in deed.[13]

All the elements of a holy death were already present: the communion of the sick woman, her preaching to her companions, and finally her testamentary dispositions which, in the case of Clare, took the form of begging the cardinal protector of the Order to intercede with the pope that he confirm the *Privilegium paupertatis*, the *Privilege of Poverty*.[14]

Once again, Clare did not die. This was fortunate because both the *Privilege*, and the Rule which went with it, met with far more difficulties than anyone had foreseen. Despite the efforts of Cardinal Rainaldo (at least according to the *Life*), the pope still hesitated for a long time before he confirmed the Rule proposed by Clare. A whole year passed in which nothing happened. Clare continued to be ill. It was not until 16 September 1252, that Cardinal Rainaldo wrote the sisters a letter, *Quia vos*, in which, in his role as protector of the Order, he agreed to their following the Rule Clare had written.[15] This was still not the papal approval which Clare had asked for. That would have to wait until the pope himself came to Assisi and visited Clare at San Damiano.

The life of Innocent IV, written by Niccolò da Calvi,[16] tells of two meetings between the pope and the saint, but the *Life* of Clare conflates them into one. In this way her biographer could better fulfil his intention of describing an exemplary death. Clare was overtaken by one of the gravest crises of her illness:

Since her sacred limbs had deteriorated with her illness, a new weakness took hold that indicated her impending call to the Lord and prepared the way for her eternal health.[17]

She prepares for her *transitus*, her passing:

She already desired and longed with all her desire to be freed from the body of this death and to see reigning in the heavenly mansions Christ, the Poor One, whom as a poor virgin on earth she followed with all her heart.[18]

Here the author of the *Life* is quoting what became almost a slogan for the poverty movements of the twelfth and thirteenth centuries: poor, to follow the Christ who was poor on earth.[19] It was an appropriate quotation; all her life Clare had made the imitation of Christ the point of reference for all her actions. Now, in her last moments, she came to a total identification with Christ poor on the cross. Her biographer, as he restructured his account to relate an exemplary death, was nearer to the reality than he might have imagined. Other episodes, not told in the *Life*, confirm that during the last months of her life Clare wanted to prepare herself for death as she gathered her sisters around her and gave them everything necessary for the future.

Here we must pause to look at what had happened in the months between the letter of Cardinal Rainaldo and the visit of Innocent IV.

CLARE AND AGNES: FRAGMENTS OF A CORRESPONDENCE

Clare was ill during all the early months of 1253. Sometime in this period she was joined at San Damiano by her sister Agnes.

This was the sister who had followed Clare to Sant'Angelo in Panzo and had endured the family's reaction to her flight. So she was not only Clare's blood-sister but also her first companion in the new way of life begun under the aegis of Francis. They had been separated for a long time because Agnes had gone to Florence in order to teach the regimen of San Damiano to the monastery of Santa Maria in Monticelli. The two women must have kept up an intense correspondence of which, unfortunately, nothing now remains except one letter from Agnes to Clare.[20]

The Rule of Ugolino provided that a sister could only leave the enclosure in order to found or reform another monastery. Agnes' exit from San Damiano to Monticelli perfectly fitted this requirement. However, her return to San Damiano was not allowed for, even though her sister was gravely ill. On the other hand, the Rule of Clare (for which Innocent's approval was awaited during those very months) decreed that one could go out of the enclosure 'for a useful, manifest and approved cause'.[21] To Clare, the return of Agnes was just such a cause. So even before they had received official approval – although we must not forget that they had had the approval of the cardinal protector – the sisters were already living by that Rule which expressed the spirit of their community.

During these months, San Damiano was a meeting-point for Franciscans from all over the world. Brothers returning from, and preparing to go to the most remote provinces, all came to seek out the first companion of the Poverello, ill though she was.

Among these were Brothers Amatus and Bonagura, who were setting out for Bohemia.[22] What better than to give them a letter for the other Agnes, daughter of the king of Bohemia who had left everything to found a monastery in Prague? This Agnes, too, had fought in the battle in defence of the *Privilege of Poverty*, which she had requested in vain from both Gregory IX and Innocent IV.[23] Although they were geographically far apart, the two women had drawn closer and closer, both spiritually and in friendship, over the years. The fourth and last letter of Clare to Agnes, which she wrote during the final months of her life, is the most personal, the most filled with expressions of affection. Clare begins by calling her 'her dearest mother and favourite daughter of all', presenting herself as 'Clare, the unworthy servant of Christ and useless handmaid of the handmaids of Christ who live in the monastery of San Damiano in Assisi'. She prays that Agnes may 'sing a new song in the company of the other most holy virgins, before the throne of God and the Lamb, and that she may accompany the Lamb wheresoever he goes'.[24] Naturally these Scripture references are by no means casual; here Clare refers to chapter 14 of the Apocalypse where it speaks of the 144,000 martyrs who sing the new song of the resurrection on the day of judgement:

They are virgins, they have not betrayed their God, they follow the Lamb wheresoever he goes. They have been taken from among men to be the first-fruits of offering to God and the Lamb and no shame is ever spoken of them for they are blameless.[25]

So, at the beginning of this last letter, Clare wishes Agnes eternal salvation among all the saints. The scriptural references give us a taste of the sort of reading the sick woman must have favoured during those days. At the same time, the other allusions which Clare makes are also interesting, for example those to Agnes the martyr:

Like that other most holy virgin Agnes, untie yourself from all the riches and vain things of this world; you have been most marvellously wedded to the Lamb without blemish who takes away the sins of the world.[26]

Clare's mind had been nourished on the lives of the saints, but this is the only explicit reference in all her writings to any saint other than Francis. The example of the courageous virgin and Roman martyr, Agnes, must have seemed particularly dear to her in the more difficult moments of her illness.

Her biographer says that Clare had wanted to follow the poor Christ, being herself poor, and the letter to Agnes confirms this. The heart of the letter is in the invitation to look at Christ as at a mirror in which one can see oneself:

In this mirror shine blessed poverty, holy humility and unutterable love as, with the grace of God, you can contemplate in the whole mirror. I tell you, think about the boundaries of this mirror, the poverty of him who was placed in a crib and wrapped in swaddling clothes. O wonderful humility, O stupendous poverty! The King of Angels, the Lord of heaven and earth lying in a manger. In the centre of the mirror, consider the humility, or at least the blessed poverty, the innumerable labours and struggles which he underwent for the redemption of the human race. Then in the depths of that mirror contemplate the unutterable love through which he chose to suffer on the wood of the cross and there to die the most shameful of deaths.[27]

Clare prepared herself for death by reflecting more and more on the cross and so identifying herself with Christ. Besides this image, however, she adds another in her letter:

More than this, contemplate his delights which cannot be told, his riches, his perpetual honour; and as you sigh in the extreme desire and love of your soul cry out:

Draw me after thee, we run in the odour of your ointment, O beloved from heaven! I run, I will never grow tired until you lead me into your wine-cellar, until your left hand is under my head and your right hand embraces me so joyously and you will kiss me with the most joyful kiss of your lips.[28]

When she was writing like this, Clare was almost sixty and for twenty-eight years had been confined to her bed with a difficult illness, yet she dreamed of running, in the words of the Song of Songs, to meet her Lord, the Beloved from heaven. If Clare saw death as identification with the Crucified, she also saw the resurrection as the ultimate embrace of her Beloved who had promised life to her.

In the conclusion of the letter, Clare joins her sisters with herself in their affection towards Agnes and her companions:

Every day I am full of love towards you and your daughters, and again and again I and my daughters in Christ recommend ourselves to you all. These same daughters, then, and especially the most prudent virgin Agnes, our sister, recommend themselves in the Lord as much as possible to you and to your daughters.[29]

All Clare's letters to Agnes end with a recommendation that they pray for each other. Each time, Clare says it in different words as if to underline that this was not just a formality but a genuine trust in the power of their spiritual solidarity. In this last letter, though, the recommendation is part of Clare's preoccupation with her approaching death. She wants to entrust the sisters at San Damiano to the best protection possible: this is why she has recourse to the prayers of Agnes.

THE SPIRITUALITY OF *TRANSITUS*: HER TESTAMENT AND BLESSING

Clare was aware that it behoved her to prepare for death. As the actual moment approached, three characteristic elements of her spirituality come into focus: her imitation of Christ in his sufferings, her desire for the eternal wedding feast of her heavenly Beloved and her maternal preoccupation with her sisters.

All these elements come out in her meeting with Innocent IV. In the light of the prophecy made by the nun of San Paolo, Clare waited for him as for Christ himself and when he arrived she behaved accordingly:

Entering the monastery, [the Pope] went to her bed and extended his hand so that she might kiss it. The most grateful woman accepted it and asked that she might (also) kiss the foot of the Pope with the greatest reverence. The Curial Lord appropriately offered her his foot which he placed on a wooden stool and she reverently inclined her face towards it, kissing it above and below.[30]

Her biographer does not underline this, but her gesture certainly recalls the attitude of Magdalen at the foot of the cross. Kissing the feet of the Crucified is a constant in the *laudes* of the Passion and in the religious art of the period.[31]

After kissing the pope's feet, Clare asked for forgiveness for her sins to which the pope replied: 'Would that my need of pardon were no more than yours!' He gave her full absolution and a solemn blessing.

The *Life* is concerned to record that Clare had received the Eucharist from the Minister Provincial on the same day and so to underline that all the actions of the liturgy of dying were now complete: confession, communion and benediction. The author, however, forgets to mention that Clare also poured out to the pope all her anxiety about the future of San Damiano and explicitly begged him to confirm the Rule which she had drawn up.

Her long agony dragged on. The sisters were around her bed, among them Agnes whom Clare promised would soon join her in Paradise:

Dearest sister, it is pleasing to God that I depart. But stop crying, because you will come to the Lord a short time after me, and before that, after I have left you, the Lord will give you great consolation.[32]

The longer her agony went on the greater grew the popular devotion. San Damiano became a shrine. After the pope, came prelates and bishops. Clare received them all; she was, as it were, at the centre of their liturgy and she gave comfort to all who sought it. Even Brother Rainaldo who urged her to have patience, received the swift response:

After I once came to know the grace of my Lord Jesus Christ through his servant Francis, no pain has been bothersome, no penance too severe, no weakness, dearly beloved brother, has been hard.[33]

Only three people were able to give Clare any actual consolation as she lay dying. These were special people: Juniper, Angelo and Leo, the three earliest companions of Francis.[34] This is the only certain exception to the enclosure recorded in detail by the sources and it is a significant exception. Juniper, Angelo and Leo, together with Clare, kept the memory of Francis green and they continued to live according to his spirit. The *Life* tells us touchingly about the last moments they spent with Clare:

Then, seeing that the Lord was very near and almost standing in the doorway, Clare wanted her spiritual brothers and priests to stay near her, and they recited the Passion of the Lord to her, and spoke holy words. Among them was Brother Juniper, his heart filled with burning words, who kindled her to new joy. She asked him if he had anything new to tell her about the Lord and he, whenever he opened his mouth, freely poured out a flaming brilliance from the furnace of his own blazing heart. And the virgin of God found immense consolation in all that he said.[35]

For their part, Angelo and Leo consoled the sisters who were drenched in tears:

Those two blessed companions of the blessed Francis were standing there: Angelo was one of them who, while mourning himself, consoled those who were mourning; the other was Leo who kissed the bed of the dying Clare.[36]

It was the supreme moment in the liturgy of her passing; they knew that the hour was near and that the moment of blessing had come:

Finally she turned to her weeping daughters to whom she recalled in a praising way the divine blessings while entrusting them with the poverty of the Lord. She blessed her devoted brothers and sisters and called down the fullest graces of blessings upon the Ladies of the poor monasteries, those in the present and those in the future.[37]

Here Thomas of Celano summarises the two documents which have come down to us, namely the Testament and the Blessing. In the Testament, Clare recalls the way in which the San Damiano community had begun on Francis' initiative and she encourages the sisters always to persevere in this same path of poverty. To this end, she recalls, she had had the *Privilege of Poverty* approved by every pope who had ruled in her lifetime.[38] In the Blessing, Clare shows all her maternal love for her sisters:

I bless you during my life and after my death as much as I can and more than I can, with all the blessings that the same Father of mercies has blessed on earth and will bless in heaven everyone of his spiritual sons and daughters, and with all the blessings which a spiritual father and mother have blessed and will bless their spiritual sons and daughters. Amen.[39]

It is unlikely that Clare dictated this document as she lay dying, even though it so accurately reflects her preoccupation with her sisters' future. Her biographer's acknowledgement of her blessing is an indirect confirmation of the importance of the document which has come down to us.

Clare's blessing is biblical, full and solemn. She not only takes words from Scripture and the liturgy but she also introduces words of her own, for instance when she calls for the inter-cession of all the saints and feels the need to add: *et sanctarum*, 'and all the women saints'.[40] This is a significant addition. For Clare, the communion of saints means women saints as well as men, she feels that the special spiritual solidarity which binds together all the living women who seek to obey the Gospel is also a bond with those who have preceded them on the road of faith.

This notion of a special rapport linking all women of faith (whether alive or dead) was the shared patrimony of all the sisters at San Damiano. The evidence given at the canonisation process serves to underline this. In particular, we recall the testimony of Sister Benvenuta di madonna Diambra di Assisi who saw, in a vision, a procession of women saints who came with Mary to pay their last respects at the bedside of Clare.[41]

In her vision Sister Benvenuta had seen no less a person than Mary the Mother of God coming to San Damiano only three days before Clare's death. How did Mary seem in this vision? She was like a feudal queen, surrounded and followed by her court of ladies. The first part of the evidence, which is not the actual vision but rather the reflections of Sister Benvenuta, is even more explicit. Mary was preparing clothes with which to reclothe the saint who was destined to go and live with her. So might Queen Guinevere receive one of the handmaids sent her by Percival and give the girl one of her own garments.[42] Clothes were a woman's most precious possession and Clare knew this well, so much so that in her first letter to Agnes of Bohemia she spends a long time describing the new spiritual clothing which Agnes had put on by renouncing the royal garments which had been hers in the world.[43] Holiness itself was seen as a kind of garment. Clare, who had always wanted to be clothed in most poor garments, was now – at the point of death – to be reclothed in garments which were the richest, the softest, the most precious, indeed she was to be clothed in the garments of the Queen of Heaven herself who came in person to bring them to her.

So Clare died, surrounded by her sisters, by the first com-panions of Francis and herself, in the house where she had lived all her life. She died like a queen, or rather, like a young bride given her trousseau by the queen mother herself in preparation for reigning together with the older queen. Before she died she received the seal on her life, that is, the stamp of approval on the Rule which she had drawn up for the Poor Sisters of San Damiano:

At the end of her life, after calling together all her sisters, she entrusted the *Privilege of Poverty* to them. Her great desire had been to have had the Rule of the Order confirmed with a papal seal and then, on the following day, to die. It all happened just as she had wanted. She learned that a brother had come with letters bearing the papal bull. She reverently took them, even though she was very close to death, and she pressed that seal to her mouth in order to kiss it.[44]

The approval was the letter *Solet annuere*, the bull of Innocent IV given at Assisi on 9 August 1253, two days before the death of Clare. In this he definitively approves the Rule of Clare. The procedure of approval must, after so many delays, have become a matter of urgency for in the top margin the pontiff himself had written in his own hand the words: *Ad instar fiat. S. Ex causis manifestis michi et protectori mon[asterii] fiat ad instar,*[45] 'So be it! For reasons which are obvious to me and to the Protector of the monastery, let it be so.'

The letter 'S' stands for Sinibaldus Fieschi, the name of Innocent IV. The 'obvious reasons' could have been none other than Clare's worsening condition. Thus the woman of Assisi received her Rule only one day before she died. It was the crown of her life; now she could hope for a future for her sisters.

TEN

The Birth of a Cult

Clare died on 11 August 1253. During her final days, San Damiano had already become the focus of popular pilgrimage and scarcely had the notice of her death gone out than all the city rushed to the little monastery. So much so, that this became a civic problem requiring the direct intervention of the *podestà* with calvary and men-at-arms.[1] The danger was immediately obvious to everybody: the need to defend Clare's body from those who might wish to steal it. In the same way, several years earlier, when the body of Francis had been moved from San Giorgio to the new basilica which had been built for it, there had been some well-attested incidents between the brethren and the citizens.[2]

THE FUNERAL AND SOLEMN TRANSLATION OF HER BODY

The pope and his court happened to be in Assisi when Clare died and he chose to stay on until the next day. It may have been a diplomatic sensitivity to the *podestà* but, whatever the reason, the pontiff decided to attend the funeral; and, as we have seen, it was during the funeral that the pope proposed to celebrate the Office of virgins rather than the Office of the dead, thus showing that he considered Clare to be a saint already.[3]

The funeral coincided with the solemn translation of Clare's body, under armed escort, from San Damiano to the church of San Giorgio within the circle of the city walls. In this same church Francis' body had also rested for a short time.

The sisters wanted to follow their mother and to establish themselves near the church of San Giorgio. For this reason, on 1 October 1253, that is barely fifty days after the death of

Clare, they opened negotiations with the chapter of San Rufino (on whom the church of San Giorgio depended) with a view to exchanging San Damiano for San Giorgio. However, the matter was not as simple as that. Next door to the church of San Giorgio was a hospital for which the canons of San Rufino were responsible and on that very day, 1 October 1253, they had obtained a bull from Innocent IV, who was still in Assisi, granting an indulgence to whoever contributed towards the costs of running the hospital.[4] Meanwhile, San Giorgio had become a shrine and the first miracles had begun to happen at the tomb of Clare. On the 19 October, in his letter to Bartolomeo, archbishop of Spoleto, the pope said:

In his saints the glorious God, who alone does and performs marvellous and great things, acknowledges his faithful after the course and passing of their lives through the wonderful declaration, in many ways, with signs that he chooses for their supreme glory and as a reward of their heavenly beatitude. He does this so that, hearing about the signs, wonders and witnesses of so many marvellous things, only possible through the power of God, One in Trinity and Three in Unity, the goodness of the Most High may be seen and His great and wonderful name more reverently adored on earth . . .[5]

THE CANONISATION PROCESSES OF INNOCENT IV AND ALEXANDER IV

A saint is only recognised by the canonisation process and offered for veneration here on earth, when God himself has already chosen a man or a woman and called them to himself in paradise. Miracles, signs and other wonders are the tangible evidence of this choice made by God. Innocent spells this out even more plainly in the next section of his letter to Bartolomeo:

From the moment that she died joyfully, and even before she departed from this mortal life, the compassionate condescension of almighty God, rewarder of every good, in the abundance of his kindness which exceeds the merits and desires of those who pray for it, grants favours for the exaltation of his ever glorious name to those who ask for them because the clear merits of the virgin Clare were interceding. God comes down to perform on earth many different miracles through her and her prayers.

It is fitting and right that she be honoured by the Church Militant. For the divine mercy because of her gifts of grace and the worth of her miracles has demonstrated that she be venerated by the faithful. Therefore we direct your Brotherhood, through apostolic letters, diligently and carefully to research her life, conversion, and manner of life, as well as the truth of all the aforesaid miracles and all their particulars according to the questions we send you included in this Bull.[6]

The pope's initiative started an inquiry into a devotion and *cultus* which Clare had attracted even before she was officially declared a new saint. The great signs to which he alludes in his letter were even happening in his own household. In September, a young man of the papal court, who was struck with a wild madness, had been taken – against his will – to Clare's tomb and there, miraculously, healed.[7]

The cult of Clare had sprung up spontaneously and was slowly spreading, along with the news of these miraculous healings. Her holiness, which the people saw primarily as a healing power coming from her body and her tomb, seemed to have an autonomy of its own, an independence even from the life of the woman of Assisi herself. There was a difference here between Innocent's attitude and that of the people. In many ways the pope shared the spontaneous devotion of the people, as is evident from his wish to count her as a saint even before the canonisation process. In other ways he clearly distanced himself from the popular cult. For the pope, the connection between the holiness of her life and the healings taking place at her tomb was fundamental. For him, the holiness which produced miracles was the same as the holiness of her life. For those around Assisi, however, the fame of miraculous healings taking place in a church in the city was quite independent of Clare's reputation for personal holiness, so much so that some of the first people to be healed at her tomb were men and women who had not even heard about her beforehand.

After the death of Innocent IV, his successor Alexander IV (the same Cardinal Rainaldo who had advised the pope against celebrating the Mass for virgins) seemed to be reluctant to raise

Clare to the honours of the altar, but he was influenced by the strength of popular devotion. The whole canonisation process took place in an atmosphere almost of suspicion, traces of which remain even in the *Life*:

At last the Pontiff, prompted by the number of so many signs as though something singular, began to consider with his cardinals her canonisation. The miracles were submitted for examination by qualified and prudent persons and the wonders of her life were also brought into discussion. Clare was found to have been, while she lived, most brilliant in the exercise of every virtue. She was found to be admired after her death for tried and true miracles.[8]

We see in this text all the caution of the curia towards popular devotion and towards those very miracles which required discreet examination in order to ascertain their authenticity. It was not just an expression of prudence towards abuses which needed to be sifted out, for many of the cases were well-attested. Rather it was a sign that in the papal court a whole new attitude towards sanctity was maturing during those years. As a result, miraculous deeds ceased to have self-evident power and the saint was more and more seen as a human being who had won the power of interceding with God through the virtue of his or her life.[9]

'MIRACLES AFTER DEATH'

Thomas of Celano made himself the spokesman of this attitude in his *Life of St Clare the Virgin*. The second part of his biography is devoted, according to form, to the miracles which Clare worked after her death and here the author, with some difficulty, develops his ideas about miracles:

These are the marvellous signs of the saints, these are the testimonies of miracles that should be honoured that rest on their foundation of holiness of character and the perfection of their deeds. Certainly John performed no signs; nevertheless, those who did were no holier than John. For this reason the proclamation of her most perfect life would be sufficient to witness to her holiness except that something more is required partly due to the tepidity of the people, partly due to their devotion.[10]

Thomas of Celano cites the passage of John: 'Many came to him and said, John worked no sign, yet all he said was true.[11] The biography balances the holiness of John the Baptist who worked no miracles, against those who worked wonders but were not, on this account, considered any holier than John. Here emerges a certain intolerance with the feeble faith of those who need extraordinary signs in order to believe in the holiness of this or that person. For Thomas, an exemplary life is the whole of holiness; it was not that he did not believe in miracles but rather that he considered them to be fruits and not sources of sanctity.

Thus, popular devotion developed along several lines. Some saw holiness as a kind of healing power spreading outwards in concentric circles so that at the centre was the body of the holy person, then the sanctuary itself where the body was buried, and lastly the circle of all those who had, in one way or another, come in contact with this saving power. With this in mind, the first miracle to occur at Clare's tomb is particularly interesting. It took place in the month of September. Giovanni di Ventura, who had been a servant in Clare's household, was the first to mention it when he gave his evidence at the canonisation process.

He saw someone from beyond the Alps who was mad or possessed, bound with ropes, brought to the tomb of the said Lady Clare, immediately cured.

Asked how he knew this, he replied that he saw the man sick with the illness and saw him there, at the tomb of the said Lady Clare, immediately cured. Asked the name of that sick man, he replied that he did not know because he wasn't from these parts.

Asked at the invocation of what saint he was cured, he replied at the tomb of the Lady Clare. This was public and well-known. Asked about the month and the day this occurred, he replied he believed it was September just passed. He said he couldn't remember the day. Asked who was present, he replied all on the piazza saw him and ran with him to the tomb of the Lady Clare.[12]

The piazza the old servant mentioned can only have been the piazza of the commune of Assisi near the church of San Giorgio. Here Giovanni di Ventura saw a procession of strangers, not

Assisi folk, carrying this madman to the tomb of 'their' saint. Giovanni followed them and was thus present at the first miracle! It is interesting to pick up on a moment of incomprehension between the servant and the commissary who asked him: 'At the invocation of what saint was the man cured?' Giovanni replied: 'At the tomb of the Lady Clare.' For him, no other invocation was necessary: the healing had taken place by the simple act of coming into the sacred space of the sanctuary; within that space the men had been touched by the healing power of the saint's body.[13]

In his *Life*, Thomas of Celano gives further details of this event, suggesting that on this occasion he had access to other sources besides the testimony already mentioned. Above all, he tells us that the young demoniac from beyond the Alps was a French youth and from the papal court. Thomas explains:

An illness of frenzy, which both took away the use of speech and made the body horribly disturbed, possessed a certain young Frenchman who was attached to the Curia. He could at least be restrained by someone but, while in the hands of those willing to restrain him, he all the more bruised himself. He was tied with ropes to a bier and carried against his will by compatriots to the church of St Clare, placed before her grave, and was immediately freed through the faith of those who had presented him there.[14]

Giovanni di Ventura had given the evidence of a man of the piazza. Thomas of Celano, for his part and writing some time later, tried to give a theological interpretation to what had happened, underlining that the cure had taken place 'through the faith of those who had presented him there'. In this he was making a precise reference to the biblical account of the paralytic who was carried by four men to be presented to Jesus. They let him down through the roof, so that Jesus, 'seeing their faith', cured him and forgave him his sins.[15] By drawing this parallel, Celano is once again stressing that faith is a necessary condition for miracles.

The second point about the demoniac which Thomas underlines is that he was a 'young' man. In this second book of the *Life*, devoted to the miracles worked after Clare's death, he recounts fourteen miracles of which six concerned children. This predilection of Clare for children is a link with the cures which took place during her life when children had also held pride of place. Many of these children were handicapped from birth. This opens a vista on to a whole world of illness aand suffering, of men and women in difficulties right from their earliest years, even though the sources say very little about the subject.[16] How were they cared for and helped? How were they viewed in a society which had such fear of anyone different and which banished its lepers?

The *Life* tells us clearly about one of these handicapped children, the shame of his family:

A citizen of Gubbio, Giacomo da Franco, having a five-year-old boy who had never walked or been able to use his weak feet, deplored that boy as a public spectacle in his house and as a disgrace to his flesh. He was accustomed to sleep on the ground, to crawl in the ashes, wanting at times to lift himself with a cane but being incapable of doing so – someone to whom nature had given the desire to walk but had denied the ability.

His parents dedicated the boy to the merits of St Clare and, to use their own words, desired that he be 'a man of St Clare' should he obtain a cure through her. Shortly after the vow had been uttered, the virgin of Christ healed 'her man' and restored the ability to walk to the boy who had been offered to her. The parents immediately hurried to the virgin's tomb with the boy and offered him, jumping up and rejoicing, to the Lord.[17]

The illness was a blot on the family itself, a deformity which should be kept hidden in the house. The testimony as it is given in the *Life* tells us volumes about the condition of such sick people in feudal society, furnished with very rough orthopedic implements (a cane) and obliged by lack of medical help to drag himself in the dust.

On the other hand the testimony also tells us volumes about the mind of the people and their attitude towards miracles. The 'vow' which the parents had made for their son had the same characteristics as the *commendatio* of vassals.[18] This was a contract for work on the farm, and in Assisi it was known as the *hominicium*, a term which echoes the promise to be *homo alicuius*, that is, a man who serves someone else.[19] The parents offered their son to Clare as her *homo*, 'her man', in other words, as her servant. By 1253 the *hominicium* had been abolished in Assisi for some time, but in the country the idea evidently lingered on in other forms. There is nothing strange in the fact that these parents should offer their son as a servant to Clare, who is here explicitly referred to as a *domina*, 'a feudal lady'.

Another, similar, case reveals a courteous competition between Francis and Clare:

There was a ten-year-old boy from the Villa of San Quirico, in the diocese of Assisi, who was crippled from his mother's womb. He had shinbones that were weak, walked crookedly with his feet turned at angles, and was hardly capable of getting up when he had fallen. His mother had offered him many times to St Francis but did not receive any help for his improvement.

Hearing, however, that the blessed Clare was radiant with new miracles, she took the boy to the saint's burial place. After a few days, when the shinbones made some noise, the limbs were restored to their correct position, and that which Francis had not granted even though he had been implored with many prayers, his disciple Clare achieved through divine power.[20]

In those days such 'competition' betwen different devotions was common, often expressing the rivalry between neighbouring cities or even between the religious Orders attached to one sanctuary or another.[21] The strange thing here is that the devotion of the two saints was nourished by the same body, namely the Friars Minor. So what was this competition about?

The author of the *Life* appears to have no answer and simply points out that in this case the 'divine will' preferred the disciple to Francis. However, in the words of the mother of the sick child, we glimpse another idea, as simple as it is concrete: the miracles of Clare were more recent. This suggests that the *virtus*, the healing power of the saint, diminished with time. There was an analogous idea about space in those days: the further and further away one was from the saint, so his or her healing power tended to diminish.

Francis had been dead for a number of years, Clare for only

a few. As it happened, Francis had never worked a great number of miracles, or perhaps he already had sufficient *homines*, men dependent upon him. Maybe, for either or both reasons, he did not hear the insistent prayers of the woman of San Quirico. In the popular mind, feudal homage alone was not enough to obtain a miracle; it was not enough to promise homage to this or that saint. What was needed was the peasant cunning to know how to choose the more powerful saint – or merely the best disposed saint.

On occasion peasant cunning even reached the level of a contract of sale:

The savage frenzy of cruel wolves frequently disturbed the countryside; they would attack the people in those areas and would frequently feed on human flesh.

Therefore a certain woman, Bona di Monte Galliano, in the diocese of Assisi, had two sons, one of whom the wolves dragged away. She had barely stopped crying when, behold, they pursued the second boy with the same ferocity. For while the mother was in the house doing some of her domestic chores, a wolf fixed his teeth into the boy who was walking outside, dragged him off by his neck and made for the woods as quickly as possible with his prey.

Some men who were in the vineyards, however, heard the cries of the boy and shouted to his mother: 'See if you have your son, because we have just heard some unusual shouts!'

The mother, learning that her son had been seized by the wolves, shouted to heaven, filled the air with her cries and called upon the virgin Clare: 'O holy and glorious Clare, return my poor son to me! Return', she said, 'return my poor little boy to his mother, because if you don't, I will drown myself.'

The neighbours ran after the wolf and found the boy who had been brought into the woods and next to him a dog that was licking his wounds. The ferocious beast had first thrust his fangs into the boy's neck; then, in order to carry off its prey more easily, it had filled its jaws with the boy's loins. But it had not left in either place any sign of its sudden attack.

After obtaining the answer of her prayers, the woman ran off with her neighbours to her helper and poured out abundant thanks to God and the holy Clare, showing everyone who wished to see the boy's various wounds.[22]

'I will drown myself if you don't!' The miracle this time was

the fruit of a genuine threat. The saint could not but come to
the rescue and save the child for fear that she would lose the
mother too. There is no question here of the *hominicium*. Rather
the poor mother's cry of grief was the imperious statement of
a right: the saint had the power and must be concerned about
the one who turned to her.

Thanks to miracles like these, the fame of the cures worked
at Clare's tomb spread throughout the surrounding countryside.
It was a very local cult. The towns named in the second book
of the *Life* – Perugia, Fratta (today called Umbertide), Spello,
Narni, Gubbio, Bevagna, Cannara – were all Umbrian towns
not far from Assisi.

The army of poor and desperate people drawn to Assisi all
made known the good news of the tomb where they had
received healing. One such was Iacobello, son of the woman of
Spoleto whose story has already been told;[23] invited in a dream
by Clare herself to come to her tomb, he there received back
his sight although he had been blind for twelve years.

The striking thing about this healing is that the blind man
knew nothing of Clare before, had never even heard her spoken
about. When he told two other blind men of his dream, they
enlightened him: 'We have heard tell of a certain woman who
died recently in Assisi and that the hand of the Lord is said to
honour her grave with gifts of healing and many miracles.'
Nobody even knew what she was called, for the fame of Clare's
miracles had outstripped the fame of her holiness, or rather it
had taken other channels, for the memory of Clare's holiness
of life had been entrusted above all to the Poor Sisters who
would continue to live according to her spirit. The fame of her
miracles, on the other hand, spread from town to town through
the beggars, the poor and the sick of every kind.

CONFIRMATION OF HER CULT

The fame of Clare's holiness reached its peak two years after
her death when the Pope Alexander IV proclaimed her a saint
at Anagni with the bull *Clara claris praeclara*.[24]

She was the first woman who was not of royal blood to be

proclaimed a saint for many centuries. She was the first of Francis' companions to be raised to the honours of the altar (with the exception, so it is said, of Antony of Padua). Thus, it seemed, the poor sister of San Damiano attained in death a celebrity which she had not attained, or even sought, during her life. The proclamation of the cult of Clare met with considerable resistance, not least from the Order. The feast of Clare was only promulgated within the Order of Friars Minor at the chapter of Narbonne in 1260, five years after her canonisation, and to have a copy of her *Life* in the library of every convent only became obligatory in 1272 at the chapter of Lyons.[25]

This is strange behaviour on the part of an Order which, among other things, wanted to assume the guidance of the new religious ferment in which women featured so prominently. It seems that the memory of Clare grew faint in the Order from the time of Bonaventure's generalate. Perhaps it was not by chance that this great son of St Francis[26] was the only early biographer of the Saint who completely forgot to mention Clare in his life of Francis. Near Clare at the end of her life were Leo, Angelo and Rufino, the three representatives of a Franciscan spirituality which was not only in conflict with the conventual branch of the Order but which also sought to guide it along the same lines as the first generation of Franciscans.[27] Was this the reason for so inexplicable a lapse of memory?

While Clare, even after her canonisation, was left in the middle distance by those responsible for her own Order, the citizens of Assisi too seemed uninterested both in the cult of their illustrious fellow-citizen and in the resettling of her spiritual daughters. After Clare's intercession had miraculously defended the city against the imperial army of Vitalis di Aversa, the commune had proclaimed a *Festa del voto* to be celebrated every 22 July in memory of the event.[28] The *podestà* and leading citizens were the same as in the early 1260s when the body of Clare had been translated from San Damiano to San Giorgio. Then Clare had been considered as the city's own saint, in some ways even more so than Francis, for his *cultus* was taken over by the Friars Minor and was out of the hands of the city authorities.

San Giorgio was a little church with a hospital attached, and at once the problem arose of whether or not to build a new basilica to house the saint more worthily. A place would also have to be found next to the basilica for the sisters of San Damiano. The transfer presented a number of problems. The hospital and church of San Giorgio belonged to the chapter of San Rufino which was composed of the aristocracy of the city. A simple exchange of a tiny country church with almost no land round it for a huge hospital near the gates of the city, together with land and revenues, was not the sort of exchange that the canons would be likely to accept. Thus, while Clare had to wait until 1260 before she was numbered among the saints of her own Order, so the sisters had to wait until the same date before they could move everything to San Giorgio. The canons only agreed when the abbot of Farfa gave the sisters another monastery, near Murorotto, together with more land. So, in exchange for San Giorgio, the chapter of San Rufino not only received San Damiano but also some land and revenues which equalled or surpassed those which they had ceded. Naturally the canons were the same devout men who had defended the body of Clare, but business is always business.[30]

In order to achieve their desired move, the sisters had to accept a number of donations which were destined, in the end, to erode that ideal of absolute poverty which Clare had so defended. Other Rules would be drawn up for the sisters, both those of the protomonastery and those scattered throughout the world.[31] In 1288 Pope Nicholas IV, in the bull *Devotionis vestrae precibus*, dated 26 March, sanctioned the right of the sisters to inherit, to acquire and retain property, as – apart from the rights of the feudal system – nuns had done for centuries. Thus the pope definitively allowed the renunciation of the *Privilegium paupertatis*, the *Privilege of Poverty*.

So the time came when the sisters took the Rule which the saint had kissed before she died and, as if it were a relic, they sewed it into Clare's clothes, and there it remained for many centuries. It was not until the end of the nineteenth century that the Rule of Clare was rediscovered, like a seed which had lain long hidden in the ground. Perhaps it is already on the point of bearing that spiritual fruit for which Clare so longed.

Notes

AF	*Analecta Franciscana*, Quaracchi 1885
AFH	*Archivum Franciscanum Historicum*, Quaracchi/ Grottaferrata 1908
AA.SS.	*Acta Sanctorum*
BF	*Bullarium Franciscanum*, ed. J.H. Sbaralea, Rome 1759
Bibliog. Franc.	*Bibliographia Franciscana*, Assisi/Rome 1931
BS	*Biblioteca Sanctorum*, Rome 1961
CF	*Collectanea Franciscana*, Assisi/Rome 1931
DF	*Dizionario Francescano. Spiritualità*, Padua 1983
DIP	*Dizionario degli Istituti di Perfezione*, Rome 1975
DHGE	*Dictionnaire d'Histoire et de Géographie Ecclésiastique*, Paris 1912
DS	*Dictionnaire de Spiritualité*, Paris 1933
Early Documents	*Clare of Assisi: Early Documents* ed. Regis J. Armstrong, Paulist Press, New York 1988
FF	*Fonti Francescane*, Assisi 1977
Leg. vers.	*Rhyming Life*, translated from Bartoli's Italian
Life of Clare	*The Legend of St Clare* in *Clare of Assisi: Early Documents* (see above)
MF	*Miscellanea Francescana*, Foligno/Rome 1886
Omnibus	*Omnibus of Sources*, Franciscan Herald Press, Chicago, Illinois 60609, 1972
PL	J.P. Migne, *Patrologia cursus completus . . . Series Latina*, Paris 1844–64
Process	*Canonisation Process*, *Early Documents* (see above)
Rule of Clare	*Rule of Clare*, Sister Frances Teresa's translation. See also *Early Documents* (above), *Writings* (below)
Test.Cl.	*Testament of Clare*, as for *Rule* above
Writings	*The Writings of Francis and Clare*, ed. Regis J. Armstrong, Paulist Press, New York 1982

Translator's Preface

1 R. Manselli, *San Francesco d'Assisi*, Rome 1980. Trans. into English by Paul Duggan, *St Francis of Assisi*, Chicago 1988.

Introduction

1 *Life of Clare* 47.
2 For the movements of Innocent IV cf. F. Pagnotti, 'Niccolò da Calvi e la sua vita di Innocenzo IV', in *Archivo della Società romana di Storia Patria* 21 (1898) 107.
3 *Life of Clare* 47.
4 In popular opinion up to the end of the Middle Ages and long after the thirteenth century, the translation of the relics was considered an official ceremony sanctioning the birth of a *cultus*. The authoritative work on this is A. Vauchez, *La sainteté en Occident aux derniers siècles du Moyen Age, d'après les procès de canonisation et les documents hagiographiques*, Rome 1981, 28–37.
5 *Life of Clare* 47; *Leg. vers.* vv. 1418–22.
6 The original of the bull *Gloriosus Deus*, dated 18 October 1253, is preserved in the archives of the protomonastery of St Clare in Assisi and was published in *BF* I, 684.
7 Cf. Z. Lazzeri, 'Il processo di canonizzazione di S. Chiara d'Assisi' in *AFH* 13 (1920) 403–507. For the process of canonisation in full, cf. *FF* 2299–383.
8 'The commissioners were supported by an important team, usually composed of religious – and very often Mendicants – who helped the commissioners with their task and guaranteed the regularity of the procedure. Notaries appeared in Italy from the year 1220 onwards, and elsewhere a little later. Their task was to put the depositions *in formam publicam*, and to write a number of copies of the whole inquiry to which the commissioners would then append their seal', Vauchez, *La sainteté en Occident* 53.
9 It must not be forgotten that after the death of Frederick II in 1250, Bartolomeo, who was archbishop of Spoleto from 1236–1271, represented both the civil and the religious authorities in the duchy. Cf. C. Eubel, *Hierarchia catholica Medii Aevi I*, Münster 1913, 461.
10 For a study of this, cf. P. Delooz, 'Per uno studio sociologico della santità' in *Agiografia altomedioevale*, ed. S. Boesch Gajano, Bologna 1976, 227–58.
11 Cf. E. Menestò, *Il processo di canonizzazione di Chiara da Montefalco*, Florence/Perugia 1984, esp. ch. IV, 'Agiografia e santità' CLIV–CLXXXII.
12 'An important step was taken during the pontificate of Gregory IX when the letters instituting an inquiry began to be accompanied by a *forma interogatorii*, that is, a stereotyped form of procedure to be used by the commissioners charged with the inquiry', Vauchez, *La sainteté en Occident* 58f.
13 For observations on this 'interrogation' spoken of in the bull of Innocent IV, see those of Z. Lazzeri, editor of the process in 'De processu canonizationis sanctae Clarae' in *AFH* 5 (1912) 645); see the whole article 644–51.
14 On Simone da Collazzone, cf. M. Faloci Pulignani, 'Il beato Simone da Collazzone e il suo processo nel 1252' in *MF* 12 (1910) 97–132.
15 Cf. Vauchez, *La sainteté en Occident* 59, n70.

16 'This dialogue is one of the critical points for research into canonised holiness. It not only allows us to define a most important moment in the development of the canonisation process, whether we see this as springing from the confluence of different mentalities and cultures (that of the ordinary people who initiated the *cultus*, with that of the dominant power, the ecclesiastics who would have accepted and developed that *cultus*), or whether we see it arising from and justified by a more linear development, simply as an expression of power. Beyond that, however, it also enables us to catch that crucial moment of transformation when the model of sanctity is caught up into history', Menestò, *Il processo* CLV.

17 For the use of hagiographic sources in reconstructing a mind-set and in analysing the various layers of understanding so as to determine the character of an historical period, the main study is J. Le Goff, *Pour un autre Moyen Age. Temps, travail et culture en Occident. 18 essays.* Paris 1977.

18 Cf. Lazzeri, 'Il processo di canonizzazione' 403–6; G. Cozza-Luzzi, 'Codice Magliabechiano della storia di S. Chiara' in *Bolletino della Società Umbria di Storia Patria* 1 (1895) 424; P. Robinson, 'Inventarium omnium documentorum quae in Archivo protomonasterii S. Clarae Assisiensis nunc asservantur' in *AFH* 1 (1908) 418 nn 5 and 3; *BF* I 684.

19 F. Pennacchi, 'Brevi note storiche' in *Legenda S. Clarae virginis*, Assisi 1910, XXV; the bull is printed on pp. 108–18.

20 Salimbene of Parma said that 'Alexander the Pope canonised Saint Clare and wrote the hymns and prayers'. Cf. G. Scalia *Cronica, Salimbene de Adam*, vol. 1, Bari 1966, 554 (trans. by J.L. Baird, G. Baglivi and J.R. Kane, *The Chronicle of Salimbene de Adam*, Binghamton, NY 1986, 385); *Life of Clare* 119–27.

21 Vauchez, *La sainteté en Occident* 58.

22 Cf. Ch. A. Lainati, 'Scritti e fonti biografiche di Chiara d'Assisi' in *FF* 2390; E. Franceschini, 'Una cattedrale di versi per Chiara d'Assisi' in *Chiara d'Assisi – Rassegna del protomonastero* 4 (1956) 157–62; *Nel segno di Francesco*, ed. F. Casolini and G. Giamba, S. Maria degli Angeli-Assisi 1988, 416–22. 'Legenda Versificata S. Clarae Assisiensis', ed. B. Bughetti, in *AFH* 5 (1912) 238–60, 459–81, 621–31.

23 It was the Bollandists who uncovered this wrongful attribution to Bonaventure; *AA.SS.* Aug. 12, t. II, 740b–741b.

24 This attribution was first made by Cozza-Luzzi, on the basis of the Magliabechiano Codex, in 'Codice Magliabechiano' 417–26. Pennacchi, in his edition of the *Life*, also attributes it to Celano on the basis of Ms. 338 in the Biblioteca Comunale di Assisi, see *Legenda S. Clarae* XIII–XXVI; cf. also E. Grau, *Leben und Schriften der hl. Klara von Assisi*, Werl/Westf. 1960, 13–16; F. Casolini, *Vita di S. Chiara vergine d'Assisi*, S. Maria degli Angeli-Assisi 1962, 6–14; certain puzzling aspects are dealt with by Lainati, 'Scritti', 2390. A definitive attribution must await a new critical edition which would collate the numerous codices of the *Life* that have come to light since 1910, the year of Pennacchi's edition.

25 *Life of Clare*, dedicatory letter 2.

26 J. Leclercq, *Nouveau visage de Saint Bernard*, Paris 1976, 13f.

27 Ibid. 16; cf. also *Agiografia altomedioevale*, ed. Boesch Gajano, bibliography on pp. 260–300.
28 The basis of all studies of women's religious movements in the thirteenth century is H. Grundmann, *Religiöse Bewegungen im Mittelelter*. 1st edn, Berlin 1935, trans. into Italian, *Movimenti religiosi nel Medioevo*, Bologna 1974. 2nd edn, revised and enlarged, Darmstadt 1961, repr. Munich 1970.
29 F. Graus. *Volk, Herrscher und Heiliger im Reich der Merowinger*, Prague, Nakladatestvi Ceskoslovenske Akademie Ved, 1965. Trans. into Italian, 'Le funzioni del culto dei santi' in *Agiografia altomedioevale*, ed. Boesch Gajano, 152.
30 The last noteworthy historical study of Clare was in 1934, by M. Fassbinder, *Die heilige Klara von Assisi*, Freiburg i. B.; one must add the work of E. Grau, including 'Ich, Klara, die kleine Pflanze des hl. Vaters Franziskus' in *Geist und Leben* 26 (1935) 267–78; A–M. Berel, *Au Creux du rocher . . . Claire d'Assise*, Paris, 1960; F. Casolini, 'Sainte Claire et les Clarisses', in *DS* V Paris 1964, 1401–22; U. Nicolini, 'Chiara d'Assisi, santa' in *DBI* XXIV, Rome 1980, 503–8; A. Blasucci, 'Chiara d'Assisi, santa' in *DIP* II, Rome 1975, 885–92; K. Ruh, 'Klara von Assisi' in *Die deutsche Literatur des Mittelalters. Verfasserlexikon* IV, Berlin/New York 1983, 1172–83; and above all the work of Ch. A. Lainati, *Santa Chiara d'Assisi. Cenni biografici di santa Agnese d'Assisi e lettere di S. Chiara alla b. Agnese di Praga*, Assisi 1969.
31 A report of works on Clare was made at the seventh meeeting of the Società Internazionale di Studi Francescani, Assisi, 11–13 October 1979, under the title: *Movimento religioso femminile e francescanesimo nel secolo XIII*, Assisi 1980; cf. also E. Grau, *Die Schriften der heiligen Klara und die Werke ihrer Biographen*; and an inventory of recent publications in *Bibliog. Franc* XIV, nn8255–331; XV, nn7957–8039.
32 The first complete edition of Clare's writings was in Spanish and Latin, ed. I. Omaechevarria, *Escritos de Santa Clara y documentos contemporáneos*, Madrid 1970; a critical edition followed, G. Boccali, *Textus opusculorum S. Francisci et S. Clarae Assisiensium*, S. Maria degli Angeli-Assisi 1976; lastly, the Sources Chrétiennes edn, *Claire d'Assise: Écrits*, Paris 1985, ed. M.-F. Becker, J.-F. Godet and Th. Matura, trans. into Italian, Vicenza 1985, not yet available in English.
33 'Clare was also – and it is a great historical "first" – the first woman to compose a Rule for women', Matura, introduction, *Écrits*. For more about women's monastic Rules, cf. J. Leclercq, 'Femminile, monachesimo' in *DIP* III, Rome 1976, 1446–51.
34 This phrase was the heart, too, of Francis' *Regula bullata* of 1223 and is also found in the *formula* which Francis composed for Clare and her sisters and which is inserted into ch. 6 of Clare's Rule.
35 Cf. Z. Lazzeri, *La vita di S. Chiara, raccolta e tradotta da tutte le fonti conosciute . . . per un frate toscano del Cinquecento*, Quaracchi 1920, ch. 36, 149.
36 For the manuscript tradition of the Testament, see also D. Ciccarelli,

'Contributi alla recensione degli scritti di S. Chiara' in *MF* 79 (1979) 347–74.

37 Cf. Godet, 'Présentation des Écrits' in *Écrits* 17.

38 This is Codex M-10 of the Library of St Ambrose which was discovered some years before by the then librarian, Achille Ratti, later Pope Pius XI: A. Ratti, 'Un codice pragense a Milano con testo inedito della vita di S. Agnese di Praga' in *Rendiconti dell'Istituto Lombardo di Scienze e Lettere*, ser. II, 29 (1896) 392–6. In 1924 W. Seton published 'The Letters from St Clare to Blessed Agnes of Bohemia' in *AFH* 17 (1924) 509–19.

39 Cf. J.K. Vyskŏcil, *Legenda Blahoslavene Anežky a čtyri listy Sv. Kláry*, Prague 1932; trans. into Italian by L. Barabas, 'Le lettere di santa Chiara alla beata Agnese di Praga' in *Santa Chiara d'Assisi. Studi e cronaca del VII Centenario 1253–1953*, Assisi 1954, 123–43; trans. into English by V. Buresh, *The Legend of Blessed Agnes of Bohemia and the four letters of Clare* Cleveland 1963.

40 L. Wadding, *Annales Minorum* IV, Ad Claras Aquas (Quaracchi) 1931, 90ff. (an. 1257, n20).

41 Cardinal Ugolino's letter is found in 'Chronica Generalium' in *AF* III, 183; his own letter, *Deus Pater*, is in *BF* I, 37; also L. Wadding, *Annales Minorum* III, Ad Claras Aquas (Quaracchi) 1931, 273 (an. 1251, n17). For Agnes' letter to Clare see 'Chronica Generalium' 175–7; see also Lazzeri, 'Il processo di canonizzazione' 496ff.

42 De Vitry's correspondence has been published several times; see R.B.C. Huygens, *Lettres de Jacques de Vitry*, Leiden 1960, 71–8.

43 For the historical importance of Celano's work, esp. his *First Life*, cf. Stanislao da Campagnola, *Francesco d'Assisi nei suoi scritti e nelle sue biografie dei secoli XIII–XIV*, Assisi 1977, 74–81; also S. Spirito, *Il francescanesimo di fra Tommaso da Celano*, S. Maria degli Angeli-Assisi 1963.

44 Celano, *First Life* 18; see also *Second Life* 13; *Legenda Maior* IV, *Legenda trium sociorum* 24 (trans. into English by Salvator Butler, *We were with St Francis*, Edizioni Porziuncola 1984).

45 *First Life* 18.

46 *Second Life* 204–7.

47 *Second Life* 204; cf. *Legenda perusina* 45 (ed. Rosalind B. Brooke, Oxford 1970, 170); *Speculum perfectionis* 90.

48 M. Bartoli, 'Chiara testimone di Francesco' in *Quaderni Catenesi di Studi Classici e medievali* 1/2 (1979) 467–98.

49 Ed. Lazzeri, 'Il processo di canonizzazione' 494–9.

50 On the debate around the *Privilegium paupertatis*, it is enough to cite the two most famous studies: P. Sabatier, 'Le privilege de la pauvreté' in *Revue d'histoire franciscaine* I (1924) 1–54; E. Grau, 'Das "privilegium paupertatis" der hl. Klara. Geschichte und Bedeutung' in *Wissenschaft und Weisheit* 38 (1975) 17–25. Cf. also Godet in *Écrits* 17–34.

51 For the first critical edition of the *Privilegium paupertatis*, with the text of Innocent III, 1216, see *Écrits* 196–9.

52 The original in the text of Gregory IX of 1228 is to be found in the protomonastery in Assisi; the most recent edition is in *Écrits* 200–13.

53 The oldest version of Ugolino's Constitutions (from the monastery of S. Engracia di Olite, Spain, can be dated 1228) is found in Omaechevarria, *Escritos* 210–32. The Rule of Innocent IV is included in the bull *Cum omnis vera religio* of 6 August 1247, *BF* I, 476–83.

54 The exception here is the Canticle of Creation for which the *Legenda perusina* 42–3 is the sole source (ed. Brooke 162–6) and the *Speculum perfectionis* 100 (ed. Sabatier 286–90) which both place the episode at San Damiano.

Chapter One. The Courtly Culture of Knighthood and Models of Sanctity

1 An exhaustive survey of the city of Assisi in the first half of the twelfth century is found in: *Assisi al tempo di San Francesco*, Atti del V Convegno Internazionale, Assisi 13–16 October 1977, Società Internazionale di Studi Francescani 1978; cf. *CF* 49 (1979) 277–89.

2 Cf. R. Manselli, 'Assisi tra impero e papato' in *Assisi al tempo* 337–57; and *Città e comuni*, ed. O. Capitani, in *Storia d'Italia* IV, Turin 1981, 22–6.

3 Cf. A. Bartoli-Langeli, 'La realtà sociale assisiana e il patto del 1210' in *Assisi al tempo*, 271–336; for another approach, cf. S. Bortolami, 'Fra "alte domus" e "populares homines": il comune di Padova e il suo sviluppo prima di Ezzelino' in *Storia e cultura a Padova nell'età di sant'Antonio*, Padua 1985, 3–73.

4 The first documented submission to the commune was that of the Lords of Serpignano in 1203: cf. A. Fortini, *Nova Vita di San Francesco*, S. Maria degli Angeli-Assisi (Perugia) 1959, III, 553ff.

5 The war with Perugia was 'the first crucial test of the new commune', D. Waley, 'Le istituzioni comunali di Assisi nel passagio dal XII al XIII secolo', in *Assisi al tempo*, 59.

6 Cf. D. Waley, *The Papal State in the Thirteenth Century*, London 1961; P.V. Riley jr., 'Francis' Assisi: its Political and Social History, 1175–1225' in *Franciscan Studies* 34 (1974) 393–424.

7 G. Mira, 'Aspetti di vita economica nell'Assisi di san Francesco' in *Assisi al tempo* 130–2.

8 Ibid., 152.

9 *Life of Clare* 1.

10 The connection between nobility of birth and holiness of life in hagiography has been well studied in R. Gregoire, *Manuale di agiologia. Introduzione alla letteratura agiografica*, Fabriano 1987, 297–303.

11 This research has been assessed by Fortini in *Nova Vita* III, appendix, 'Assisi al tempo del santo – gli archivi assisiani – I documenti'; and in 'Nuove notizie intorno a S. Chiara di Assisi' in *AFH* 46 (1953) 3–43. On the value as well as the limitations of Fortini's great work, see A. Bartoli-Langeli, 'La realtà sociale', 274 n2, 281 n118; and Stanislao da Campagnola, *Le origine francescane come problema storiografico*, Perugia 1979, 254ff.

12 Cf. A. Bartoli-Langeli, 'La realtà sociale', 287ff.

13 G. Duby, *L'arte e la società medievale*, Bari 1977, 49.

14 There is a vast bibliography on the family of the Middle Ages, but for an introduction see: *Forme di potere e struttura sociale in Italia nel Medioevo*, ed. G. Rossetti, Bologna 1977 (bibliography on pp. 413–15); *Famiglia e comunità: Storia sociale* and, above all, *Famille et parenté au Moyen Age*, Acts of the International Convention in Paris 1974, publ. Rome. 1980.

15 Cf. A. Fortini, *Nova Vita di San Francesco*, 2nd edn. Rome 1981, 56–105 (trans. into English by Helen Moak, *Frances of Assisi*, New York 1981, 45–84).

16 The fullest analysis of the historical and social events which led to the signorial palace is to be found in Duby, *L'arte*, 240–345.

17 On the palace where Clare lived, cf. Fortini, *Nova Vita*, 409ff; G. Abate, *La casa paterna di S. Chiara e falsificazioni storiche del sec. XVI e XVII intorno alla medesima santa e a S. Francesco d'Assisi*, Assisi 1946, and *Nuovi studi sull'ubicazione della casa paterna di Chiara d'Assisi*, Assisi 1954.

18 Cf. G. Duby, *Matrimonio medievale*, Milan 1981.

19 *Life of Clare* 1.

20 *Process* 1, 4.

21 R. Manselli, 'La religiosità popolare del medio Evo: problemi e metodi' in *Il secolo XII: religione popolare ed eresia*, Rome 1983, 17ff. The basic work on pilgrimages is that of A. Dupront, 'Pélerenages et lieux sacrés' in *Mélanges F. Braudel* II, Paris 1973, 189–206.

22 B. Matteucci, 'Bona di Pisa' in *BS* III, Rome 1963, 234–6.

23 The observations made of Ch. de La Roncière are also valid for Clare's family, see 'La vita privata dei notabili toscani' in *La vita privata dal feudalesimo al rinascimento*, ed. Ph. Ariès and G. Duby, Bari 1987, 132–251 (even though this refers to the next century).

24 Cf. I. Magli, *Donna. Un problema aperto*. Florence 1969.

25 Cf. *Prediche alle donne del secolo XIII*, ed. C. Casagrande, Milan 1978.

26 There is plenty of evidence of this dichotomy between aristocratic women and those of the 'middle class'. Cf. S. de Beauvoir, *Le Deuxième Sexe*, Paris 1949 (trans. into English, *The Second Sex*).

27 Clare's family was in exile in Perugia at least from 1203 until 1205. Cf. A. Fortini, 'Nuove notizie' 17–19.

28 Thomas of Celano, *Second Life* 4.

29 Cf. Duby, *L'arte*, 49ff.

30 Ibid. 154ff.

31 Cf. S. Folema, 'Tradizione e cultura trobadorica nelle corti e nelle città venete' in *Storica della cultura veneta* I, 'Dalle origini al Trecento' Vicenza 1976, 453–562, with a full bibliography.

32 Cf. J. Frappier, 'Vues sur les conceptions courtoises dans les littératures d'oc et d'oil au XIIIe siècle' in *Cahiers de civilisation médiévale* 2 (1959) 135; also R.R. Bezzola, esp. 'La transformation des moeurs et le role de la femme dans la classe féodale du XIe au XIIe siècle' in his *Les origines et la formation de la littérature courtoise en Occident (500–1200)* II/2, Paris 1960, 461–84.

33 E. Koehler, 'Observations historiques et sociologiques sur la poésie des troubadours' in *Cahiers de civilisation médiévale* 7 (1964) 35; cf. Koehler *Sociologia della fin'amour. Saggi trobadorici*, trans. into Italian by M. Mancini, Padua 1976; cf. also J. Frappier, *Amour courtois et table ronde*, Geneva 1973.

34 G. Duby, 'Convivialità' in *La vita privata* 66.

35 Cf. D. Régnier-Bohler, 'Esplorazione di una letteratura' in *La vita privata*, 225–336.

36 Cf. Gilbert of Tournai, 'Ad virgines. Sermo secundus' in *Prediche alle donne* 105ff.

37 Cf. B. Migliorini and A. Duro, *Prontuario etimologico della lingua italiana*, Turin 1953.

38 Cf. A. Fortini, *Assisi nel medioevo. Leggende–avventure–battaglie*, Rome 1940, 29–77.

39 This is preserved for us in G. Di Costanzo, *Disamina degli scrittori e dei monumenti riguardanti San Rufino vescovo e martire di Assisi*, Assisi 1797, 113–19.

40 Fortini, *Assisi nel medioevo* 62.

41 Ch. A. Lainati, *Santa Chiara d'Assisi. Cenni biografici di santa Agnese d'Assisi e lettere di S. Chiara alla b. Agnese di Praga*, Assisi 1969, 101–25; A. Brunacci, 'Agnese di Assisi', in *BS* I, Rome 1961, 369ff.

42 A good introduction to this subject is M.C. de Matteis, *Idee sulla donna nel medioevo: fonti e aspetti giuridici, antropologici, religiosi, sociali e letterari della condizione femminile*, Bologna 1981.

43 A. Vauchez, *Les laïcs au Moyen Age. Pratiques et expériences religieuses*, Paris 1987, 187–249.

44 *Test.Cl.* 6, 8.

45 Galatians 1:15–16; cf. Jeremiah 1:5; Isaiah 49:1–5; Luke 1:15; Romans 8:29.

46 *Process* 6, 12.

47 Ibid. 12. 1.

48 Ibid. 20, 1–5.

49 On the role of domestic servants, see Ch. de La Roncière, *La vita privata*, 180–90.

50 For a definition and discussion of *fama publica*, cf. R. Manselli, *San Francesco d'Assisi*, Rome 1980, 34, trans. into English by Paul Duggen, *St Francis of Assisi*, Chicago 1988, 26–7.

51 Cf. L. Genicot, *Le XIIIe siècle européen*, Paris 1968; J.L. Flandrin, *La famiglia. Parentela, casa, sessualità nella società preindustriale*, Milan 1979, 249–51; P. Feuchère, 'La noblesse du Nord de la France' in *Annales E.S.C.6* (1951) 315–18; J.C. Russel, *British Medieval Population*, Albuquerque 1948, 176–86.

52 Cf. J. Hoppenot, *Le crucifix dans l'histoire, dans l'art, dans l'âme des saints et dans notre vie*, Lille 1905; H. Leclercq, 'Croix et Crucifix' in *Dictionnaire d'Archéologie chrétienne et de Liturgie* III/2, Paris 1914, 3045–131; cf. J. de Vitry, *Vita Mariae oigniacensis* in *AA.SS.* 23 June, t V, Paris-Rome 1867, 547a–572b.

53 Cf. G. Duby, *L'anno mille*, Turin 1976, 51; P. Brezzi, *La civiltà del medioevo europeo* I, Rome 1978, 248.

54 *Process* 6, 12; 3, 28 and *Life of Clare* 2.

55 A. Fortini, 'Nuove notizie' 11–15.

56 *Process* 1, 2.

57 On Benvenuta da Perugia, see A. Fortini, 'Nuove notizie' 17–19. On the family of Leonardo de Gliserio see Fortini, *Nova vita* (1st edn see above n4) I, 158ff.

58 *Process* 17, 4.

59 'The place held by windows in the plots of these romances, is notable; for the unhappily married woman it brought dreams of freedom', G. Duby in *La vita privata* 54.

60 The exact relationship between Clare and Amata (and Balvina) is uncertain.

61 *Process* 4. 2.

62 Ibid. 3, 2.

63 The *fama sanctitatis* was essential if a canonisation process was to go forward. Thus Gregory IX writes 'not only through witnesses but also through reputation and authentic writings', in the letter *Patri luminum* of 16.2.1233 (ed. B. Haureau, *Gallia christiana in provincias ecclesiasticas distributas*, t. XVI Paris 1865, 213ab) and in the letter *Licet quicquid* of 17.2.1233 (cf. L. Auvray, *Les registres de Gregoire IX*, Paris 1890–1955, n1098).

64 *Process* 18, 1.

65 Ibid 19, 1–2.

66 For an introduction to this theme, see *Agiografia altomedioevale*, ed. S. Boesch-Gajano, Bologna 1976; C. Leonardi, 'Dalla santità "monastica" alla santità "politica" in *Concilium* 15 (1979) 84–97; E. Menestò, *Il processo di canonizzazione di Chiara da Montefalco*, Florence/Perugia 1984, CLIV–CLXIX.

67 *Life of Clare* 1–2.

68 Cf. H. Grundmann, *Movimenti religiosi nel Medioevo*, Italian trans. Bologna 1974 (for German edns see above Introduction n28), 147–302.

69 For a general bibliography see A. Mens, 'Beghine, Begardi, Beghinaggi' in *DIP* I Rome 1974, 1165–80.

70 On the evolution of the idea of feminine holiness in the thirteenth century, see A. Vauchez, *La sainteté en Occident aux derniers siècles du Moyen Age, d'après les procès de canonisation et les documents hagiographiques*, Rome 1987, 427–46.

71 The tree can be told by its fruit (Matthew 12:33) and the fruit is recommended by the tree (*Life of Clare* 2).

72 *Life of Clare* 1.

73 Ibid.

74 Ibid.

75 *Process* 1, 3; 17, 14; 18, 1–5; 20, 3–5.

76 Ibid. 17, 7.

77 Job 31: 18 and Proverbs 31: 20.

78 Proverbs 31: 20, 30–1.

79 *Life of Clare* 3; cf. Job 31:17.
80 *Process* 20, 4; cf. Lainati, *Santa Chiara d'Assisi* 16.
81 Leviticus 1-2.
82 Hebrews 10:11-14.
83 R. Manselli, *Il soprannaturale e la religione popolare nel Medio Evo*, Rome 1985, 57-74.
84 Cf. Romans 13:14; Galatians 3:27; *Life of Clare* 4.
85 *Process* 20, 4.
86 Cf. R.M. Bell, *Holy Anorexia*, Chicago 1985.
87 *Life of Clare* 4.

Chapter Two. The Search for an Alternative

1 Cf. F. Pennacchi, *Legenda S. Clarae virginis*, Assisi 1910, X.
2 *Process* 12 and 17.
3 'De noticia et familiaritate beati Francisci; Qualiter per beatum Franciscum conversa de saeculo ad religionem transivit; Qualiter a consanguineis impugnata firma perseverantia stetit.'
4 *Testament of Francis* 1, *Writings* 154.
5 'Francis began to seem more and more oppressed by a profound inner crisis. We know nothing of its origins because it seems that he made no confidences but kept it all enclosed within the silence of his own conscience. We only know that he became increasingly disquieted and that this disquiet, filled as it was with uncertainty, with vacillations and perplexity, led to that decisive moment of conversion which was to determine his future', R. Manselli, *San Francesco d'Assisi*, Rome 1980, 58 (trans. into English by Paul Duggan, *St Francis of Assisi*, Chicago 1988). For a discussion of all the problems around Francis' conversion, see J.G. Bougerol, 'Conversione, fuga dal mondo' in *DF* 227-40; F. De Beer, *La conversion de saint François selon Thomas de Celano. Étude comparative des textes relatifs à la conversion en Vita I et Vita II*, Paris 1963.
6 Cf. St Athansius, *Life of St Anthony*, PL 26, 835-970; G.Cassiano, *Collationes* III, PL 49, 557-84; St Gregory, *Dialogorum book II: Vita S. Benedicti*, PL 66, 125-214
7 Cf. I. Magli, *Gli uomini della penitenza*, Milan 1977, 42-7.
8 *We Were with St Francis*, trans. Salvator Butler, Edizioni Porziuncola 1984.
9 Clare's cousin, Rufino, had been drawn to Francis before her and had thrown in his lot with Francis. Cf. A. Fortini, *Nova Vita di San Francesco*, S. Maria degli Angeli-Assisi (Perugia) 1959, I/1, 420 and II, 315-49 (where there is full documentation about Clare's family).
10 *Test.Cl.*, 25.
11 *Life of Clare* 5.
12 *Process* 12, 2.
13 Ibid 17, 2.
14 *Process* 17, 7.
15 Celano's *Second Life* 57.

16 For an introduction on the theme of the *status* of women in medieval law, cf. 'La Femme', *Recueils de la Société Jean Bodin* XII/2, Brussels 1962.

17 *Process* 17, 2.

18 Cf. I. Noye, 'Miséricorde (oeuvres de)' in *DS* X, Paris 1980, 1328–49.

19 *Test.Cl.*, 24–5.

20 *Life of Clare* 5.

21 Ibid.

22 Ibid.

23 Ibid.

24 *Regula non bullata* 12, 4.

25 Ibid. 12, 5 and 6.

26 *Process* 17, 3.

27 Ibid. 18, 2; 19, 2.

28 *Life of Clare* 4.

29 The *Life of Clare* says that she left 'with a virtuous companion' who is traditionally identified as Pacifica di Guelfuccio, sister of Bona (who was away on pilgrimage at that moment). Pacifica, who later became the second 'sister' at San Damiano, does not mention this important flight in her testimony. On the other hand, the *Rhyming Life* (vv. 280–1) describes Clare's flight as 'alone'. Perhaps Celano's 'virtuous companion' can be identified as Francis' brothers who accompanied Clare along the road. Cf. Ch. A. Lainati, 'Scritti e fonti biografiche di Chiara d'Assisi' in *FF* 2308.

30 *Life of Clare* 8.

31 *Process* 17, 5.

32 *Life of Clare* 7.

33 This would date her flight as 28 March 1211 (Z. Lazzeri, F. Casoloni and Ch. A. Lainati). Others date it a year later, 18 March 1212 (D. Cresi, L. Hardwick, A. Terzi). See also L. Di Fonzo, 'Per la cronologia di San Francesco. Gli anni 1182–1212' in *MF* 82 (1982) 100–2.

34 Cf. *Études de pastorale liturgique*, Paris 1944, esp. J. Leclercq, 'Dévotion privée, piété populaire et liturgie au Moyen Age' 156–69.

35 *Life of Clare* 7.

36 Ibid. 8.

37 *Process* 12, 4. The *Life* (7) is more general: at the hands of the brothers, her hair was cut off.

38 Bull *Clara claris praeclara* n5.

39 Sabatier seems to have been the first to realise how extremely unusual this was on Francis' part. Cf. P. Sabatier, *Vie de Saint François d'Assise*, 3rd edn Paris 1926, 172; trans. into English by L.S. Houghton, *Life of St Francis of Assisi*, London 1894, 151.

40 It is probable that at that time Francis was not even a deacon. Cf. Di Fonzo, 'Per la cronologia' 96, n153, 100–2.

41 The event at Greccio was particularly important. It too, was a liturgy which Francis had thought about beforehand. There are several details which the two episodes have in common: the night, the lighted torches, the sense of joy. Cf. Celano, *First Life* 84–6.

42 *Life of Clare* 9.

43 Bull *Clara claris praeclara* n7 (Pennacchi, *Legenda S. Clarae* 110).
44 *Process* 13, 10.
45 Cf. M. Parisse, *Les nonnes au Moyen Age*, Le Puy 1983, with bibliography.
46 *Process* 12, 3–4.
47 D. Owen Hughes, 'Famiglia e successione ereditaria nell'Europa medioevale' in *Famiglia e comunità*, monograph 33 *Quaderni Storici* (1976) 932ff.
48 Cf. M. Fassbinder, *Die heilige Klara von Assisi*, Freiburg i. B., 66ff.
49 *Life of Clare* 13.
50 Cf. G. Miccoli, *S. Francesco d'Assisi e la povertà* in *Seguire Gésú povero*, Magnano 1984, 119–97, which synthesises the study in *Studi medievali* 24 (1983) 17–73 ('La proposta cristiana di Francesco d'Assisi. Un problema di lettura').
51 *Testament of Francis* 16–17, *Writings*.
52 There can be no need to stress that we are again confronted by the courtly culture of knighthood here, and that the *viltà*, the wretchedness of Clare, must be contrasted with *gentilezza*.
53 For full information on San Paolo delle Abbadesse, see A. Fortini, 'Nuove notizie intorno a S. Chiara di Assisi', in *AFH* 46 (1953) 29–33.
54 Cf. J. Leclercq, 'La spiritualità del medioevo (VI–XII secolo). Da S. Gregorio a S.Bernardo' in *Storia della spiritualità*, 4/a, Bologna 1986, 174.
55 Celano, *First Life* 16.
56 *Process* 12, 4.
57 Ibid. 20, 6.
58 *Life of Clare* 9.
59 See n24 and 25 above.
60 *Test.Cl.* 27–8.
61 *Process* 13, 1.

Chapter Three. The Privilege of Living without Privileges

1 Cf. A. Fortini, 'Nuove notizie intorno a S. Chiara di Assisi' in *AFH* 46 (1953), 29–33. The monastery of San Paolo delle Abbadesse, about 4km from Assisi, was under the jurisdiction of the bishop of the city.
2 The 1354 register of religious groups in the commune of Assisi estimated the property of San Paolo delle Abbadesse at 53.290 librae per year and those of the bishop at 43.812 (a libra is an old Roman measurement, about 327g. *Trans.*). This document is more than a century later than the time under consideration but 'historical investigations in other areas suggest that the rural districts of the mid thirteenth century were not very different then from the way they were a century later, this is particularly true of ecclesiastical property', A. Grohmann, 'Per una tipologia degli insediamenti umani del contado di Assisi' in *Assisi al tempo di San Francesco*, Atti del V Convegno Internazionale, Assisi 13–6 October 1977, Società Internazionale di Studi Francescana 1978, 198–203. For a description of the register cf. A. Fortini, *Nova Vita di San Francesco*, S. Maria degli Angeli-Assisi (Perugia) 1959, III 234; C. Cenci, 'Documentazione di vita assisana 1300–1448', *Spicilegium bonaventurianum* X, Grottaferrata 1974, 19 n21.

3 *Life of Clare* 9; *Process* 12, 4.
4 *Process* 12, 5; *Life of Clare* 10.
5 See above, ch. 2.
6 Cf. *L'eremitismo in Occidente nei secoli XI e XII*, Atti della II Settimana internationale di Studio, Mendola 1962.
7 For a discussion of this concept of evangelical poverty, which was unique to Francis until Clare came, see R. Manselli, *Evangelismo e povertà*, Bologna 1974, 153–92.
8 *Life of Clare* 10.
9 Cf. A. Fortini, 'Nuove notizie intorno' 29–33; F. Santucci, *S. Angelo di Panzo presso Assisi* in *Atti Accademia Properziana del Subasio* 13 (1986) 83–112.
10 The same inventory of 1354 mentioned above (n2) estimates the possessions of S. Angelus Pacii at 10.591 librae, and puts the monastery in seventh place, economically speaking, of religious houses of the diocese.
11 M. Sensi, 'Incarcerate e recluse in Umbria nei secoli XIII e XIV: un bizzocaggio centro-italiano?' in *Il movimento religioso femminile in Umbria nei secoli XIII–XIV*, ed. R. Rusconi, Florence/Perugia 1984, 87–121.
12 H. Grundmann, *Movimenti religiosi nel Medioevo*, Bologna 1974 (for German edns see above Introduction n28), 147–70.
13 A. Mens, 'L'Ombrie italienne et l'Ombrie brabançonne. Deux courants religieux parallèles d'inspiration commune' in *Études Franc.* 17 (1967) suppl.
14 This is the opinion of M. Sensi in *I frati penitenti di S. Francesco nella società del Due e Trecento*, ed. Mariano D'Alatri, Rome 1977, 305 n41.
15 Cf. 'Chronicle of the XXIV Generals' in *AF* III, 175.
16 The account of Agnes' flight and the family's even more violent reaction is only told in the *Life of Clare* (24–6) where the details are very exact (seven days after the conversion of Clare). For more about Agnes, cf. Ch. A. Lainati, *Santa Chiara d'Assisi. Cenni biografici di santa Agnese d'Assisi e lettere di S. Chiara alla b. Agnese di Praga*, Assisi 1969, 101–9.
17 *Life of Clare* 24.
18 Ibid. 25.
19 Ibid. 26.
20 Cf. Sensi, 'Incarcerate e recluse in Umbria' 93f.: 'The vocation of Clare of Assisi developed out of two antithetical currents, when Benedictine monasticism and the urban, penitential movement of reclusion were already in existence. The movement of *Poor ladies* guided by Clare transcended even as it synthesised these two movements: that is, traditional monasticism and the new style of religious life.'
21 *Locus* is the word which Francis seems to have preferred to indicate the brethren gathered around him, cf. G. Bove 'Luogo, cella, casa, costruzione' in *DF* 902–18.
22 The novitiate was introduced to the Friars by the bull *Cum secundum consilium* of Honorius III, 22 September 1220, *BF* I, 6; cf. S. Di Mattia, 'La bolla "Cum secundum consilium" of Onorio III' in *Annali Libera Università della Tuscia* 5 (1973/4) 1–15.

23 *Test.Cl.* 33.

24 Cf. C. Gennaro in *Movimento religioso femminile e francescanesimo nel XIII secolo*, Assisi 1980, 171 ff.: 'This group . . . had lived for years without feeling the need for a rule: the *formula vitae* which Francis had given them . . . placed the Gospel life and Francis' own care for them right at the heart of the venture at San Damiano.'

25 *Rule of Clare* ch.6: 3; cf. *Test.Cl.* 29.

26 Cf. A. Sanna, 'Professione, voti, promessa, dono' in *DF* 1472–8 ('La professione di Chiara e della sua fraternità').

27 *Rule of Clare* 2, 13.

28 Ibid. 7: 1.

29 *Regula bullata* of 1223 ch. 5: 1–2.

30 *Rule of Clare* 7: 3.

31 Not by chance, this phrase was also used by Jacques de Vitry in his famous letter of 1216: 'Mulieres vero iuxta civitates in diversis hospitiis simul commorantur; nichil accipiunt, sed de labore manuum vivunt', R.B.C. Huygens, *Lettres de Jacques de Vitry*, Leiden 1960, 76.

32 *Process* 1, 11.

33 *Testament of Francis* 19–21, *Writings.*

34 *Regula non bullata* ch. 7: 1–3.

35 *Process* 1, 11.

36 Bull *Clara claris praeclara* n16 (ed. F. Pennacchi, *Legenda S. Clarae Virginis*, Assisi 1910, 114).

37 Cf. *Process* 2, 12; 6, 14; 3, 4.

38 Work with wool has been the characteristic domestic occupation of women from antiquity. Preachers were also very concerned about it. Cf. Gilberto of Tournai, 'Sermones ad Status' f.177r in *Prediche alle donne del secolo XIII*, ed. C. Casagrande, Milan 1978, 68.

39 It is noteworthy that during those years the 'art of wool' underwent more development than ever before and the advent of small shops raised this handcraft – often performed by women – almost to the level of a small industry. Cf. J. Le Goff, *La civiltà dell' Occidente medievale*, Florence 1969, 362f.; on work in the Middle Ages, see *Lavorare nel medioevo. Rappresentazioni dell' Italia dei secc. X–XIV*, Centre of Studies in Medieval Spirituality, XXI, Todi 1983.

40 *Legend of Perugia* 62.

41 Cf. *Rule of Clare* ch. 6, 12–15; *Test.Cl.* 53 and 54.

42 See nn35 and 36 above.

43 For the importance of work in the experience of the Humiliati, cf. L. Zanoni, *Gli Umiliati nei loro rapporti con l'eresia, l'industria della lana ed i comuni nei secoli XII e XIII*, Milan 1911.

44 The main source for this period is always Grundmann, *Movimenti religiosi* 273–302.

45 See n31 above.

46 *Process* 1, 11.

47 *Life of Clare* 28.

48 Cf. A. Lehmann, *Le rôle de la femme dans l'histoire de France au moyen âge*, Paris 1952.

49 Cf. J. Le Goff, *Pour un autre Moyen Age. Temps, travail et culture en Occident*, Paris 1977, 363.

50 *Life of Clare* 12.

51 *Rule of Clare* 8, 16.

52 Cf. P. Galtier, 'Conversi' in *DS* II/2, Paris 1950, 2218–24.

53 See n30 above. Here I follow the interpretation of Sister Chiara Augusta Lainati, 'Scitti e fonti biografiche di Chiara d'Assisi' in *FF* 2258, rather than that of L. Iriarte, *La regola di santa Chiara*, Milan 1976, 143.

54 Clare's rule provides that the sisters who serve outside the monastery (as they were always called) had the same formation as the other sisters when they entered the monastery (*Rule* 2, 21) except that they were not obliged to fast (3, 10) nor were they bound to silence when outside the monastery (5, 1). Cf. Iriarte, *La regola*, 183–7.

55 In the prologue to *Vita Mariae Oigniacensis* in *AA. SS.* 23 June, t. V, 549.

56 Cf. Mens, 'L'Ombrie' 60–2.

57 Cf. Huygens, *Lettres* 76.

58 The problem of interference, both ecclesiastical and lay, is particularly relevant for all communities of religious women. Cf. G. Di Mattia 'Giurisdizione e vicende legali dei monasteri benedettini femminili di Assisi prima del Concilio di Trento' in *Le Abbazie nullius*, Conversano 1984, 233–79 and, above all, 248.

59 'As early as 1235, Gregory IX had repeatedly charged bishops and German canons to protect the Beguines from the conflict and molestation of clerics, monks and laity and to punish the culprits', Grundmann, *Movimenti religiosi* 278.

60 This is Constitution XIII, *Ne nimia religionum diversitas*: cf. J.D. Mansi, *Sacrorum conciliorum nova et amplissima collectio*, XXII, Venice 1878, 1002; *Conciliorum oecumenicorum decreta*, Bologna 1962, 218.

61 Cf. Grundmann, *Movimenti religiosi* 171–271.

62 We still lack a full biography of Ugolino dei Conti di Segni, but can, meanwhile, consult S. Sibilia, *Gregorio IX (1227–1241)*, Milan 1961.

63 Cf. bull *Litterae tuae* of Honorius III, sent to Cardinal Ugolino on 27 August 1218, cf. *BF* I, 1. On the problems of the Rule of the second Franciscan Order, there is a rich literature which rests, basically, on L. Oliger, 'De origine regularum ordinis Sanctae Clarae' in *AFH* 5 (1912) 181–209; see also I. Omaechevarría, 'La "regle" y las reglas de la orden de Santa Clara' in *CF* 46 (1976) 93–119.

64 The oldest manuscript of Ugolino's Constitutions, dated 1228, comes from the monastery of S. Engracia de Olite, cf. I. Omaechevarria, *Escritos de Santa Clara y documentos contemporáneos*, Madrid 1970, 210–32.

65 The first of the two writings of Francis for the sisters at San Damiano date from this period. Clare inserted this one into her Rule and quoted it in her Testament. It is generally known as the *Forma vivendi*. Cf. *Rule of Clare* 6, 3–4; *Test.Cl.* 29.

66 *Process* 1, 6.

67 Cf. L.A. Redigonda, 'Domenicane' in *DIP* III, Rome 1976, 780–93.
68 *Life of Clare* 12.
69 Cf. *Le Abbazie nullius* n58.
70 Cf. Sensi, 'Incarcerate e recluse in Umbria' 101 ff.
71 There are a great many studies of the *Privilege of Poverty*. Among them, see Z. Lazzeri, 'Il "Privilegium paupertatis" concesso da Innocenzo III e che cosa fosse in origine' in *AFH* 11 (1918) 270–6; E. Grau, 'Das Privilegium paupertatis Innozenz III' in *Franz. Stud.* 31 (1949) 337–49, and above all P. Sabatier, 'Le privilège de la pauvreté', in *Revue d'histoire franciscaine*, 1 (1924) 1–54.
72 *Clare of Assisi, Early Documents* 83.
73 1 Celano 33; 2 Celano 17; *Legenda Maior of Bonaventure* 3, 10; *Legend of the Three Companions* 49–51.
74 It is worth underlining the verbal parallels between this document and the Testament of Francis where he describes the life of the first companions: 'Those who came to receive life gave to the poor everything which they were capable of possessing, and they were content with one tunic...' *Testament of Francis* 16–17, *Writings*, 155.
75 For a survey of the debate about the authenticity of the Testament of Clare, see J.-F. Godet in *Clare d'Assise: Écrits*, Paris 1985; also Ch. A. Lainati, 'Testamento di santa Chiara' in *DF* 1827–46.
76 *Life of Clare* 14.
77 *Test.Cl.* 41–43.
78 *Process* 3, 14; cf. also 3, 32 and 12, 6.

Chapter Four. The Space of Sanctity: Enclosed and Open to the World

1 *Comuni e signorie: istituzione, società e lotte per l'egemonia*, Turin 1981, esp. the contribution of G. Cherubini, 'Le campagne italiane dall'XI al XV secolo'; also *Agricoltura e società rurale nel medioevo*, Florence 1972; *Signori, contadini, borgesi. Ricerche sulla società italiana del basso medioevo*, Florence 1974.
2 For a bibliography on the theme of the medieval city, see E. Ennen, *Storia della città medievale*, Bari 1975 (original edn. Gottingen 1972).
3 A. Fliche, *Storia della Chiesa*, Turin 1967, vol. X: A. Fliche, Ch. Thouzellier, and Y. Azais, *La cristianità romana (1198–1274)*, ed. Mariano D'Alatri.
4 Cf. vols. 48 and 69 *Statuti della provincia romana* (Fonti per la Storia d'Italia), ed. F. Tommasetti, V. Fedrici and P. Egidi, Rome 1910; and the vol. ed. by V. Federici, Rome 1930.
5 Cf. *Il movimento religioso femminile in Umbria nei secoli XIII–XIV*, ed. R. Rusconi, Florence/Perugia 1984.
6 Cf. *L'eremetismo in Occidente nei secoli XI e XII*. Acts of the 2nd Study Week, La Mendola, Milan 1975, esp. the papers of G. Tabacco (73–119), O. Capitani (122–63), K. Elm (491–559); also J. Sainsaulieu, 'Ermites: II. En Occident' in *DHGE* XV, Paris 1963, 771–87.

7 For a study of the religious awakening of the thirteenth century, cf. R. Manselli, *Il secolo XII: religione popolare ed eresia*, Rome 1983.

8 There were recluses and hermits even in the time of Gregory the Great: cf. *Dialogorum* book III, ch. 16 (*PL* 77, 257–62).

9 Cf. J. Hubert, 'Les recluseries urbaines au Moyen Age', in *L'eremitismo in Occidente* 485–87.

10 A. Vauchez, *Les laïcs au Moyen Age*, Paris 1987, 169–86.

11 For a general presentation of this new concept of sanctity, cf. A.I. Galletti, 'I francescani ed il culto dei santi nell'Italia centrale' in *Francescanesimo e vita religiosa dei laici nel '200*, Atti dell' VIII Convegno Internazionale, Assisi 16–18 October 1980, publ. Assisi 1981, 311–63.

12 Cf. Manselli, *Il secolo XII* esp. 311–31, 'Profilo della storia religiosa italiana nel secolo XII'.

13 As in the case of Mary of Oignies, cf. Jacques de Vitry, *Vita Mariae Oigniacensis* in *AA.SS.* 23 June, t. V, 547a–572b. For a panoramic survey cf. G. Casagrande, 'Il movimento penitenziale nei secoli del basso Medioevo. Nota su alcuni recenti contributi' in *Benedictina* 30 (1983) 217–33.

14 Cf. M. Sensi, 'Incarcerate e recluse in Umbria nei secoli XIII e XIV: un bizzocaggio centro-italiano?' in *Il movimento religioso femminile in Umbria* 87–121.

15 Bull *Litterae tuae nobis* of Honorius III, 27 August 1218, in *BF*, I, 1.

16 Cf. Ch. A. Lainati, 'La clausura di santa Chiara d'Assisi e delle prime "Sorelle Povere" di S. Damiano nella legislazione canonica e nella pratica' in *Forma Sororum* 17 (1980) 45–76. Trans. into English, 'The enclosure of St Clare and the first Poor Clares in canonical legislation and practice' in *The Chord* 28 (1978) 4–15, 47–60. Also E. Grau, 'Die Klausur im Kloster S. Damiano zu Lebzeiten der heiligen Klara' in *Studia historico-ecclesiastica, festgabe für Prof. Luchesius G. Spätling OFM*, Rome 1977, 311–46.

17 Cf. L. Auvray, 'Les registres' 2408, *BF* I, 145 n153; A. Potthast, *Regesta Pontificum Romanorum I*, Berlin 1874–74, 837 n9829. There is abundant documentation on Gregory IX, the classic work being J. Vossius, 'Gesta et monumenta Gregori IX pontificum romanorum. Vita Gregorii IX papae' in *Rerum Italicarum Scriptores* III/1, 575–87.

18 H. Grundmann, *Movimenti religiosi nel Medioevo*, Bologna 1974 (for German edns see above Introduction n28), esp. 171–270.

19 The *Rule of Ugolino, Early Documents* 87. For the Latin text cf. I. Omaechevarría, *Escritos de Santa Clara y documentos contemporáneos*, Madrid 1970, 210–32. This is the oldest text known to us, preserved at the monastery of S. Engracia di Olite, collated in the light of an unpublished text in the Monastery of S. Catalina di Saragoza. The first is dated 1228, the second 1230.

20 *Rule of Ugolino* n4, *Early Documents* 89.

21 Ibid. 89.

22 Cf. J.-M. Bienvenu, 'Robert d'Arbrissel' in *DS* XIII, 704–13; also J. Smith, *Robert d'Arbrissel* in *Medieval Women*, London 1978.

23 J. Leclercq, 'Il monachesimo femminile nei secoli XII e XIII' in *Movimento religioso femminile e francescanesimo nel secolo XIII*, Assisi 1980, 83.

24 M. de Fontette, *Les religieuses à l'âge classique du droit canon. Recherches sur les structures juridiques des branches féminines des ordres*, Paris 1967; J.H. Canivez, *'Statuta capitulorum generalium ordinis cisterciensis ab anno 1116 ad annum 1786'* in *Bibliothèque de la revue d'histoire ecclésiastique* fasc. 9–14b (Louvain 1933) I, 1213, 59. On enclosure, see also J. Leclercq, 'La clôture. Points de repère historique' in *Coll. Cist.* 43 (1981) 366–76; O. Schmucki, 'Secretum solitutidinis' in *CF* 39 (1969) 51–4 – trans. into English by Sebastian Holland, 'Place of Solitude: an essay on the external circumstances of the prayer life of St Francis of Assisi' in *Greyfriars Review* 2 (Jan. 1988) 103–6; Schmucki, 'Speculum S. Francisci in S. Clara' in *CF* 41 (1971) 402 and n35.

25 *Rule of Ugolino* 6; I. Omaechevarria, *Escritos* 221; *Early Documents* 90. Cf. R. van Waefelghem, 'Le premiers statuts de l'ordre de Prémontré' in *Analecta Ordinis Praemonstratensis* 8 (1913) 63.

26 *Rule of St Benedict* ch. 6.

27 Ibid.

28 Ibid. ch. 42.

29 *Rule of Ugolino* 11, *Early Documents* 94.

30 This same prohibition also characterised the early Cistercian nuns. Cf. the Life of Stefano d'Aubazine, bk. 2, n4, 159; E. Jombart and M. Viller, 'Clôture' in *DS* II/1, 990–1007.

31 Cf. E. Pásztor, 'San Francesco e il cardinal Ugolino nella "questione francescana"' in *CF* 46 (1976) 209–39. Trans. into English by Patrick Colbourne, 'St Francis, Cardinal Hugolino, and the "Franciscan Question"' in *Greyfriars Review* 1 (Sept. 1987) 1–29.

32 'Chronica XXIV Generalium Ordinis Minorum' in *AF* III, 183.

33 Cf. *Early Documents* 97.

34 Ibid.

35 Cf. de Fontette, *Les religieuses* 32.

36 Cf. the formulary of Marino de Eboli, vice-chancellor of the Roman curia from 1244 to 1251, the authenticity of which is discussed in E. Grau, *Leben und Schriften del hl. Klara von Assisi*, Werl/Westf. 1960, 29. See also L. Wadding, *Annales Minorum* III, 273, an. 1251, n17.

37 Cf. G. Boccali, 'San Damiano, santuario' in *DF* 1583–1604.

38 For Francis' dealings with the priests at San Damiano, see *Legenda trium sociorum* 16, 21–22 (trans. in to English by Salvator Butler, *We were with St Francis*, Edizione Porziuncola 1984); cf. *AFH* 67 (1974) 101f., 106f.

39 Cf. *Lo Spazio dell' umiltà*, Atti del convegno di studi sull'edilizia dell'ordine dei minori, Fara Sabina, 5–6 November 1982, publ. Fara Sabina 1984.

40 Cf. L. Pellegrini, 'L'esperienza eremitica di Francesco e dei primi francescani' in *Francesco d'Assisi e francescanesimo dal 1216 al 1226*, Assisi 1977, 279–313.

41 The *Legenda perusina* 43, ed. F.-M. Delorme, Paris 1926 (trans. into English in *Omnibus* 959ff.); this is the source of the tradition that the Canticle was composed at San Damiano; also the *Speculum perfectionis*

100, ed. P. Sabatier, Manchester 1928 (trans. into English in *Omnibus* 1105).

42 *Process* 1, 14.

43 Cf. Ch. A. Lainati, 'Scritti e fonti biografiche di Chiara d'Assisi' in *FF* 2227–9.

44 *Test.Cl.* 9–14.

45 2 Celano 13.

46 Bull of canonisation, Alexander IV, 19 October 1255; cf. edn of F. Pennacchi, *Legenda S. Clarae Virginis*, Assisi 1910, 109 n4.

47 *Life of Clare* 10–11.

48 On the value given to example in Franciscan tradition, cf. G. Boccali, 'Esempio, testimonianza, scandalo' in *DF* 493–512. For example in preaching and thirteenth-century popular religion, cf. P. Adnès, 'Exemple' in *DS* IV/2, Paris 1961, 1878–85, and above all R. Cantel and R. Ricard, 'Exemplum: II. Au moyen âge' in *DS* IV/2, 1892–5.

49 R. Manselli, *San Francesco d'Assisi*, Rome 1980, 232; trans. into English by Paul Duggan, *St Francis of Assisi*, Chicago 1988, 227–8.

50 *Test.Cl.* 19. For the meaning of the word *speculum* in thirteenth-century culture, cf. M. Schmidt, 'Miroir' in *DS* X, Paris 1980, 1290–303.

51 Cf. C. Gennaro, 'Chiara, Agnese e le prime consorelle' in *Movimento religioso* 171.

52 See n37 above.

53 Cf. Francisci Bartholi de Assisio, *Tractatus de indulgentia S. Mariae de Portiuncula*, ed. P. Sabatier, Paris 1900.

54 S. Nessi, *La basilica di San Francesco e la sua documentazione storica*, Assisi 1982.

55 Cf. M. Bartoli, 'Gregorio IX, Chiara d'Assisi e le prime dispute all'interno del movimento francescano' in *Rendiconto dell'Accademia nazionale dei Lincei. Classe di scienze morali, storiche e filosofiche* 35 (1980) 97–108.

56 *Life of Clare* 37.

57 *Process* 6, 6.

58 Ibid. 7, 2.

59 G. Odoardi, 'Berardo, Pietro, Ottone, Accursio e Adiuto' in *BS* II, Rome 1962, 1271f., with bibliography.

60 The first to draw attention to the importance of Francis' contact with the Moslems was L. Massignon, *Les trois prières d'Abraham. Seconde prière*, Tours 1935; cf. too G. Basetti-Sani, *L'Islam e Francesco d'Assisi*, Florence 1975; Basetti-Sani, *Per un dialogo cristiano musulmano*, Milan 1969.

61 *Legenda Maior* 9, 8 (*Omnibus* 615); cf. G. Basetti-Sani, 'Saraceni' in *DF* 1647–72.

62 Cf. Giordano da Giano, 'Chronica' nn7–8, in *AF* I, 3f; ed. H. Boehmer, Paris 1908, 7.

63 Odoardi, 'Berardo . . .' 1272.

64 *Regula non bullata*, 1221, ed. K. Esser, *Opuscula*, Grottaferrata 1978, 268f., Armstrong *Writings of Francis and Clare* 121.

65 The literature on the crusades is endless. A good general summary is found in the 'Idea of the Crusades' session of the 10th Congresso di Scienze

Storiche, Rome 1955, *Relazioni*, vol. 7, Florence 1955: III, 543–652; VI, 158–61; VII, 243–53. Cf. P. Alphandéry and A. Dupront, *La chrétienté et l'idée de Croisade*, Paris 1959.

66 On the impact of Frederick II on the concept and reality of the crusades, see F. Cardini, *Le crociate tra il mito e la storia*, Rome 1971, 135–42.

67 In the letters to Agnes, there are no terms indicative of enclosure (hermitage, caves, remoteness, etc.) just as the hagiographical references are not to holy nuns but to martyrs who Clare could have learned about from the Breviary.

68 According to the Chronicle of Nicolas Glassberger (*AF* II, Quaracchi 1887, 57) Clare would have played an active part in establishing the Prague monastery because five sisters went from San Damiano, travelling through Trent, in order to *informare* ('train') the sisters at Prague.

69 Third letter to Agnes 19; cf. Augustine, *De sancta virginitate*, ch. 5 n5 (*PL* 40, 398f.).

70 *Regula non bullata* of 1221, 22, 27, *Writings* 128.

71 *Test.Cl.*, 54.

72 Ibid. 56–7.

73 Ibid. 54–5.

74 There are some fascinating pages on the choice of poverty in H. Roggen, *Lo spirito di S. Chiara*, Milan 1970 (trans. into English by J.P. Oligny, *The Spirit of St Clare*, Chicago 1971); see also E. Grau, 'Das Leben der hl. Klara in Armut im kulturellen und religiösen Umfeld ihrer Zeit' in *Wissenschaft und Weisheit* 46 (1983) 175–92; on the rapport with the brethren, cf. L. Hardwick, *La spiritualità di S. Chiara*, Milan 1975, 31–40.

75 The juridical life of the San Damiano community has been mapped by L. Oliger, '*De origine regularum Ordinis S. Clarae*' in *AFH* 5 (1912) 181–209, 413–47. On the links between San Damiano and the other foundations promoted by Ugolino, there is a restrictive and a wide view, between R. Rusconi and R. Manselli in *Movimento religioso* 263–313 ('L'espansione del francescanesimo nel secolo XIII') and 239–62 ('La chiesa e il francescanesimo femminile').

76 On his return from the Holy Land in 1219, Francis accepted the Rule of Ugolino for the Poor Ladies. The bull *Angelis gaudium* of Gregory IX to Agnes of Prague, 11 May 1238 (*BF* I, 242–4) explicitly states this. Cf. Lainati, 'The enclosure of St Clare' 9 n19.

77 Cf. Th. Matura, introduction, *Clare d'Assise: Ecrits*, Paris 1985.

78 *Rule of Clare* 11, 3; cf. the observations of Lainati in 'The enclosure of Clare' 56. During that same year there was an analagous development towards a restrictive interpretation in the case of the Dominican nuns: *Costitutiones* of 1259, ch. XXVIII (cf. Balme-Leladier, *Cartulaire ou histoire diplomatique de Saint Dominique*, Paris 1893, 1897, 1901), cited in de Fontette, *Les religieuses* 112.

79 Bull of Gregory IX, *Ad audientiam* of 21 March 1241 (*BF* I, 290); the condemnation was repeated by Innocent IV in 1250 (*BF* I, 541–2), and Alexander IV in 1257 (*BF* II, 183–184) and in 1261 (*BF* II, 417).

80 *Rule of Clare* 2, 12.

81 Ibid 5, 1.
82 Ibid. 5, 3–4.
83 Ibid. 8, 19.
84 Ibid. 5, 10.
85 Ibid.

Chapter Five. A Woman of Penance

1 M. de Fontette, *Les religieuses à le'âge classique du droit canon. Recherches sur les structures juridiques des branches féminines des ordres.* Paris 1967.
2 *Process* 7, 3.
3 Ibid. 2, 9.
4 Ibid. 10, 3.
5 *Test.Cl.* 61.
6 *Rule of Clare* 3, 1–4.
7 *Regula non bullata* (1221) 3, 10; *Regula bullata* (1223), 3, 3. *Writings.*
8 *Rule of Innocent* IV 4, *Early Documents* 112.
9 Francis' Letter to the Entire Order, 41, 42, *Writings* 60.
10 *Process* 10, 8.
11 *Test.Cl.* 24.
12 Th. Matura, introduction, *Clare d'Assise: Ecrits*, Paris 1985.
13 *Process* 1, 7.
14 Ibid. 14, 2.
15 Ibid. 6, 3; 4, 4.
16 Cf. E. Franceschini, 'Il volto di Chiara' in *Chiara d'Assisi – Rassegna del Protomonastero* 1/2 (1953) 19–22, and *Nel segno di Francesco*, S. Maria degli Angeli-Assisi 1988, 362–66.
17 *Life of Clare* 20.
18 *Process* 2, 17.
19 Cf. A. Vauchez, *La sainteté en Occident aux derniers siècles du Moyen Age, d'après les procès de canonisation et les documents hagiographiques*, Rome 1981, 509–11, which in its turn refers to Raymond of Capua, *Legenda maior S. Catherinae Senensis* in *AA.SS.* 30 April, t. III, Paris 1866, 940b; and the canonisation process of Clare of Montefalco in ASV *Riti, Proc.* 2929, f.140 and f.434 (these two folios were not included in the critical edition of the process, but ed. E. Menestò, Perugia/Florence 1984).
20 *Process* 1, 9.
21 Ibid. 1, 9.
22 Ibid. 1, 7.
23 Ibid. 8, 2–3.
24 Cf. Matthew 4:17.
25 Cf. R. Pazzelli, 'Penitenza, mortificazione' in *DF* 1271–96.
26 Cf. G.G. Meersseman, *Dossier de l'Ordre de la pénitence au XIIIe siècle*, Fribourg 1961; *L'Ordine della penitenza di San Francesco d'Assisi nel sec. XIII*, Atti del 1° Convegno di Studi Francescani (Assisi 3–5 July 1972); *I frati penitenti di San Francesco nella società del Due e Trecento*, Atti del 2° Convegno (Rome 12–14 October 1976); *Il movimento francescano*

della penitenza nella società medioevale, Atti del 3° convegno (Padua 25–27 September 1979); *La 'Supra montem' di Niccolò IV (1289): genesi e diffusione di una regola*. Atti del 5° Convegno (Ascoli Piceno 26–27 October 1987).

27 Cf. I. Magli, *Gli uomini della penitenza. Lineamenti antropologici del medioevo italiano*, Milan 1977, 39.

28 *The Little Book of Angela of Foligno*, 'Instruction II'; cf. A.M. Pompei, 'Concetto e practica della penitenza in Margherita da Cortona e Angela da Foligno' in *La 'Supra montem' di Niccolò IV* 381–423.

29 Jacques de Vitry, *Vita Mariae Oigniacensis*, 23 AA.SS. 23 June, t. V, 552a.

30 Margaret of Cortona, for instance, ended up by mutilating herself. Cf. Pompei, 'Concetto e pratica' 392.

31 *Process* 2, 5; cf. C. Carozzi, 'Une béguine joachimite: Douceline, soeur d'Hugues de Digne' in *Franciscains d'Oc. les spirituels, ca. 1280–1324* (Cahiers de Fanjeaux 10), Toulouse 1975, 183.

32 I. Magli, *Gli uomini della penitenza* 47.

33 Ibid. 42f.

34 Cf. A. Vauchez, 'La sainteté féminine dans le mouvement franciscain' in *Les laïcs au Moyen Age* Paris, 1987, 194.

35 *Process* 10, 7.

36 Ibid. 4, 5; see also 3, 5; 6, 4.

37 *Ibid.* 1, 8; *Life of Clare* 18.

38 Fasting, or not eating, is one of the most interesting problems of women's penance in the Middle Ages; cf. R.M. Bell, *Holy Anorexia*, Chicago 1985, 145f.

39 In fact, throughout history there has never been a univocal concept of the body (as there has with the separate members, the arm or the hand), so much so that one can almost speak of a Greek body, a medieval body, a contemporary body, meaning that these concepts or ideas of the body are layered one upon the other. Cf. M. de Certeau, 'Histoires de corps' in *Esprit* 62 (1982) 179–87; A. Ghisalberti, 'La rappresentazione del corpo nel pensiero medievale' in *Communicazioni sociali* 2/3–4 (1980) 19–32.

40 J. Le Goff, 'Franciscanisme et modèles culturels' in *Francescanesimo e vita religiosa dei laici nel '200*, Assisi 1981, 121.

41 Cf. Matthew 15:18–19; Mark 7:23; Second Letter to all the Faithful, 37.

42 Admonition X, *Writings* 30.

43 'The term "body" or "flesh" here does not mean the body in the biological or psychological sense but the egoistic thoughts of a man. In the end, it is the person himself who must bear responsibility for his own acts. He sins because he is the slave of his body; our enemy is not primarily the devil but our own body in the sense of our 'I' with its egocentric tendencies', N. Nguyen-van-Khanh, *Gesú Cristo nel pensiero di san Francesco secondo i suoi scritti*, Milan 1984, 165.

44 Admonition V, *Writings* 29. For an analysis of this text, cf. Nguyen-van-Khanh, *Gesú Cristo*, 104–11.

45 *Admonition V, Writings* 29.

46 2 Celano 126.

47 2 Celano 126; *Legend of Perugia* 24; St Bonaventure, *Legenda Maior* 5, 11; *Omnibus* 466, 1001, 682 and 686.
48 Cf. 2 Celano 116.
49 Cf. R. Manselli, *San Francesco d'Assisi*, Rome 1980, 324f. Trans. into English by Paul Duggan, *St Francis of Assisi*, Chicago 1988.
50 Cf. Pompei, 'Concetto e practica' 421.
51 Ibid. 391f.
52 *Process* 2, 7.
53 *Test.Cl.* 27–8.
54 The text which reveals most about how hard those days were at San Damiano is the letter of notification of the death of St Clare, *Early Documents* 122.
55 *Process* 2, 4.
56 *Life of Clare.* 38; *Process* 8, 3.
57 *Rule of Clare* 8, 12–13; Exhortation of St Francis to the Poor Ladies of San Damiano, *Early Documents* 250; *Legend of Perugia* 45, *Omnibus* 1024.
58 *Process* 3, 9.
59 Ibid. 2, 3; *Life of Clare* 38.
60 *Process* 2, 3; 3, 9.
61 *Life of Clare* 38.
62 *Process* 10, 11 (translator's version).
63 Cf. A. Thier and A. Calufetti, *Il libro della beata Angela da Foligno*, Grottaferrata, 1985, 242, 132–6.
64 *Process* 1, 17.
65 *Life of Clare* 28.
66 *Process* 1, 11.
67 *Life of Clare* 14.
68 Salvator Butler, *We were with St Francis*, Edizioni Porziuncola, ch. 2.
69 *Testament of Francis* 3, *Writings* 154.
70 Ibid. 16.
71 *Regula non bullata* 9, 2.
72 Matthew 5:5.
73 *Legend of Perugia* 24.
74 Letter of James 1:2–4.
75 The episode is in the *Fioretti* ch. 8; see also 2 Celano 213; *Legend of Perugia* 43; *Mirror of Perfection* 100.
76 2 Celano 128.
77 *Regula non bullata* 7, 16.
78 For this kind of spirituality, the prime reference can be no other than the *De Contemptu Mundi* of Lotario di Segni, that is Pope Innocent III.
79 *Test.Cl.* 10.
80 First letter of Clare 19, 22, 25.
81 *Process* 2, 7.
82 Ibid. 2, 6.

Chapter Six. The Theology of Clare

1 Cf. E. Gilson, 'La philosophie franciscaine' in *Saint François d'Assise, son oeuvre, son influence 1226–1926*, Paris 1927, 147–75.

2 Cf. N. Nguyen-van-Khanh, *Gesú Cristo nel pensiero di san Francesco secondo i suoi scritti*, Milan 1984, 23.

3 *Test.Cl.* 19–20.

4 Cf. K. Esser, 'Der heiligen Kirche Bild und Spiegel. Zur Siebenhundertjahrfeier des Todes der hl. Klara von Assisi' in *Wissenschaft und Weisheit* 16 (1953) 81–9; trans into Italian, 'S. Chiara d'Assisi immagine e specchio della santa Chiesa' in *Temi spirituali*, Milan 1981, 211–30.

5 On the importance of example in the spirituality of Francis and his companions, see G. Boccali, 'Esempio, testimonianza, scandalo' in *DF* 493–512.

6 Fourth letter of Clare, 14–18.

7 The motive of imitating Christ which is only mentioned in the Life of Francis, is spelt out much more explicitly by Clare: cf. L. Hardick, 'Erläuterungen 7. Die Nachfolge Christi' in *Leben und Schriften der hl. Klara von Assisi*, 5th edn. Werl/Westf. 1980, 182–6; in Italian, *La spiritualità di S. Chiara. Commento alla vita e agli scritti della santa*, Milan 1975, 78.

8 *Process* 9, 4.

9 Ibid. 9, 10.

10 Ibid. 10, 8.

11 Ibid.

12 Ibid.

13 Cf. G.B. Montorsi, *Chiara d'Assisi maestra di vita*, Padua 1985, 76–9.

14 *Process*, 3, 30.

15 Ibid. 7, 9.

16 *Life of Clare* 29.

17 *Fioretti* 25. For reconstruction of this episode, cf. E. Franceschini, 'La notte di Natale del 1252' in *Chiara d'Assisi – Rassegna del Protomonastero* 2 (1954) 69–74.

18 *Process* 4, 16.

19 *Rule of Clare* 2, 24.

20 There is an affective crescendo; Francis began with Isaiah 9:6, added 'most holy and beloved', cf. Office of the Passion XV, 7, while Clare turned it into 'most holy and most beloved'.

21 Cf. I. Omaechevarria, 'Croce, crocifissione, crocifisso, passione' in *DF* 301–12; Hardick in *La spiritualità di S. Chiara*; K. Esser and E. Grau, *La risposta all'amore*, Milan 1978, 41–55 (trans. into English by I. Brady, *Love's Reply* Chicago 1963, 22–31); and, above all, Oktavian von Rieden (Schmucki), 'Das Leiden Christi im Leben des hl. Franziskus von Assisi. Eine quellenvergleichende Untersuchung im Lichte der zeitgenössischen Passionsfrömmigkeit' in *CF* 30 (1960) 5–30, 129–45, 241–63, 353–97. Trans. into English by Ignatius McCormick, 'The Passion of Christ in the life of St Francis of Assisi. A comparative study of the sources in the light

of the devotion to the Passion practised in this time', *Greyfriars Review* 4 (1990) 1–101.

22 *Process* 11, 2.

23 Ibid. 10, 3.

24 Ibid. 14, 8.

25 *Life of Clare* 30.

26 Cf. E. Franceschini, 'Note sull' "Ufficio della Passione del Signore" ' in *Quaderni di spiritualità francescana* 4 (1962) 42–62; repr. in *Nel segno di Francesco*, S. Maria degli Angeli-Assisi 1988, 146–69, which also includes the *Riflessioni conclusive sull'Ufficio della Passione* 164–9.

27 For the observations which follow, see Oktavian von Rieden (Schmucki), *Das Leiden Christi; Preghiera liturgica secondo l'esempio e l'insegnamento di san Francesco d'Assisi*, Rome.

28 On the office of the Passion, see K. Esser, *Die Opuscula des hl. Franziskus von Assisi. Neue textkritische Edition*, Grottaferrata 1976, 322–53; D. Gagnan, 'Office de la Passion, prière quotidienne de saint François', in *Antonianum* 55 (1980) 3–86; J. De Schampheleer, *L'Office de la Pâque*, Paris, 1963.

29 Cf. Nguyen-van-Khanh, *Gesú Cristo*, 200.

30 *Life of Clare* 30; *Process* 10, 10.

31 Cf. von Rieden, 'Das Leiden Christi' 390 ('The Passion of Christ' 94); Nguyen-van-Khanh, *Gesú Cristo* 145.

32 Z. Lazzeri, 'L'orazione delle cinque piaghe recitata da S. Chiara' in *AFH* 16 (1923) 246–9.

33 *Life of Clare* 30; *Process* 10, 10 (translator's version).

34 *Life of Clare*, 30.

35 The study which best throws this originality of Clare into relief is that of Th. Matura, introduction, 'Le contenu des écrits', in *Claire d'Assisi: Écrits*, Paris 1985.

36 'Of the eight passages which treat of spiritual experience, the last five are devoted to this nuptial union ... obviously it is here that we best catch the echoes of her personal experience as applied to Agnes', ibid.

37 Cf. Esser and Grau, *La risposta all'amore* 208–13; *Love's Reply* 129–41.

38 There is a large bibliography on the position of women in medieval culture and society; for an introduction, see M. Bartoli, 'Donna e società nel tardo medioevo. Guida bibliografica' in *Cultura e scuola* 73 (1980) 81–8, and the more recent contributions in M.C. De Matteis, *Idee sulla donna nel medioevo*, Bologna 1981. A less negative impression is found in the writings of J. Leclercq, *I monaci e il matrimonio. Un'indagine sul XII secolo*, Turin 1984, which ignores the very real misogyny of medieval men. Cf. G. Duby, *Il cavaliere, la donna e il prete*, Bari 1982 (trans. into English by Barbara Bray, *The Knight, the Lady and the Priest*, London 1985).

39 *Life of Clare*, dedicatory letter.

40 Cf. for example J. Leclercq, 'Il monachesimo femminile nei secoli XII e XIII,' in *Movimento religioso femminile e francescanesimo nel secolo XIII*, Assisi 1980, 98. Interesting, because this argument is close to the letter of Jacques de Vitry cited by Duby in *Il cavaliere* ... 187f. (*The Knight* ... 212)

where two unedited sermons are mentioned: *Bibliothèque Nationale 17509; 3284, Cambrai 534.*

41 St Augustine, *De sancta virginitate* XI 11 (*PL* 40, 401).

42 This link found its strongest expression in St Bernard; cf. J. Leclercq, *Le mariage vu par les moines au XIIe siècle*, Paris 1983, 113; also A. Vauchez, *Les laïcs au Moyen Âge*, Paris 1987, esp. part IV, 'La femme entre le mariage et les noces spirituelles', 187–236.

43 Cf. Th. Matura, introduction, *Ecrits* 65–7.

44 First letter of Clare, 5–7.

45 The account of St Agnes' martyrdom, parts of which are included in the Office of the feast of the saint, was wrongly attributed to St Ambrose. It is given in *PL* 17, 735–42.

46 First letter of Clare, 12–13.

47 Cf. A. Dufourcq, 'Agnès, sainte' in *DHGE* I, Paris, 1912, 971f; E. Josi, 'Agnese, santa, martire di Roma' in *BS* I, Rome 1961, 382–407.

48 Ch. A. Lainati, *Santa Chiara d'Assisi. Cenni biografici di santa Agnese d'Assisi e lettere di Santa Chiara alla b. Agnese di Praga*, Assisi 1969, 101–25; A. Brunacci, 'Agnese di Assisi', in *BS* I, Rome 1961, 369f.

49 Fourth letter of Clare 7–8.

50 See ch. 4 nn57–66 above.

51 Antiphon: Sancta Maria in the Office of the Passion I, 2; cf. *Writings*, 82.

52 See n46 above.

53 Cf. Hardick in *La spiritualità di S. Chiara* 125–33; R. Ch. Dhont, *Claire parmi ses soeurs*. Paris 1973; trans. into English, *Clare among her sisters*, New York 1987.

54 Third letter of Clare, 18–19.

55 Blessing of St Clare 1–4, 6–13. The last lines are slightly different from Armstrong's trans., *Writings*, 231–2.

56 On the Marian spirituality of Bernard of Clairveaux, cf. J. Leclercq, *La donna e le donne in San Bernardo*, Milan 1985, 80f.

57 The so-called 'last will' mentioned by Clare in the *Rule* (6, 7–8), *Writings* 46.

58 *Rule of Clare* 2, 24; cf. n19 above.

59 Ibid. 8, 5.

60 Ibid. 12, 13.

61 See ch. 5 nn52 and 61–4 above.

Chapter Seven. Clare as Another Francis

1 This idea of Clare as an *alter Franciscus* is a natural development of the idea of Francis as an *alter Christus*. On this, see Stanislao da Campagnola, *L'angelo del sesto sigillo e l' 'alter Christus'. Genesi e sviluppo di due temi francescani nei secoli XIII–XIV*, Rome 1971.

2 *Test.Cl.*, 79.

3 M. Bartoli, 'Gregorio IX, Chiara d'Assisi e le prime dispute all'interno del movimento francescano' in *Rendiconti Accademia Nazionale dei Lincei* 35 (1980) 97–108.

4 *Process* 2, 22.

5 *Life of Clare* 14.

6 E. Pásztor, 'San Francisco e il cardinale Ugolino nella "questione frances-cana"' in *CF* 46 (1976) 209–39. Trans. into English by Patrick Colbourne, 'St Francis, Cardinal Hugolino, and the "Franciscan Question"' in *Greyfri-ars Review* (Sept. 1987) 1–29.

7 *Privilegium paupertatis* (1228), *Early Documents* 103.

8 In that same year, 1230, problems about poverty were also to arise in the monastery of Monticelli near Florence, if we are to judge by the letter Clare's sister Agnes wrote to her from there. Cf. Z. Lazzeri, 'Il processo di canonizzazione di S. Chiara d'Assisi' in *AFH* 13 (1920) 496f, where the Latin text is given along with those of Wadding and the Chronicle of the XXIV Generals.

9 Cf. Thomas of Eccleston, *On the coming of the Friars Minor to England*, ed. A.G. Little and J.R.H. Moorman, Manchester 1951, 65–7.

10 For the importance of the 1230 chapter, see R. Brooke, *Early Franciscan Government. Elias to Bonaventure*, Cambridge 1959, 130; Gratien de Paris, *Histoire de la fondation et de l'évolution de l'Order des Frères Mineurs au XIIIe siècle* (bibliography updated by M. D'Alatri and S. Gieben), Rome 1982, 111–20; J. Moorman, *A History of the Franciscan Order from its origins to the year 1517*, Oxford 1968, 89–91; D. Nimmo, *Reform and Division in the Medieval Franciscan Order*, Rome 1987, 56–64.

11 E. Lempp, *Frère Elie de Cortone. Étude biographique*, Paris 1901, 69–100, had pointed out the inconsistency in Eccleston's account, whereby Elias, aspiring to be General, alienated those who would have to elect him. See also G. Barone, 'Frate Elia' in *Bull. Ist. Stor. Ital. per il Medioevo e Arch. Muratoriano*, 85 (1974–75) 89–114; A. Pompei, 'Frate Elia nel giudizio dei contemporanei e dei posteri' in *MF* 54 (1954) 539–635.

12 The fundamental study with a critical edition of this bull is that of H. Grundmann, 'Die Bulle *Quo elongati* Papst Gregors IX in *AFH* 54 (1961) 1–25.

13 Gregory IX, *Quo elongati* 3 in *FF* 2197 n2731.

14 Gregory went so far as to affirm that even had Francis written his Testa-ment while General of the Order, it would still not be binding on his successors because he did not have *imperium par in parem*. This juridical formula was particularly 'modern' having been first used by Innocent III in 1200: cf. Grundmann, 'Die Bulle' n4 and W. Ullmann, *Medieval Papal-ism, The Political theories of medieval canonists*, London 1949, 155.

15 Gregory IX, *Quo elongati* 11 in *FF* 2201f. n2739.

16 'The juridical rigour of such a decision must have been like a grievous wound in the hearts of many of his sons', de Paris, *Histoire de la fondation* 119.

17 *Life of Clare* 37.

18 L. Hardick in *La spiritualità di S. Chiara. Commento alla vita e agli scritti della santa*, Milan 1975, 31f.

19 R. B. Brooke, *Scripta Leonis, Rufini et Angeli sociorum S. Francisci*, Oxford 1970, 4–6, text of the letter 86–9.

20 A general introduction to the problem of the Franciscan sources and the *Florilegium* in particular is found in Stanislao da Campagnola, *Francesco d'Assisi nei suoi scritti e nelle sue biografie dei secoli XIII–XIV*, Assisi 1977, 67–123 esp. 81–9.

21 2 Celano 204.

22 *Rule of Clare* 6, 2–5.

23 M. Bartoli, 'Chiara testimone di Francesco' in *Quaderni catanesi di studi classici e medievali* 1/2 (1979) 467–98.

24 2 Celano 207.

25 On the many references to folk culture in the attitudes of Francis, see R. Manselli, *San Francesco d'Assisi* Rome 1980, esp. 88–91 (trans. into English by Paul Duggan, *St Francis of Assisi*, Chicago 1988, 79–83); Manselli, 'Appunti sulla religiosità popolare in Francesco d'Assisi' in *Pascua Mediaevalia. Studies voor Prof. Dr. J.M. De Smet*, Louvain 1983, 295–311: on this particular episode cf. Manselli, 'Il gesto come predicazione per san Francesco' in *CF* 51 (1981) 5–16; trans. into English by Patrick Colbourne and Edward Hagman, 'Gesture as Sermon in St Francis of Assisi' in *Greyfriars Review* 6 (1992) 37–48.

26 *Life of Clare* 23.

27 *Dicta B. Aegidii Ord. Min*, n73 in *AA.SS.* 23 April t. III, Paris 1866, 238b–239a; a reconstruction of this episode can be found in J. Joergensen, *Saint Francis of Assisi*, 1966.

28 *Life of Clare* 12; 18; 31. It is interesting to note that each of these three times concerns an episode in which Francis opens Clare to a new attitude (on her election as abbess and on fasting).

29 *Process* 3, 29.

30 Cf. J. le Goff, 'I sogni nella cultura e nella psicologia dell'Occidente medievale' in *Tempo della Chiesa e tempo del mercante*, Turin 1977, 284n.

31 'Here we have an aspect which – perhaps through lack of material – has not played much part in studies of medieval monastic culture; namely that of the ways and forms in which women, whether abbesses or simple nuns, gave themselves to work for each others' salvation, by preaching, instructions, through explaining their own mystical experiences and even their dreams', E. Pásztor, *S. Chiara da Montefalco nella religiosità femminila del suo tempo*, Perugia/Florence 1985, 203.

32 For a study of the problems of women's mysticism in the thirteenth and fourteenth centuries, see *Temi e problemi della mystica femminile trecentesca*, Convegni del centro di studi sulla spiritualità medievale XX, Todi 1983.

33 Cf. Pásztor, *Chiara da Montefalco* 245.

34 Cf. C. Frugoni, 'Le mistiche le visioni e l'iconografia. Rapporti ed influssi,' in *Temi e problemi* 137–79.

35 For Rose of Viterbo, apart from A.M. Vacca, *La mente e la croce. S. Rosa da Viterbo*, Rome 1982, see F. Casolini, 'Rosa da Viterbo' in *BS* XI, Rome 1968, 413–25; G. Abate, *S. Rosa da Viterbo terziaria francescana. Fonti*

storiche della vita e loro revisione critica, Rome 1952; also ch. 8 n53 below.

36 On visions in general see E. Benz, *Die Vision*, Stuttgart 1969; P. Dinzelbacher, *Vision und Visionliteratur im Mittelalter*, Monographien zur Geschichte des Mittelalters 23, Stuttgart 1981.

37 *Test.Cl.*, 9–14.

38 *Life of Clare*, 2.

39 *Process* 6, 12.

40 Ibid. 3, 28.

41 Ibid. 3, 25.

42 *Life of Clare*, 31.

43 Note the difficulty of distinguishing between sleeping and waking in almost all ecstatic experiences. Purely as an example from a different cultural context than that of Clare, we cite the case of Angela of Foligno, ten to twelve years after Clare's death, which is a very interesting text: 'At one time I was shown those eyes . . . *I do not know whether I was asleep or awake* but I found myself in the midst of this immense and inexpressible joy', *The book of God's love*, Rome 1973, 67.

44 Cf. A. Vauchez at the Meeting in Assisi: *Movimento religioso femminile e francescanesimo nel secolo XIII*, Assisi 1980; also M. Bartoli, 'Analisi storica e interpretazione psicanalisi di una visione di S. Chiara d'Assisi' in *AFH* 73 (1980) 449–72 – trans. into English by M. Balestrieri, 'Historical analysis and psychoanalytic interpretations of a vision of Clare of Assisi' in *Greyfriars Review* 6/2 (1992) 189–209.

45 We see better how to value the evidence given at a canonisation process when we compare it with literary works properly so called which are taken from the evidence. The *Life* is an example. Cf. J.-C. Schmitt, 'La parola addomesticata. San Domenico, il gatto e le donne di Fanjeaux' in *Quaderni Storici* 41 (May–Aug. 1979) 416–39.

46 *Process* 4, 1 and 16.

47 *Legend of Perugia* 42–5; *Compilatio Assisiensis* 83–5; *2 Celano* 213; *Speculum Perfectionis* 91–100; all in *Omnibus*.

48 The bibliography on the language of dreams and the language of vision is vast. For a start: Bianca e Franco Fornari, *Psicanalisi e ricerca letteraria*, Milan 1974; A. Besançon, 'Vers une histoire psychanalytique' I and II in *Annales E.S.C.* 3–4 (1969) 594–616 and 1011–33.

49 Cf. S. Freud, *The Interpretation of Dreams*.

50 It is this characteristic which makes dream language into symbolic language. 'In the language of symbol, the interior experience is expressed as if it were a sense experience, that is, as if it were something which had happened or been undergone in the external world. Here the exterior world is a symbol of the interior one, a symbol of our souls and our minds', E. Fromm, *The Forgotten Language*, New York 1951.

51 *Life of Clare* 3.

52 Ibid. 37.

53 Clare's writings show a good knowledge of the New Testament and at

least a working familiarity with several books of the Old, especially the Song of Songs.

54 Clare's Rule shows familiarity with earlier monastic rules. As regards hagiography, which formed the bulk of that preaching Clare so loved to hear, we must remember that here we are meaning a hagiography which was primarily Franciscan.

55 Francis, *Canticle of the Creatures*.

56 John 13:4–5.

57 St Bonaventure, *Legenda Maior*, 2, 6 (*Omnibus* 643).

58 This is recorded at least four times during the canonisation process.

59 *Process* 10, 6.

60 Cf. E. Bertaud and A. Rayez, 'Échelle spirituelle' in *DS* IV/I, Paris 1960, 62–86.

61 *Rule of St Benedict* 7, 5–7, trans. by Abbot Justin McCann, London 1952.

62 Cf. C. Cargnoni, 'Umiltà, umilazione' in *DF* 1869–902.

63 2 Celano 123; cf. also *Legenda maior* 6, 6; *Legend of Perugia* 23.

64 Cf. *Process* 6, 13.

65 Cf. L. Reau, *Iconographie de l'art chrétien* III/I Paris 1958, 209f.

66 2 Celano 199.

67 Celano, *Treatise on the Miracles* 182 (*Omnibus*).

68 Cf. M. Schmidt, 'Miroir' in *DS* X, Paris 1980, 1290–1303.

69 H. Grabes, *Speculum, Miror und Looking-Glass. Kontinuität und Originalität der Spiegelmetapher in den Buchtiteln des Mittelalters und der englischen Literatur des 13. bis 17. Jahrhunderts*, Tubingen 1973.

70 *Test.Cl.* 38.

71 Cf. *Temi e problemi* (n 32 above) and *Vita e spiritualità della beata Angela da Foligno*, ed. P. Clement Schmitt, Perugia 1987.

Chapter Eight. Mother of the Sisters and Defender of the City

1 St Augustine, *De util. cred.* XVI, 34 (*PL* 42, 89f).

2 Cf. U. Fracassini, 'Miracolo' in *Enciclopedia Italiana* XXIII, Rome 1934, 432–25; also A. Michel, 'Miracle' in *Dictionnaire de Théologie Catholique* X/2, Paris 1929, 1798–859.

3 Cf. J. le Goff, *Il meraviglioso e il quotidiano nell'Occidente medievale*, Bari 1983.

4 Cf. P. A. Sigal, *L'homme et le miracle dans la France médiévale (XI–XII siècle)*, Paris, 1985, 293; M. Goodich, *Vita Perfecta: The Ideal of Sainthood in the Thirteenth Century*, Stuttgart 1982; cf. *CF* 53 (1983) 426–9.

5 Cf. A. Vauchez, 'L'efficacité de la sainteté. Rèflexion sur le rôle des saints dans la piété chrétienne des origines au Moyen Age' in *Saints d'hier et sainteté d'aujourd'hui. Recherches et débats du Centre catholique des intellectuels français*, Paris 1966.

6 Cf. A. Vauchez, *La sainteté en Occident aux derniers siècles du Moyen Age, d'après les procès de canonisation et les documents hagiographiques*, Rome 1981, 499–502; Sigal, *L'homme et le miracle* 17.

7 There is a vast literature on this subject; see, as an introduction, P. Brown, *The Cult of the Saints*, Chicago 1981.

8 Sigal, *L'homme et le miracle* 18; for Thomas à Becket see R.C. Finucane, *Miracles and Pilgrims. Popular Beliefs in Medieval England* London 1977.

9 Cf. Vauchez, *La sainteté*, 450–55 and 583.

10 Thomas Aquinas, *Summa Theologica* I q. 105, art. 7.

11 *Life of Clare* II, 49.

12 For this distinction, see Sigal, *L'homme et le miracle* esp. 289–93.

13 Originally, 'miracles' and 'biography' were two distinct literary *genres* which were rarely brought together into one book. Cf. Sigal, *L'homme et le miracle* 289f. We see the same distinction in the Franciscan context in, for example, Thomas of Celano's *Treatise on Miracles*.

14 For this link between holy women and new urban developments, we must refer to A. I. Galletti, 'I francescani ed il suo culto dei santi nell'Italia centrale' in *Francescanesimo e vita religiosa dei laici nel '200*, Assisi 1981, 313–63; also A. Benvenuti Papi, 'Una terra di sante e di città. Suggestioni agiografiche in Italia' in *Il movimento religioso femminile in Umbria nei secoli XIII–XIV*, ed. R. Rusconi, Florence/Perugia 1984, 183–202.

15 Cf. the table of miracles during her life on pp. 174–5.

16 Cf. Sigal, *L'homme et le miracle* 18; for miracles in the Gospels, a good introduction is J. Jeremias, *The Theology of the New Testament* I, 'The Preaching of Jesus'.

17 Visions were considered to transcend corporal and spatial limits in the experiences common to women religious of the thirteenth century. An outstanding example is Margherita da Città di Castello who was 'blind as to her bodily eyes but clear and luminous in her mind', *Life* ch. II 24, ed. in *Analecta Bollandiana* 19 (1900) 21–36; cf. C. Frugoni, 'Su un "immaginario" possibile di Margherita da Città di Castello' in *Il movimento religioso femminile in Umbria nei secoli XIII–XIV*, 203–216.

18 *Process* 13, 1.

19 *Life of Clare* 7.

20 *Process*, 14, 6; 15, 2.

21 *Rule of Clare*, 5, 11–13.

22 *Life of Clare*, 14.

23 *Process* 1, 15; 2, 14; cf. 3, 26.

24 Cf. Sigal, *L'homme et le miracle* 30.

25 *Life of Clare* 16.

26 Gregory the Great, *Dialogorum* book II, chs 28–9 (*PL* 66, 186ff.).

27 There is a vast literature on the concept of poverty but we must acknowledge the research of M. Mollat, esp. his 'La notion de la pauvreté au Moyen Age' in *Revue d'histoire de l'église de France* 52 (1966) 5–23; cf. G.S. Polica, 'Storia della povertà e storia dei poveri' in *Studi medievali* 17 (1976) 363–91. For the most recent bibliography on Franciscan and Poor Clare poverty, see L. Hardick, 'Povertà, povero' in *DF* 1375–412.

28 *Process* 6, 16.

29 Cf. Matthew 14:13–21; Mark 6:32–44; Luke 9:10–17; John 6: 1–13.

30 Cf. Sigal, *L'homme et le miracle* 272.

31 *Life of Clare*, 15.
32 *Process*, 3, 13.
33 See the table on p. 174.
34 *Life of Clare*, 32.
35 *Process* 1, 18.
36 Ibid. 9, 7.
37 Ibid. 3, 11; 4, 7.
38 Ibid. 11, 1.
39 Ibid. 7, 12.
40 *Life of Clare*, 32.
41 Ibid. 35.
42 *Process* 14, 5.
43 Ibid. 4, 11.
44 See, for example, the life of Mary of Oignies by Jacques de Vitry: 'When the Lord did anything good through her, she would attribute it to the merits of someone else. She never sought her own glory but referred everything to him from whom all good things come', *Vita Mariae Oigniacensis* V, n46, *AA.SS.* 23 June t. V, 558a.
45 *Process* 3, 15; 9, 6.
46 Ibid. 2, 18.
47 In the second book of the *Life*, devoted to miracles after her death, there are fourteen miracles detailed of which six were worked for children.
48 Clare even inserted a mention of the Child Jesus into her Rule, to invite the sisters to wear poor clothes as he did (*Rule of Clare* 2, 24). Devotion to the Child in the crib is typically Franciscan; we recall Greccio, 1 Celano 84–7. See also ch. 7 nn 8–20 above.)
49 *Process* 9, 4.
50 Cf. Jacques de Vitry VI, n55.
51 *Process* 16, 4.
52 Cf. *Legend of Perugia* 44.
53 On Umiliana de' Cerchi, see A. Benvenuti Papi, 'Umiliana dei Cerchi' in *Studi Francescani* 77 (1980) 87–117. For Rose, see Mariano D'Alatri, 'Rosa da Viterbo' in *Italia Franc.* 44 (1969) 122–30; D'Alatri, 'Rosa da Viterbo tra mito e storia' in *Lunario Romano 1979*, Rome 1979, 345–54; also the works of A. M. Vacca, *La menta e la croce*, Rome 1982; cf. *CF* 55 (1985) 183.
54 *Process* 1, 4–5; *Life of Clare* 1.
55 See A. Benvenuti Papi, 'Margherita filia Jerusalem. Santa Margherita da Cortona e il superamento mistico della crociata' in *I. Italia, Orient, Mediterraneo. Toscana e terrasanta nel medioevo*, ed. Alinea, 117–37.
56 The Portiuncola Indulgence is a particularly interesting example here; the debate among scholars about its origin is still open; cf. L. Canonici, *Porziuncola*, in *DF*, 1335–54.
57 The most important study of devotion to the Eucharist is *Studia Eucharistica (DCC Anni a condito festo Sanctissimi Corporis Christi 1246–1949)*, Anversa 1946, with bibliography. See also F. Calley, *Le origini della festa*

del Corpus Domini, Rovigo 1958; E. McDonnel, *The Beguines and Begards in Medieval Culture, with special emphasis on the Belgian scene*, New Brunswick/New Jersey 1954, 299–319.

58 *Process*, 2, 20; 3, 18; 4, 14; 6, 10; 7, 6; 9, 2; 10, 9; 12, 8.

59 The prototype here is St Leo the Great, see the bibliography on him in G. Zannoni, 'Leone I, papa' in *BS* VIII, Rome 1966, 1232–78.

60 *Life of Clare* 21, 22.

61 *Process* 9, 2.

62 Cf. E. Franceschini, 'S. Chiara e i Saraceni' in *Chiara d'Assisi – Rassegna del Protomonastero* 1 (1955) 147–57; Franceschini, 'I due assalti dei Saraceni a S. Damiano e ad Assisi' in *Aevum* 27 (1953) 289–306; also cf. Franceschini, *Nel segno di Francesco*, S. Maria degli Angeli-Assisi 1988, 381–405.

63 *Life of Clare*, 21.

64 Genesis 18:16–33.

65 *Process* 9, 2.

66 Ibid. 3, 19; 9, 3.

67 An example of this rapport is studied in G. Casagrande, 'Forme di vita religiosa femminile nell'area di Città di Castello nel sec. XIII' in *Il movimento religioso femminile in Umbria*, 125–57. A few years later the same words of prayer are found on the lips of Chiara da Montefalco in reference to Spoleto, in M. Faloci-Pulignani, 'La vita di S. Chiara da Montefalco scritta da Berengario di S Africano' in *Archivio storico per le Marche e l'Umbria* 2 (1885) 262.

68 Cf. A. Benvenuti Papi, 'Una terra di sante e di città' in *Il Movimento religioso femminile in Umbria*, 183–202.

69 Cf. A. I. Galletti, 'I francescani' 313–63; Vauchez, *La sainteté en Occident*, 559–608.

70 Cf. F. Casolini, *Il protomonastero di S. Chiara in Assisi*, Milan 1950, 33–50.

71 For the documentation of the transformation of the church of San Giorgio into the Basilica of S. Chiara, cf. M. Bihl, 'Documenta inedita Archivi Protomonasterii S. Clarae Assisi' in *AFH* 5 (1912) 663f.

Chapter Nine. The Liturgy of the 'Transitus'

1 *Process* 9, 10.

2 Cf. J.-F. Godet, introduction, *Clare d'Assise: Écrits*, Paris 1985.

3 Cf. Z. Lazzeri, *La vita di S. Chiara, raccolta e tradotta da tutte le fonti conosciute . . . per un toscano del Cinquecento*, Quaracchi 1920, ch. 36, 149.

4 *Life of Clare* 39–48.

5 Cf. Ph. Ariès, *L'homme devant la mort*, Paris 1977, 13–16; Ariès, *Essais sur l'histoire de la mort en Occident du Moyen Age à nos jours*, Paris 1975.

6 *Life of Clare* 39; on illness in Clare's life, cf. O. Schmucki, 'Infermità' in *DF* 731–45.

7 *Leg. vers.* vv. 1167–394, ed. B. Bughetti, in *AFH* 5 (1912) 467–73.

8 *Rule of Innocent IV 1247, Early Documents* 109f.

9 'Clare was also – and it is a great historical "first" – the first woman to compose a Rule for women', Th. Matura, introduction, *Écrits.*

10 *Life of Clare* 39.

11 Ibid. 40.

12 There was just such a circle around Clare of Montefalco; cf. E. Pásztor, *S. Chiara da Montefalco nella religiosità femminila del suo tempo*, Perugia/Florence 1985, 185f.

13 *Life of Clare* 40.

14 Cf. *Il dolore e la morte nella spiritualità dei secoli XII e XIII*, V Congress of Centro di studi sulla spiritualità medievale, Todi, 7–10 October 1962, publ. Todi 1967.

15 *Quia vos* was inserted in full into the bull *Solet annuere* of 9 August 1253 in which Innocent IV approved the Rule of Clare. Cf. *Early Documents* 61f.

16 F. Pagnotti, *Niccolò da Calvi e la sua vita di Innocenzo IV*, in *Archivio della Soc. Romana di Storia Patria* 21 (1898) 107.

17 *Life of Clare* 41.

18 Ibid.

19 Cf. G. Miccoli, 'S. Francesco d'Assisi e la povertà' in *Seguire Gesú povero*, Magnano 1954, 139; Miccoli, 'La proposta cristiana di Francesco d'Assisi' in *Studi medievale* 24 (1983) 42 and n62.

20 *Early Documents* 105f.

21 *Rule of Clare* 2, 5.

22 We know nothing of these two brothers beyond what we can conclude from the reference in Clare's fourth letter to Agnes.

23 Cf. J. Nemec, *Agnese de Boemia*, S. Maria degli Angeli-Assisi 1982, 22f.

24 Fourth letter of Clare 1–3.

25 Apocalypse 14:4–5.

26 Fourth letter of Clare 8.

27 Ibid. 18–23.

28 Ibid. 28–32.

29 Ibid. 37–8.

30 *Life of Clare* 41.

31 Ch. Frugoni, *La morte propria, la morte degli altri*, in *Storia vissuta del popolo cristiano*, ed. J. Delumeau, Turin 1985, 349f.

32 *Life of Clare* 43.

33 Ibid. 44.

34 The *Rhyming Life* adds that Clare wanted Angelo, Leo and Juniper near her in order to read the Passion of the Lord to her, *Leg. vers.* vv. 1316–39; *AFH* 5 (1912) 471.

35 *Life of Clare* 45.

36 Ibid. 45.

37 Ibid. 45; *Leg. vers* vv. 1329f.

38 *Test.Cl.*, 42–3.

39 Blessing of Clare, 11–13.

40 Ibid. 7; also 2 Corinthians 1:3; Ephesians 1:3.
41 *Process* 11, 4; cf. *Life of Clare* 46.
42 Chrétien de Troyes, *Perceval*.
43 First letter to Agnes, 10–11.
44 *Process* 3, 32. The silence of Celano on this matter is inexplicable unless, knowingly, he wanted Clare's Rule to be forgotten.
45 Cf. P. Robinson, 'Inventarium omnium documentorum quae in Archivo protomonasterii S. Clarae Assisiensis nunc asservatur' in *AFH* 1 (1980) 417.

Chapter Ten. The Birth of a Cult

1 *Life of Clare* 47.
2 Cf. Thomas of Eccleston, *On the coming of the Friars Minor to England*, ed. A.G. Little and J.R.H. Moorman, Manchester 1951, 65f.
3 *Life of Clare* 47.
4 For all this, see F. Casolini, *Il protomonastero di S. Chiara in Assisi*, Milan 1950, 1–67.
5 Innocent IV, *Gloriosus Deus*, 18 October 1253. The Latin original is preserved in the *Bullarium Franciscanum* while a translation into the old Umbrian dialect is placed at the start of the canonisation process; cf. *AFH* 13 (1920) 439.
6 Ibid. 440.
7 *Process* 20, 9.
8 *Life of Clare* 62.
9 The definitive work on this is A. Vauchez, *La sainteté en Occident aux derniers siècles du Moyen Age, d'après les procès de canonisation et les documents hagiographiques*, Rome 1981, esp. 491–622.
10 *Life of Clare* 49.
11 John 10:41.
12 *Process* 20, 9; cf. n7 above.
13 On the sanctuary as a 'sacred space', see *Culto dei santi, istituzioni e classi sociali in età preindustriale*, ed. S. Boesch Gajano and L. Sebastiani, Rome 1984.
14 *Life of Clare* 52.
15 Mark 2:1–12.
16 The authoritative work on the condition of children in the Middle Ages is Ph. Ariès, *Padri e figli nell'Europa medioevale a moderna*, 2 vols., Bari 1976.
17 *Life of Clare* 57.
18 Cf. P.-A. Sigal, *L'homme et le miracle dans le France médiévale (XI–XII siècle)*, Paris 1985, 80f.
19 The importance of this Assisian institution was shown by A. Bartoli Langeli, *La realtà sociale assisana e il patto del 1210*, in *Assisi al tempo di san Francesco*, Assisi 1978, esp. 295–8.
20 *Life of Clare* 56.

21 Cf. A.I. Galletti, 'I francescani ed il culto dei santi nell'Italia centrale' in *Francescanesimo e vita religiosa dei laici nel '200*, Assisi 1981, 313–63.

22 *Life of Clare* 60.

23 Ibid. 52–3.

24 Ibid. 62; the bull is dated between August and October 1255 and is printed in *Early Documents* 176.

25 Cf. L. Wadding, *Annales Minorum* IV.

26 On the role of Bonaventure in the history of the evolution of the Order, see *S. Bonaventura francescano*, Todi 1974; G. Odoardi, 'L'evoluzione istituzionale dell'Ordine codificata e difesa da san Bonaventura' in *MF* 75 (1975) 137–85; R. Manselli and T. Gregory, 'Bonaventura da Bagnoregio, santo' in *DBI* XI Rome 1969, 612–30; A. Pompei, 'S Bonaventura da B.' in *DIP* I, Rome 1974, 1504–8; Gratien de Paris' always valid, *Histoire de la fondation et de l'évolution de l'Ordre des Frères Mineurs au XIIIe siècle*, Rome 1982, 266–320; also the brief but well-documented *Dalla intuizione alla istituzione*, ed. Th. Desbonnets, Milan 1986, 171f. (trans. into English by Paul Duggan and Jerry Du Charme, *From Intuition to Institution*, Chicago 1988, 127f.).

27 For the rapport between Clare and the first Franciscans, see M. Bartoli, 'Gregorio IX, Chiara d'Assisi e le prime dispute all'interno del movimento francescano' in *Rendiconti Accademia Nazionale dei Lincei* 35 (1980) 107f.

28 Cf. E. Franceschini, 'I due assalti dei saraceni a S. Damiano e ad Assisi' in *Nel segno di Francesco* S. Maria degli Angeli-Assisi 1988, 381–405; Ch. A. Lainati, 'Scritti di Chiara d'Assisi' in *FF* 2331, n52.

29 Cf. L. Bracaloni, 'La chiesa di San Giorgio in Assisi' in *CF* 8 (1938) 493–511.

30 For this reconstruction, see Casolini, *Il protomonastero*, 33–67.

31 For the history of Second Order legislation, see L. Oliger *De origine regularum Ordinis S. Clarae* (1912); F. Casolini, 'Sainte Claire et les Clarisses' in *DS* V, Paris 1964, 1404–22.

Index

Index

Index

Index

Index

Index

Index

Rufino of Assisi, companion of
Francis 38; 137; 199
Ruh K. 204 n30
Rules *see* Augustine, Benedict,
Clare, Innocent, Ugolino
Rusconi R. 216 n5; 220 n75; 231 n14
Russel J.C. 208 n51

Sabatier P. 72f; 205 n50; 206 n54;
211 n39; 218 n41; 219 n53
Sainsaulieu J. 216 n6
Salimbene de Adam da Parma OFM
203 n20
San Michele sul Gargano sanctuary 15
Sanna A. conv. 214 n26
San Paolo delle Abbadesse OSB
(monastery) 46–52; 53; 57; 71;
177; 212 n53
Sant'Angelo in Panzo (church) 54–7;
74; 181
Santucci F. 213 n9
San Verecondo OSB (monastery) 54
Saragoza, S. Catalina PC
(monastery) 217 n19
Scalia G. 203 n20
Schampheleer J. de OFM 225 n28
Schmidt M. 219 n50; 230 n68
Schmitt Cl. OFM 230 n71
Schmitt J-C. 229 n45
Schmucki O. CAP 218 n24; 224 n21;
225 nn27, 31; 233 n6
Sebastiani L. 235 n13
Sensi M. 213 nn11, 14, 20; 216 n70;
217 n14
Seton W. 205 n38
Sibilia S. 215 n62
Sigal P. 230 nn4, 6; 231 nn8, 12, 13,
16, 24; 235 n18
Silence 79–82; 95
Silvester of Assisi, companion of
Francis 84; 87
Simone of Collazzone OFM 3; 202 n14
Sisters who serve 80; 110
Smith J. 217 n22
Speculum perfectionis 205 n47; 206
n54; 218 n41; 223 n75; 229 n47

Spiritual motherhood 92; 128–31
Stanislao da Campagnola CAP 205
n43; 206 n11; 228 n20
Stefano d'Aubazine 218 n30

Tabacco G. 216 n6
Terzi A. OFM 211 n33
Thomas Aquinas OP 159; 231 n10
Thomas à Becket 159
Thomas of Ecclestone OFM 227 nn9,
11; 235 n2
Thouzellier Ch. 216 n3
Tommasetti F. 216 n4

Ugolino de Pietro Girardone 168
Ugolino di Segni 7; 10; 11; 69f; 71;
79–85; 220 n75
Constitutions of 79–82; 181; 206
n53; 217 nn20, 21; 218 nn25,
29; 220 n76
Letter to Clare 112–14; 205 n41
see Gregory IX
Ullmann W. 227 n14
Umiliana de'Cerchi 232 n53
Upsala 7; 9

Vacca A. 228 n35
Vallingegno *see* San Verecondo
Vauchez A. 202 nn4, 8, 12, 15; 203
n21; 208 n43; 209 n70; 217
n10; 221 n19; 222 n34; 226
n42; 229 n44; 230 nn5, 6; 231
n9; 235 n9
Virgin Mary 128–31; 187
Vision of Francis 141–5
Vitalis of Aversa 172–3
Vyskočil J.K. 205 n39

Wadding L. 205 nn40, 41; 218 n36;
227 n8; 236 n25
Waefelghem R. van 218 n25
Waley D. 206 nn5, 6

Zannoni G. 233 n59
Zanoni L. 214 n43